Festivals *of* Lite

KOSHER COOKBOOK

Festivals *of* Lite

KOSHER COOKBOOK

Gail Ashkanazi-Hankin

PELICAN PUBLISHING COMPANY

Gretna 1999

*The word "Pelican" and the depiction of a pelican are trademarks
of Pelican Publishing Company, Inc., and are registered in the
U.S. Patent and Trademark Office.*

Library of Congress Cataloging-in-Publication Data

Ashkanazi-Hankin, Gail.
    Festivals of lite kosher cookbook / Gail Ashkanazi-Hankin.
       p.   cm.
    Includes index.
    ISBN 1-56554-334-3 (hc. : alk. paper)
    1. Cookery, Jewish. 2. Low-fat diet—Recipes. 3. Low-cholesterol
diet—Recipes. 4. Low-calorie diet—Recipes. I. Title.
TX724.A83 1999
641.5'676—dc21
                                    99-18520
                                           CIP

Illustrations by the author

Printed in the United States of America

Published by Pelican Publishing Company, Inc.
1000 Burmaster Street, Gretna, Louisiana 70053

In loving memory of my father,
Bernard Ashkanazi
1924-97

Cooking for him and creating recipes with him were among my great joys.
Together, we learned that special-needs diets can be delicious.

Contents

Acknowledgments..9

Introduction..11

Lite and Healthy Tips..15

Time- and Money-Saving Tips 19

Our Holidays...23

Appetizers...53

Salads...73

Breads..93

Soups...99

Fish...123

Meat Entrees..139

Vegetarian Entrees...165

Vegetables..187

Potatoes...201

Rice and Grains...211

Kugels 221

Condiments and Sauces...229

Fruit Dishes..237

Desserts...247

Passover 275

Index 303

Acknowledgments

The best thing about writing this book was the opportunity to meet and receive recipes from some wonderful Jewish cooks from all over the world. In the course of collecting recipes and researching Jewish food history, I called upon old friends as well as strangers who became new friends. All are treasured. I am indebted to the following generous recipe contributors: Zendra Ashkanazi, Alisa Vardi Benabu, Etta Chaya Brummel, my daughter Jennifer Hankin, my sister-in-law Joelle Hankin, Yaffa Hanouna, Felicia Herscovici, my sister Janis Hoover, Sara Kishoni, Cantor Isaac and Zahava Koll, Jeannette Male, Bernard and Marilyn Mendoza, Marcelle Morgan, Emilia Novoseletsky, Lucie Prenzlau, Sofiya Sandler, Carol Joy Shaffer, Dr. Gratia Meyer Solomon, and Bernice Tarley.

Two cooking enthusiasts graciously volunteered to test many recipes. I thank Shana R. Goldberg and Mira Zevin for their time and feedback, and I thank their families for tasting their experiments on my behalf.

Speaking of tasters, my family and friends have been very generous with their opinions on many occasions: the Galemba Family, my husband and son Larry and Michael Hankin, my Brazilian "son," Benny Goldstein, the Reaven Family, Dr. Bill Silvers, and David and Gratia Solomon and their Shabbat guests.

I would like to thank the entire staff at Pelican Publishing Company for their professional expertise in making my first book, *Passover Lite Kosher Cookbook,* a success and their patience and guidance in the production of this book.

I want to thank all my friends who have had a patient ear and have listened to me as I've thought out loud, worried, and tried to put together the giant jigsaw puzzle that became *Festivals of Lite.*

I want to thank my mother, Bernice Ashkanazi, who has tested recipes and been my cheerleader, not only all the way through this project but through my entire life.

And finally, my husband, Larry, has been my assistant, typist, and partner in creating, testing, and tasting.

Introduction

This book, *Festivals of Lite,* combines three of my passions: healthy cooking, international Jewish cuisine, and Jewish observance. They are intertwined.

Jewish cooking can be healthy, and with today's concern of eating smaller amounts of fats, sugars, and meat—either by choice or due to health problems—many Jews are looking for ways to keep our culinary traditions on our holidays while maintaining healthier lifestyles.

I have heard many people rationalize that "it only comes but once a year, so why not splurge?" But there are numerous Jewish holidays, and many revolve around home-cooked traditional dishes that are high in fat, cholesterol, salt, and sugar. So yes, Passover is only once a year but so are Rosh Hashanah, Sukkot and Chanukah (two more weeklong holidays), Purim, and Shavuot—all featuring foods traditionally laden with calories, not to mention Shabbat, which comes every week.

Between Friday-night dinner and *Havdalah* Saturday night, one could top off the scales and destroy what he or she has been trying to accomplish healthwise all week.

All that is needed is moderation. Many traditional dishes can be kept. After all, they are delicious.

Combining a healthier way of eating with kashrut, the Jewish dietary laws, can be, at times, another hurdle. Since more and more people are adding kashrut to their lives, I hope to contribute to this trend by helping people make the transition, showing them how easy it can be to combine these two lifestyle disciplines.

The 1980s saw a surge of both Jewish cooking and interest in keeping kosher—and the trend is still going strong. In this book, there are choices from Ashkenazic and Sephardic cuisines as well as contemporary dishes inspired by these cuisines that are all kosher, according to the dietary laws.

Evidence of the "kosher revolution" is everywhere. An example is the ever-growing kosher-wine industry. No longer is the perception of kosher wine limited to heavy, sweet sacramental wines. Today's kosher wines include award-winning sophisticated vintages, both dry and sweet.

This blossoms from the ever-expanding selections of kosher products available in the grocery stores, not only in the kosher-food aisle, but integrated throughout all the departments. The kosher-food industry has grown to include virtually every type of convenience food, including kosher versions of popular American foods and food trends.

New chefs are contributing fresh ideas for menus and recipes for Rosh Hashanah, Chanukah, and Passover in newspapers and gourmet magazines every year.

This book evolved into a sampler, skimming the surface of traditional foods from the diverse Jewish communities. Some no longer thrive in their host countries but their remnants come together in Israel and in parts of the Diaspora to form the world of Jewish cuisine. There are so many dishes from which to choose, but I have tried to include a variety of tastes from the different communities that could easily translate into low-fat variations.

While researching the differences of the communities, I have also noticed that the holidays sometimes unify the cultures. Cholent, associated with Shabbat as the main meal on Saturday, is always recognized, not because of the ingredients, but because of the method of cooking, which creates a stewed mixture of meats and vegetables.

During Sukkot, stuffed vegetables are served in virtually every *sukkah* anywhere in the world. The items stuffed vary according to availability in different countries and include cabbage leaves, grape leaves, bell peppers, onions, leeks, pumpkins, squashes of nearly all kinds, eggplants, carrots, and even fruits.

On Chanukah, most Jews eat fried foods—sweet or savory—to remember the olive oil miraculously burning in the Temple. Dairy foods are also traditional.

For Purim, it seems that sweets and pastries are popular everywhere.

Passover is more complex with many differences in choices of foods, but the unifying ingredient in this holiday, of course, is the Jewish soul food, matzah, baked unleavened bread. The traditional dishes are always with us, but Jewish women, with our wit and creativity, continue to invent ways to dress up this mainstay for the week.

For Ashkenazim and Sephardim, Shavuot is associated with dairy dishes. The ultimate dairy dessert for Ashkenazim is cheesecake, dating back to 350 B.C.E. when Greece occupied Palestine (Israel). Other Ashkenazic specialties include dairy kugels, cheese blintzes, cheese kreplach, and borscht with sour cream. Some Sephardic specialties include cheese pastries, cheese fillings in dough or phyllo, and rice puddings.

The 2,000-year separation of a nation of people from their homeland and each other understandably brought about the different cuisines. When I began researching Jewish cuisine, the more I studied the foods of the different countries, the more vivid it became how food choices have been affected by historical and political developments, and how neighboring countries affect each others' cuisines.

Because of historical events that resulted in countries dominating other countries and Jews fleeing from one country to another, the same dish could be found in each of the Jewish communities in the region, only with slight variations on a seasoning. For example, I found one dish of green beans, tomatoes, and onions everywhere from Spain to Tunisia to Egypt. Many Spanish Jews fleeing the Inquisition brought their recipes with them and adapted them to their new host countries.

Dishes from Eastern Europe and northern regions of Russia revolved around cabbage and root vegetables such as beets, potatoes, and carrots. These foods have become traditional at Ashkenazic holiday tables because of geographical influences: potato kugels, carrot kugels, stuffed cabbage, beet salads.

Where lamb recipes might be on a holiday table in the Mediterranean region, chicken and beef are more associated with the Ashkenazic Jews, again due to the geographical differences.

Many appetizers and salads appear together in this book because of Sephardic influences. Sephardic and Oriental Jews (from Middle Eastern and Asian countries) have a custom of eating *mezza,* or many appetizers, before the main course. Most of these *mezza* are vegetable salads, often cooked. These can be made healthfully by reducing the amount of oil.

A typical Sephardic Shabbat meal or other special occasion begins with a proud display of many cooked vegetable salads presented the traditional way—in small amounts across the table. I have been told by Sephardim that eating all of these delicious salads before the main course is so filling that it leaves little room for the heavier meat main dish yet to come.

Of course, the high calorie count comes at dessert time with both Ashkenazic and Sephardic menus. While Ashkenazic desserts are based on cakes and strudels laden with oil and sugar, Sephardic desserts are fried pastries, most loaded with nuts. The majority of these delicious, tempting desserts can be somewhat modified without compromising their character. The exception is fried desserts, and I didn't want to change their very essence, so, in moderation, enjoy them as they are. I didn't want the theme of this book to be a fear of food, just an awareness, and a guide to modification.

American Jews are accustomed to the fusion way of cooking because of the variety of cultures in the United States and the popularity of ethnic restaurants. It is no surprise that Middle Eastern food has become quite popular. Hummus, pita, and baba ghanouj have become so much a part of the American palate that they are available readymade in neighborhood supermarkets.

Broadly speaking, Sephardic cooking is part of the popular Med-Rim culinary trend in the United States. It encompasses the flavors of the Levant (Greece, Turkey, Syria, Lebanon, Israel, Jordan, and Egypt) and the Maghreb (Morocco, Algeria, and Tunisia) as well as the more familiar Italian and French cuisines, although they are quite different from each other.

Chefs are taking advantage of this desire to expand our palates, and are creating new tastes by combining the different cultures' seasonings and foods. It has worked its way into many Jewish communities. In my *shul,* at the *Kiddush,* salsa is served alongside gefilte fish as a condiment.

Israel is truly the quintessential fusion of cultures, including foods. Until recently, the different communities of Jews in Israel remained "culinarily segregated." Now with more and more cross-cultural marriages (Ashkenazic and Sephardic) and generational assimilation, fusion cuisine has affected the average home kitchen in Israel. The Yemenite who marries a Jew from Poland, for example, will combine the foods of both families in an effort to please.

Israeli grocery stores have packaged foods and condiments from Russia to Morocco, all on one shelf. But as many cultures as Israel has absorbed, it is still influenced by neighboring countries. This is why falafel, pita, hummus, tahini, and baklava are mainstays.

The fusion style of eating can add interest to your own meals. Create your own fusion cuisine, by mixing and matching. In each chapter, there are choices of Ashkenazic, Sephardic, some Oriental, and contemporary dishes that are updated to fit into a healthy lifestyle. Many of the suggested holiday menus in this book blend tastes and textures gleaned from different Jewish communities for memorable meals.

In choosing recipes for this book, I tried to take into account how they can be used for holidays as well as every day, and their ease of preparation, with some dishes being made several days in advance or frozen. I've tried to keep many dishes pareve so they can blend into meat and dairy meals.

The recipes in this book were analyzed for nutrition using *Micro Cookbook 4.0 for Windows* (Pinpoint Publishing, 1993). If you have picked up *Festivals of Lite* to help make your particular diet easier to calculate, or if you are identifying with Jews worldwide by keeping kosher and observing the holidays, and are always searching for new ideas, I am sure you will benefit from this collection.

Lite and Healthy Tips

- Reduce the amount of meat in your recipes. Traditional cholent, for example, can be made with just a little meat, along with a larger amount of flavorful vegetables, grains, herbs, and spices for a lower-fat Shabbat treat.

- To include a small amount of brisket in your meat dishes, choose a square-end piece over a pointed end. According to *Prevention* magazine, the square end of the brisket has less fat content.

- Substitute crumbled "veggie burgers" or unflavored soy protein crumbles for ground meat in recipes. Besides lowering the fat and eliminating the cholesterol, this turns a meat dish into a pareve dish, so you can serve dairy side dishes and desserts if you desire.

- I included just a few dishes with red meat. As of this writing, though, a company, Better Beef, is breeding beef cattle that will have less cholesterol and fat than poultry, and plans are being made for kosher production and marketing of Better Beef. If you do consume red meat, this will be a big boon to your diet.

- Do not eat charred food. Grilling is the number-one way to prepare meats in the North African Jewish communities. For beef, lamb, and chicken, it has been suggested to reduce grilling time by partially cooking the seasoned meat in the microwave before grilling. This lessens the exposure to the carcinogens from the flame.

- Grill all kinds of vegetables from sweet potatoes and peppers to tomatoes and onions without brushing on oil or sauce. Toss with a variety of lettuces. The flavors of the vegetables are enough—no salad dressing is needed. You can also cut up the grilled vegetables and stir them into hot vegetable or chicken broth for a quick and simple soup. Finally, you can top a plate of a pasta with the grilled vegetables—simple, elegant, healthy, and delicious.

- Try to use fresh herbs. They always give a little "extra" to any dish, especially parsley and cilantro. (Cilantro is a synonym for fresh coriander.) Just by intensifying the seasonings, you can automatically reduce the oil, salt, or sugar.

- Remember that if you do not have a fresh herb on hand (except parsley and cilantro) use 1 teaspoon dried herbs for every tablespoon of fresh herbs called for in a recipe.

- To store fresh parsley and cilantro, wash the herbs and shake off the excess water. Wrap loosely in paper towels and keep in an opened plastic bag. A suggestion from one of my recipe contributors, Yaffa Hanouna: Store the washed herbs in zipper storage bags, and freeze. This will make it easier to mince and use them in cooking.

- Save half the fresh herbs called for in the recipe, and add them 10 minutes before the dish is done.

- Add new spices and seasonings to your collection, and try new combinations of spices and foods. Spices used in the Western world for sweetening desserts, such as cinnamon, cloves, and nutmeg, are used by the Jews of Iraq, Iran, and Afghanistan to flavor meats and other nonsweet foods. Middle Eastern desserts are perfumed with rosewater or orange-blossom water, rather than spiced with cinnamon, cloves, and nutmeg.

- Take advantage of the variety of grains (rice, pasta, bulgur wheat) and legumes (peas, lentils) and different root vegetables such as beets, parsnips, and rutabagas. It's just as easy to cook a pot of bulgur wheat as it is to cook rice for a side dish.

- There is a variety of flavored nonstick cooking-oil sprays on the market, referred to in this book simply as "cooking spray." I mention butter-flavored, garlic-flavored, and olive-oil cooking sprays, but there are so many varieties from which to choose. If you are interested in creating your own flavor of oil, you can purchase a simple spray bottle or an aerosol dispenser designed specifically for this purpose. This can be a money-saving step as well.

- When I call for oil in a recipe, I recommend canola oil. It is low in saturated fats. Many recipes call for a small amount of olive oil, which is high in monounsaturated fat and is considered to be beneficial in cutting cholesterol.

- For Passover, use Passover oil, which is lowest in saturated fats and highest in polyunsaturated fats. Make your own Passover cooking spray.

- Recipes calling for olive oil have all been tested with extravirgin olive oil. It is stronger tasting, so the food needs less for full flavor.

- To sauté, make sure the nonstick skillet is hot first, then coat it with cooking spray just before adding the ingredients, or heat a little broth and 1 teaspoon oil to create more liquid for sautéing.

- When freezing green bell or other peppers, blanch them first in boiling water to preserve their texture and freshness.

- You will find in this book many recipes containing red bell peppers. They are rich in vitamin C and beta carotene.

- Calcium-fortified soy milk or rice milk is a great substitute for milk for pre- and postmenopausal women and lactose-intolerant individuals.

- Soft tofu can replace sour cream. Add 1 tablespoon vinegar per cup of pureed tofu for a sour-cream effect.

- If you are restricted to a low-sodium diet, use low-sodium canned products in these recipes. Use either a low-sodium broth or Vegetable Broth (see index). The nutritional analyses of most recipes calling for canned tomato products have been calculated with the low-sodium versions.

- For a fried taste to potatoes, steam the potatoes first until tender. The potatoes can be coated (with dry herbs, or see index for Crusty Browned Potatoes recipe), then baked at 450 degrees or broiled.

- The best foods in any diet—whether for losing weight or due to medical restrictions—are those lower in fat but rich in vitamins and minerals and high in fiber.

- To cook dry beans, soak the beans overnight in enough water to cover. Drain and rinse. Add water to the beans to cover and bring to a boil. Reduce heat. Cover and simmer 1½ hours or until fork tender.

- To prepare potatoes for latkes and kugels, a tip from Denver cooking maven Jackie Frazin: Soak the potatoes in salt water and add 2 tablespoons flour. Cover and refrigerate overnight. Drain well the next day. This will keep the potatoes very white.

- To roast garlic, snip the tops off the cloves of 5 heads of garlic, or 4 shallots. Spray the garlic with olive-oil spray. Bake at 350 degrees 50 minutes. Cool. Squeeze the garlic out of the sacs. It can be mashed and used as a spread on bread or in recipes. Makes 1 cup. You can store it in the refrigerator in a covered container up to one week.

- To make yogurt cheese, do not start with yogurt made with gelatin. It will not drain properly. Obtain a yogurt drainer. If you do not have one, you may use a colander. Line the colander with two layers of cheesecloth. Set the colander in a large bowl to collect the liquid. Dump the plain yogurt in the colander, cover with plastic wrap, and place in the refrigerator from 24 hours to 4 days. As it drains, empty the liquid that accumulates. Draining only 6-12 hours will give you sour cream. This is a good alternative in cheesecakes and recipes calling for nonfat sour cream and cream cheese. Add seasonings to make spreads and dips.

Time- and Money-Saving Tips

- Plan ahead . . . general wisdom. Work out a menu and a list of ingredients needed. Many of these recipes can be made a day or two in advance, and some can be frozen.

- The simplest everyday cooking method for chicken is to grill it, or slice it into stir-fry strips and prepare it with vegetables and rice.

- Obtain a few good knives: a chef knife, paring knife, and bread knife. Learning how to use a good, sharp knife for chopping will make it easier and quicker to chop more than 1 or 2 ingredients. After all, who wants to drag out the food processor every time you cook? In many of my recipes, I refer to the food processor, but skillfully chopping by hand can be just as easy. Some say it's even therapeutic!

- Keep a wide variety of seasonings and spices in your collection so they will always be there when you want to make a recipe in this book.

- Mince fresh herbs with scissors for speed.

- For recipes calling for large amounts of broth, use bouillon cubes, granules, or powders dissolved in water if you're not on a sodium-restricted diet.

- Greek or Spanish olive oil is less expensive than Italian olive oil.

- To extract more juice from a lemon, microwave the lemon 20 seconds, then roll it back and forth on the counter with your hand to soften it. Cut the lemon, then squeeze it or use a handheld wooden lemon reamer. This will significantly increase the amount of juice you get.

- Keep nonfat dry milk on hand for baking. It is less expensive than fresh milk, and will save you trips to the store.

- To cool a cake hot from the oven, place the pan on a wet towel. This way, the cake is less likely to stick to the pan. Another timesaver is to place the cake directly in the refrigerator.

ABBREVIATIONS

STANDARD			METRIC		
tsp.	=	teaspoon	ml.	=	milliliter
tbsp.	=	tablespoon	l.	=	liter
oz.	=	ounce	g.	=	gram
qt.	=	quart	kg.	=	kilogram
lb.	=	pound	mg.	=	milligram

STANDARD METRIC APPROXIMATIONS

⅛ teaspoon	=	.6 milliliter		
¼ teaspoon	=	1.2 milliliters		
½ teaspoon	=	2.5 milliliters		
1 teaspoon	=	5 milliliters		
1 tablespoon	=	15 milliliters		
4 tablespoons	=	¼ cup	=	60 milliliters
8 tablespoons	=	½ cup	=	118 milliliters
16 tablespoons	=	1 cup	=	236 milliliters
2 cups	=	473 milliliters		
2½ cups	=	563 milliliters		
4 cups	=	946 milliliters		
1 quart	=	4 cups	=	.94 liter

SOLID MEASUREMENTS

½ ounce	=	15 grams		
1 ounce	=	25 grams		
4 ounces	=	110 grams		
16 ounces	=	1 pound	=	454 grams

Festivals *of* Lite

KOSHER COOKBOOK

Our Holidays

SHABBAT

Sabbath, Day of Rest
Every week
Sundown Friday to Sunset Saturday

Shabbat ("to rest") is the separation from the rest of the week. We rest physically and mentally while we reflect, through thoughts and prayers, in synagogue. Relaxing with friends and family helps us to recharge for the week to come. More and more, people are learning and appreciating why this holiday is so necessary in our busy lives.

The seventh day is a day of rest but all part of the Creation, and it is the focal point of the week for Jews. This is why Jews all over the world make this day special with family and favorite meals while making sure that the laws regarding the prohibition of certain kinds of work are upheld. This has led to the uniquely prepared Jewish dish, cholent or hamin, a long, slow-cooked stew with different names. Ashkenazim call it cholent. Sephardim call it hamin, s'keena, or d'fina, depending on the community.

TRADITIONS AT THE TABLE

- The Friday-night Shabbat dinner is more lavish than meals served the rest of the week—that's part of the separation. Shabbat is welcomed like a bride and we greet her with songs (*zimrot*), delicious food, and our finest table settings. A fine white tablecloth adorns the table and the best dishes and silverware are spread upon it.

- All of the meals for Friday night, Saturday afternoon, and the small meal, Seudah Shlishit, are made ahead of time, as no cooking is permitted on the Sabbath. With advanced preparation, and freezing, you can begin Shabbat without being exhausted.

- Two braided challah loaves are always placed on the table.

MENUS

Recipes included in this book appear in **boldface**.

ASHKENAZIC-STYLE FRIDAY NIGHT DINNER

Meat

Wine
Challah
Baked Salmon Gefilte Fish
Chicken Soup with noodles
Roasted Turkey Tzimmes
Zahava's Marinated-Vegetable Salad
Root-Beer Spice Cake

VEGAN FRIDAY NIGHT DINNER

Pareve

Wine
Etta Chaya's Back-to-Nature Eggless Challah
Lentil Pâté
Carrot-Beet Salad "Bi Tahini"
Lucie Prenzlau's Vegetable Soup
Polenta-Stuffed Peppers
Broccoli in Lemon-Soy Sauce
Felicia's Romanian Chocolate Potato Balls

AUTUMN FRIDAY NIGHT DINNER

Meat

Wine
Challah
Algerian Lentil Vegetable Soup
Chicken with Artichokes and Olives
Egyptian Rice Pilaf
Braised Carrots and Leeks
Apple-Plum Crisp

SEPHARDIC-STYLE WINTER FRIDAY NIGHT DINNER

Pareve

Wine

Challah

Moroccan Carrot Salad
Grilled-Pepper Salad
Hummus with Peppers
Vegetarian Moroccan Harira Soup
Fish in Tomato-Cumin Sauce with Eggplant
Roasted-garlic-flavored instant couscous
Flower-Scented Fruit Compote
Anisette Cookies
Mint Tea

CONTEMPORARY SEPHARDIC-STYLE VEGAN FRIDAY NIGHT DINNER

Wine
Challah
Grilled-Pepper Salad
Moroccan-Style Beet Salad
Baby Ghanouj with **Spice-of-Life Chips**
Vegetable Rice Soup
Vegetarian Seneyeh with Apricot-Tomato Chutney
Steamed bulgur wheat
Lemon Cream Pudding
Anisette Cookies

BRAZILIAN-INSPIRED FRIDAY NIGHT DINNER

Dairy/Pareve

Wine
Etta Chaya's Back-to-Nature Eggless Challah
Cream of Artichoke Soup or **Brazilian Black Bean Soup**
Bahian Fish Muqueca
Arroz Brasileiro
Green lettuce layered with tomato slices, yellow onion slices,
and hearts of palm slices with any low-fat vinaigrette
Truffles (Kartoshka)
Orange Sponge Cake

SUMMER SHABBAT LUNCH

Dairy

Bagels with **Confetti Smoked Whitefish Spread**
Herbed Cucumber-Fennel Salad
Sephardic Portuguese Zucchini Soup
Cherry Dairy Kugel
Summer's Fruit in a Cloud

WINTER SHABBAT LUNCH

Meat

Cold Apple-Beet Borscht
The Tax Chazzan's Great Cholent, Adobe Cholent, or cholent of choice
Russian Sweet and Sour Zucchini Salad
Chocolate or Cinnamon Mandelbroit

SEUDAH SHLISHIT

Dairy

Zahava's Marinated-Vegetable Salad
Pickled Tuna Salad
Rye bread, challah, or bagels
Picnic Potato Salad
Fruit Tray with **Honey-Almond Sauce**

ROSH HASHANAH

New Year
1st and 2nd of Tishri
September

Rosh Hashanah literally means "head of the year" and is also sometimes referred to as the Day of Remembrance or Day of Judgment (Yom Hadin), when G-d evaluates our deeds of the previous year. This is a time of introspection, spiritual renewal, and prayer as Jews prepare to stand in judgment before G-d.

Rosh Hashanah is symbolized by the shofar. Relatives and friends gather to exchange greetings. A fairly recent custom has been the sending of New Year greeting cards. Many people save their cards and use them to decorate their sukkahs.

TRADITIONS AT THE TABLE

- The holiday is traditionally celebrated by eating sweet foods to remind us of the sweetness of a new year to come.

- Honey is used as a symbolic sweet dip and is in many recipes for Rosh Hashanah.

- The meal begins with dipping apples in honey and reciting blessings.

- Round challah studded with raisins to symbolize sweetness of life is traditional to Ashkenazic Jews at this time. It is round to express our hope for a new year without problems—a smooth year. Sometimes the challah is shaped like a ladder or a bird to symbolize directing our prayers to heaven.

- Ashkenazic Jews sprinkle challah with poppy or sesame seeds to symbolize fruitfulness, and dip it in honey, instead of salt as is customary on Shabbat.

- It is traditional to serve a fruit that we have not eaten during the previous year on the second night of Rosh Hashanah. Some Jews deny themselves one type of fruit all year so as to fulfill this custom.

- Fruit is found throughout Rosh Hashanah. Fruits named in the Bible such as grapes, figs, dates, and pomegranates all have symbolic meanings and have a place on our holiday menus. Pomegranates, for example, are meaningful because they are said to contain 613 seeds, the number of commandments set forth in the Torah.

- Sephardim like to have seven types of vegetables, which symbolize wishes and prayers for the new year. For example, leeks symbolize the desire to cut off one's enemies. My daughter in Israel observed a Moroccan family's custom of the host screaming his desire to cut off our people's enemies while cutting an onion into tiny pieces.

- In ancient times, there was a sheep's head on the Rosh Hashanah table, symbolizing the desire to be in the "head" of life, not the "tail." It is still an active custom with Sephardic Jews in Israel.

- Today, menus often begin with a fish head, either to be eaten or simply as a symbol for the wish for success. And fish is now a popular choice for an appetizer.

- The table for Rosh Hashanah is covered with a white tablecloth, and includes round challahs with the Kiddush cup and candles nearby.

MENUS

Recipes included in this book appear in **boldface**.

ASHKENAZIC

Meat

Wine
Etta Chaya's Back-to-Nature Eggless Challah
Apple slices with honey for dipping
(on the second night, serve a new fruit along with the apples)
Vegetable-Stuffed Tomatoes
Baked Salmon Gefilte Fish
Chicken Soup with **Gourmet Matzah Balls**
Sweet and Savory Chicken or **Latke Chicken**
Broccoli in Lemon-Soy Sauce
South African Vegetable Tzimmes or **Glazed Sweet Potatoes**
Pineapple Honey Cake or **Sweet Apples in Date Sauce**

SEPHARDIC

Meat
Challah
Grilled-Pepper Salad
Mediterranean Eggplant Salad
Black-Eyed-Pea Salad
North African Poached Fish
Moroccan Chicken with Almonds and Prunes
Steamed couscous
Moroccan Oranges Rimonim
Orange Sponge Cake

ECLECTIC

Pareve
Challah
Carrot-Beet Salad "Bi Tahini"
Vegetable Broth with **Gourmet Matzah Balls** or **Chilled Apple Soup**
Sea Bass in Tomato Sauce
Orzo Rice Pilaf or **Sweet Pumpkin and Chickpeas**
Indian Carrot Curry
Flower-Scented Fruit Compote or **Pineapple Honey Cake**

VEGAN

Pareve
Etta Chaya's Back-to-Nature Eggless Challah
Avocado-Grapefruit Salad
Grilled-Pepper Salad
Five-Vegetable Stew with Couscous
Sweet Apples in Date Sauce or **Moroccan Dates Dipped in Chocolate**

YOM KIPPUR

Day of Atonement
10th of Tishri
September-October

Yom Kippur is the most solemn day of the Jewish calendar.

As God's judgment of a person and his or her fate is made on Rosh Hashanah, the final verdict is given 10 days later on Yom Kippur. The period between the two holidays is devoted to repentance and self-evaluation. Jews atone for their sins and for the sins of the world. Before they can ask for forgiveness from G-d they must ask forgiveness from people against whom they have sinned.

During the day itself, Jews fast and pray. All the restrictions of Shabbat and more apply to Yom Kippur. One may not consume any food or drink. Fasting is not optional, except for children under Bar and Bat Mitzvah age and people who are ill and for whom fasting would present a physical danger.

The fast is from sundown on the eve of Yom Kippur until sundown on the next day, which concludes Yom Kippur.

The end of the Ne'ilah service completes the fast. The end of Yom Kippur is signified by one long, uninterrupted blast of the shofar and the call of "next year in Jerusalem." Many people then gather to break the fast as a community with some challah and honey cake and wish each other a sweet new year before going home.

TRADITIONS AT THE TABLE

To prepare for the fast, do not binge on eating. More than 50 percent of your prefast meal should be complex carbohydrates such as pasta, potatoes, rice, and other grains. This, combined with water, will retain the fluids your body will need the next day for a more comfortable fast. If you consume only proteins, you will lose the water. (The current diet trend is just that—high protein, low carbohydrates, quick weight loss due to the loss of water.)

Unlike Rosh Hashanah, there are no traditional meals before the fast or to break the fast, although some people have boiled or baked chicken and rice before the fast. Drink a lot of water the day before the fast. Refrain from salty or sweet foods or beverages.

Do not eat high-fat, high-calorie meals after the fast. They might stay with you longer than you want. Because of the food your body did not have for 26 hours, your metabolism slows down—your body is protecting itself in the starvation mode.

For break-the-fast, make the meal a day ahead. It is easiest, of course, to lay out bagels and cream cheese. Another common practice is to break the fast with fruit juice and a piece of challah dipped in honey or a piece of honey cake. As for the main meal at this point, most people have dairy and fish dishes.

Foods that contain water, such as fruit juices and hot vegetable soups or broths, will rejuvenate and soothe you after a trying day of fasting.

Keep your intake in small proportions after the fast. Remember, it takes 15 minutes before your stomach signals the brain that you've had food.

MENUS

Recipes included in this book appear in **boldface**.

PRE-YOM KIPPUR MEAL (*SEUDAT HA-MAFTEKET*)

Meat

Brazilian Black Bean Soup
Green salad with fat-free dressing
Brazilian-Style Arroz con Pollo
Steamed zucchini with lemon and dill
Chocolate or Cinnamon Mandelbroit or **Apple Cake**

Vegan

Vegetarian Mushroom Barley Soup
Syrian Mejadarra with **Caramelized Onions**
or **Stuffed Eggplant** or **Broccoli in Lemon-Soy Sauce**
Israeli Baked Apples

BREAK-THE-FAST

Dairy

Watermelon-ade or any fruit juice
Challah and honey
Vegetable Rice Soup
Bagels with **Smoked-Salmon Cream Cheese** or **Olivada**
Creamy Egg Salad
Caramel Rolls or **Chocolate Mandelbroit**

BREAK-THE-FAST—CHOICES FOR A CROWD

Dairy

Orange juice
Individual challah rolls
Sarah's Spinach Pie or **Pasta Salad Col D'Var**
Pickled Tuna Salad with bagels and/or rye bread
Pita Blintzes with Syrup or **Peaches 'n' Cream Kugel**
Lemon Poppy-Seed Cream-Cheese Bars
Sour-Cream Coffeecake

SUKKOT

Festival of Booths
15th of Tishri
September-October

Sukkot comes two weeks after the first day of Rosh Hashanah; five days after Yom Kippur. It is a harvest festival, lasting for eight days.

A sukkah ("booth") is built to represent the temporary shelters in which the Israelites lived for 40 years while wandering in the desert after the exodus from Egypt. Today we build these in our yards or synagogues and decorate them with fruits, vegetables, posters, and mobiles. Families' imaginations add individual character to each regulated sukkah.

All meals are served in the sukkah for the eight days of Sukkot and, weather permitting, it is a *mitzvah* to also sleep in it. In Denver, we do not have too many opportunities for this, due to some chilly autumn nights in Colorado. It has snowed here more than once during Sukkot. For others this is the rainy season.

Part of the fun of Sukkot is to go sukkah hopping, getting together with other families during the week of Sukkot.

It is a *mitzvah* also to invite people who do not have a sukkah.

TRADITIONS AT THE TABLE

No particular food is required for Sukkot, but it is traditional to eat stuffed vegetables, in recognition of the harvest festival. Hot vegetable soup is a welcomed first course for people in cooler climates during this autumn season.

MENUS

Recipes included in this book appear in **boldface.**

Meat
Challah
Vegetarian Moroccan Harira Soup
Salad tray with sliced bell peppers of all varieties
Moroccan Carrot Salad
Stuffed Tomatoes Syrian Style
Festive Couscous
Steamed mixed harvest vegetables
Apple Cake

Meat
Ashkenazic Split-Pea Soup
Vegetable-Stuffed Tomatoes
Dafna's Chicken
Herbed Bread
Roasted-Garlic Potato Kugel
Steamed green beans
Root-Beer Spice Cake

Meat or Pareve
American Spaghetti in a Bread Bowl
Raw vegetable tray
Large green salad
Carol Joy's Microwaved Fruit Compote
Quick Chocolate-Chip Cherry Ring

Pareve/Vegetarian
Turkish Salad (Salsa)
California Hummus
Raw vegetable tray
Vegetarian Seneyeh with Apricot-Tomato Chutney
Egyptian Rice Pilaf or **Rice-Stuffed Zucchini**
Moroccan Dates Dipped in Chocolate
Fresh fruit tray

Dairy or Pareve/Vegetarian
Vegetable Rice Soup
Polenta-Stuffed Peppers
Roasted Vegetables with a Sephardic Taste
Cranberry-Apple Kugel topped with low-fat frozen yogurt
or pareve equivalent

Dairy or Pareve/Vegetarian
Etta Chaya's Back-to-Nature Eggless Challah
Vegetable Broth with **Gourmet Matzah Balls**
Greek Salad
Lentil and Rice Stuffed Peppers
Caramelized Onions
Baked sweet potatoes with cinnamon, sugar, and cardamom,
served with butter replacement
Moroccan Oranges Rimonim
Felicia's Romanian Chocolate Potato Balls or
Pineapple-Apricot Strudel

SIMCHAT TORAH

Rejoicing of the Torah
23rd of Tishri
October

Taking place the day after Sukkot ends, Simchat Torah, the joyous and final day of the High Holiday season, is celebrated in a happy frenzy at the synagogue. Concluding the annual cycle of reading the entire Torah, the final verses are completed, and are immediately followed by the opening verses of Genesis to show that there is no end to learning or teaching. It is a cycle.

Children parade around the synagogue carrying flags, and are often given apples, sometimes caramel apples, as a treat. There is much dancing and singing as the Torah is carried seven times around the synagogue. Drinking whiskey or liqueurs and eating sweets is part of the merriment.

TRADITIONS AT THE TABLE

There are no particular traditions associated with the meals, although it is customary to have festive dinners and luncheons on Simchat Torah.

MENUS

Recipes included in this book appear in **boldface.**

Meat
Mixed Green Salad with Honey-Mustard Dressing
Best Mediterranean Chicken
Orzo Rice Pilaf
Fruit 'n' Carrot Salad
Cinnamon Mandelbroit
Israeli Baked Apples or **Lemon Cream Pudding**

Pareve/Vegetarian
Brazilian Black Bean Soup
South African Malaysian Vegetable Curry
Steamed rice
Bowls of bananas, raisins, and chutney
Anisette Cookies

CHANUKAH

Festival of Lights
Eight days, 25th of Kislev-1st of Tevet
November-December

Chanukah is called the Festival of Lights.

This holiday is a celebration of a historic event. A long struggle proved successful for the Jews to keep our culture intact. Jews were not allowed to observe the Shabbat and were forced to practice paganism. Hellenism spread rapidly to various nations, including Israel, but then it was forced upon the Jews. In the process, Jewish practices such as circumcision and dietary laws were to be destroyed so that all could assimilate.

As history tells us, it was the Maccabees who led the revolt. When the Temple, which had been defiled, was regained by the Maccabees, they proclaimed an eight-day holiday. The oils in the Temple had been desecrated. According to the rabbis, only one flask was found—barely enough for one day, yet it lasted eight. This miracle brought spirituality to this historical holiday.

Chanukah, a minor holiday, became more popular in the 19th century and continues to be popular today. The message of Chanukah should not be forgotten.

 This holiday is commemorated by placing colorful candles in a *chanukiah,* a special menorah or candelabrum for Chanukah. Blessings are sung and candles are lit after sundown each night of Chanukah, starting with one candle the first night, two the second night, and so on. There may be family gatherings throughout the week to play the traditional game "Spin the Dreidel" (a four-sided top) and eat latkes with music and song.

TRADITIONS AT THE TABLE

Chanukah foods traditionally include anything that reminds us of the oil that burned in the Temple for eight days. This can be disastrous for "fat watching." Usually, anything fried goes—vegetables are grated or mashed and fried as pancakes. In Sephardic communities, festive couscous with nuts and fruits is traditional as well.

In Israel, fried jelly doughnuts, *sufgoniot,* are everywhere. A recent variation includes caramel filling. In Russian communities, kasha varnishkes are eaten during the week.

The first night of Chanukah is traditionally a dairy meal. Your favorite vegetable grated or mashed in the form of a pancake (latkes), fried on a nonstick skillet coated with cooking spray, is an appropriate choice. If you are watching your cholesterol, replace eggs in the recipes with the equivalent amount of egg substitute.

If Rosh Hashanah is one of the most formal of the holiday dinners, then Chanukah is as informal as it gets. Have a party making different kinds of latkes. Just add simple salads, maybe a big pot of soup, and a fruit dessert. The latkes are the stars of the menu in my house.

MENUS

Recipes included in this book appear in **boldface.**

Pareve
Vegetarian Mushroom Barley Soup
Low-Fat Classic Potato Latkes or **Broccoli Latkes**
Carol Joy's Microwaved Fruit Compote

Dairy or Pareve/Vegan
Algerian Split-Pea Soup or **Ashkenazic Split-Pea Soup**
Cornmeal Latkes (dairy or vegan version)
Sweet Apples in Date Sauce or applesauce
Truffles (Kartoshka)

Dairy
Salmon in Phyllo
Festive Couscous
Coleslaw with Lime and Cilantro
Quick Chocolate-Chip Cherry Ring or **Apple-Plum Crisp**

Meat
Chicken Kasha Soup
Pareve latkes of choice
Applesauce

Meat
The Tax Chazzan's Meatballs over spaghetti or **Garlic Mashed Potatoes**
Broccoli Latkes
Israeli Baked Apples or **Pineapple-Apricot Strudel**

TU BISHEVAT

New Year of the Trees
15th of Shevat
January-February

Tu Bishevat is not a historic or religious holiday, but a reminder holiday to show us the responsibility we have of caring for the land. For Jews in the Diaspora it is a minor holiday, but in Israel it is very relevant. In Israel, this season is the time when the rains cease and the rebirth of the plants and saplings begin.

The holiday is not mentioned in the Bible, but was established in the Mishnah. The rabbis wrote that it is mandatory for the Jewish people to plant trees in the their homeland of Israel.

TRADITIONS AT THE TABLE

- Followers of Rabbi Isaac Lurie in the 16th century created a Tu Bishevat Seder, based on the Passover Seder. Four cups of wine are drunk and symbolic foods are eaten. The foods are based on the fruits, nuts, and seeds mentioned in Deuteronomy and grown in Israel. Use fruits and nuts for centerpieces on your table.

- In some Tu Bishevat Seders, four categories are present: nuts; fruits that are eaten whole, such as grapes and figs; fruits with pits, such as plums; and fruits with inedible skins, including oranges or pomegranates. Other Seder practices call for a variety of nuts and fruits in any form, including fresh, dried, frozen, or canned.

- Lunch is served after the Seder. It can and should be very casual. It can be a fun time for children.

MENUS

Recipes included in this book appear in **boldface.**

Pareve or Dairy
Round Challah
Greek Salad
Tunisian Pasta with Tuna
Moroccan Dates Dipped in Chocolate
Flower-Scented Fruit Compote or
Lemon Poppy-Seed Cream-Cheese Bars

Pareve/Dairy
Mediterranean Broccoli Salad
Fruit tray or **Lemon Waldorf Salad**
Cinnamon Mandelbroit

Dairy
Pickled Tuna Salad on rye bread
Raw vegetables with **Roasted Pepper Dip**
Peaches 'n' Cream Kugel
Low-fat brownies from a mix

PURIM

Feast of Lots
14th of Adar
February-March

Like Chanukah, Purim is a minor holiday, but the message is not.

The Jews of Shushan, Persia, were saved from a massacre by Queen Esther, a Jewish woman married to the king of Persia. Queen Esther foiled the king's advisor Haman from carrying out his evil plans. It is a timeless story of the Jews triumphing over the threat of annihilation.

Purim is not a Torah holiday. In the synagogue we listen to the *megillah* (the Book of Esther) being read and listen for the name of the evil Haman so that we can shake our *greggors* (noisemakers) and stamp our feet to blot out his name.

Purim's story is the basic story of good over evil. Amalekites, before the Nazis, were the most evil of all peoples toward the Jews. Amalek became synonymous with evil. On Purim, we symbolically blot out our enemies.

However, children love this holiday. It is a joyful time during which we exchange food baskets and gifts. In Israel, costume parades take place in the streets. In the Diaspora, children and many adults dress up in costumes and attend carnivals, usually at synagogues.

The Purim meal is in the late afternoon and usually dairy. Both Ashkenazim and Sephardim have triangular cookies and pastries representing the three-cornered hat worn by Haman, or Haman's ears. These cookies are eaten for dessert and are included in *shalach manot*.

In the United States, many synagogues and organizations are popularizing the practice of *shalach manot* by delivering baskets to the needy. It's a beautiful tradition that is growing stronger all the time.

To give *shalach manot* privately, people fill ready-made baskets or creatively made assorted containers with hamantaschen, candies, fruits, small bottles of wine, and other snacks, and give them to individuals or families.

There are special requirements for *shalach manot*. Send at least two "portions" of ready-to-eat foods to friends. Boxed and store-bought packaged items are common in the baskets. Certification symbols on the packages ensure that they are kosher. But kosher homemade items are even more special.

TRADITIONS AT THE TABLE

- One custom is to eat legumes for the Purim afternoon meal, in commemoration of Queen Esther, who ate them in her efforts to maintain the Jewish dietary laws while in court.

- Russian and German Jews fill their hamantaschen with poppy seeds (*Mohn*) while Sephardic Jews eat deep-fried pastries (*ozeni Haman*), some with sugar syrup, and candies.

MENUS
Recipes included in this book appear in **boldface**.

PURIM DINNER
Dairy
Sara's Spinach Pie
Orzo Salad or **Syrian Mejadarra**
Melon Fruit Salad
Coleslaw with Lime and Cilantro or **Romanian Coleslaw**
Hamantaschen
Lemon Poppy-Seed Cream-Cheese Bars

SHALACH MANOT BASKET
Pareve
Pumpkin-Filled Hamantaschen or your choice of filling
Anisette Cookies
Chocolate-Almond Macaroon Minibites
Whole fresh fruits such as apples or oranges
Small boxes of raisins or low-fat kosher candies, such as hard candies
Small bottle of wine or fruit juice

PESACH

Passover—Feast of Unleavened Bread
15th-22nd of Nisan
March-April

This historical holiday celebrates our Jewish ancestors' escape from Egypt and the birth of the Jews as a people under the leadership of Moses. It is an eight-day festival (seven days in Israel and for Reform Jews). To prepare for this holiday we thoroughly clean the house and kitchen. We remove all leavened products, and pots, pans, dishes, and utensils that are used every day of the year are replaced with kitchenware that will be used only during Passover.

Pesach is the oldest of all holidays of Jews as a nation. The first two nights, Diaspora Jews have a Seder. Israelis have one. The Seder is the service around the dinner table during which the story of the exodus from Egypt is told through the Haggadah. The Haggadah relates the story of G-d's intervention, which resulted in our deliverance to freedom. The Sephardic custom is to have everyone read a part of the story from the Haggadah; at Ashkenazic Seders, the leader usually reads the Haggadah. The Sephardic custom is gaining popularity in the U.S. in an effort to make the Seder more participatory.

Although families all over the world may have different customs, the order of the service and the story never change.

TRADITIONS AT THE TABLE

- Matzah is the soul food of the Jews. During Pesach, everything revolves around matzah and its derivatives—matzah meal, farfel, and, in the U.S., matzah cake meal. And no trace of *chometz* (leavened foods, such as bread, grains, and their derivatives) must remain in one's possession, let alone in our diets, on Passover.

- For those wanting to eat healthily, Pesach can be another disastrous holiday because of the dietary restrictions of the festival. Jewish women, once again, prevail. Health-conscious people are relying more on the basics of fruits and vegetables and downplaying the high-cholesterol red meats, eggs, and saturated fats.

- Sugar, in large quantities, seems to have found its way into Passover cooking, but there is really no reason to eat more sugar during this week than any other—not with all of the vegetables and fruits available to us now. In Europe, Ashkenazic Jews did not have the choices because Passover arrived too early for many vegetables to be available, but Sephardic Jews prepare many Passover salads because, in the Mediterranean regions, spring comes earlier.

MENUS

Recipes included in this book appear in **boldface**.

SEDERS

Meat
Baked Salmon Gefilte Fish with **Russian Beet Salad**
Chicken Soup with **Gourmet Matzah Balls**
Zahava's Marinated-Vegetable Salad
Moroccan Eggplant
Roasted Turkey Tzimmes
Steamed asparagus
Roasted-Garlic Potato Kugel
Toasted Macaroon Cake Delite
Fresh fruit

Meat
Springtime Chicken Soup with **Gourmet Matzah Balls**
Sweet and Savory Chicken or **Latke Chicken**
Garlic Mashed Potatoes or **Roasted Vegetables with Sephardic Taste**
Basil-Zucchini Kugel
Cinnamon Macaroons
Fresh strawberries with **Raspberry Coulis**

Passover Dinners through the Week

Dairy

Grilled fish
Broccoli and Cheese Kugel
Baby spinach salad, cherry tomatoes, and other assorted vegetables
Passover Fruit Crisp

Dairy

Fish and Vegetable Platter
Sephardic Farfel Puffs
Passover Chocolate Cake Roll

Dairy

Baked potato topped with **Austrian Mushroom Sauce**
Greek Salad
Melon Fruit Salad
Chocolate Brownies

Pareve/Dairy

Austrian-Hungarian Eggplant Goulash
with mashed potatoes or steamed spaghetti squash
Sautéed spinach
Melon Fruit Salad
Chocolate-Spice Angel Food Cake with **Cocoa Cinnamon Topping** or
Dairy Chocolate Sauce

Pareve

Creamy Potato Chili Soup
Tunisian Pasta Salad with Tuna
(replace the pasta with steamed spaghetti squash) or
Fried Matzah with Chili and Tomatoes
Grilled-Pepper Salad
Fruit 'n' Carrot Salad
Apple-Plum Kugel

Meat

Herb Chicken in Tomato Sauce
Garlic Mashed Potatoes
Natural applesauce
Steamed broccoli
Chocolate Torte

YOM HAATZMA'UT

Israel Independence Day
5th of Iyar
April-May

Yom HaAtzma'ut is a very important date in the history of the Jewish people. The State of Israel was established May 14, 1948. After 2,000 years in the Diaspora, after being forced to live in hostile country after country, Jews were finally free to choose their own destiny.

It was a struggle from the beginning. Many neighboring Arabs didn't want a Jewish state, and the struggle continues to this day. Many Jews have died in the struggle. In Israel, the day prior to Yom HaAtzma'ut is Yom Hazikaron, Memorial Day. Everything comes to a halt, and a countrywide blast of sirens is followed by a moment of silence in memory of the fallen soldiers and victims of war.

Mourning then gives way to celebration, as the country remembers why the soldiers gave their lives for the Jewish nation. Festivities abound throughout Israel on its independence day, and Diaspora Jews celebrate as well, usually on the community level, although families may also commemorate the miracle of Israel's rebirth with their own special meals or parties.

TRADITIONS AT THE TABLE

- Israeli foods are most appropriate for this day, falafel being the best known.

- This is a time of warmer weather and informal picnic meals are traditional. Rather than having hot dogs and potato salad, eat like Israelis for the day—pita sandwiches, hummus, tabbouleh, shashlik, and of course some sort of eggplant salad.

MENUS

Recipes included in this book appear in **boldface.**

Meat or Pareve
Israeli Salad
Hummus with Peppers
Kibbeh (meat) or **Falafel** (pareve) in pita with **Harissa Salsa**
Melon Fruit Salad
Chilled **Lemon Cream Pudding**

Meat or Pareve
Dolmas
Smoked Eggplant Caviar or
Shashlik with Harissa Seasoning or grilled fish with **Harissa Seasoning**
Romanian Coleslaw
Chickpea Salad or corn on the cob
Fresh fruit

Pareve
Grilled Veggie Sandwich
Tabbouleh
Coleslaw with Lime and Cilantro or
Russian Sweet and Sour Zucchini Salad
Moroccan Dates Dipped in Chocolate

LAG B'OMER

The 33rd Day of Counting the Omer
18th of Iyar
May

The Omer starts on the second day of Passover and is a seven-week mourning period between Pesach and Shavuot. There are no parties, weddings, or celebrations of any kind except on the 33rd day of this period, Lag b'Omer.

Lag b'Omer is an ancient folk festival with several stories connected to it. One tale has it that this is the day that Bar Kokba and his Jewish followers recaptured Jerusalem from the Romans. They lit bonfires to signal villages of the victories. The villagers set their own bonfires to inform villages farther away in the country. Bonfires are now part of the celebration in Israel along with picnics and outdoor activities. These days, potatoes are thrown into the fires and have become the food associated with this holiday.

In Israel, this is the busiest day of the year for weddings or parties, making it a welcome break from the seven-week mourning period.

TRADITIONS AT THE TABLE

- Lag b'Omer is a day of picnics and cookouts, weather permitting.

MENUS

Recipes included in this book appear in **boldface.**

Pareve
Grilled Halibut in a Citrus Vinaigrette
Picnic Potato Salad or baked potato
Russian Sweet and Sour Zucchini Salad
Chocolate Mandelbroit

Pareve
Grilled Veggie Sandwich or grilled veggie burger in a pita with relish
Spice-of-Life Chips
Hummus with Peppers or **Baba Ghanouj**
Israeli Salad
Chocolate Mandelbroit

Meat
Shashlik with **Harissa Seasoning** or **Tunisian Tabil Mix**
Baked potatoes
Zahava's Marinated-Vegetable Salad

SHAVUOT

Feast of Weeks
6th of Sivan
May-June

The word *shavuot* means "weeks." The holiday of Shavuot takes place seven weeks after the second day of Passover. As Passover is known as the birth of the Jews as a nation, Shavuot holds the nation together with the Torah that was given to the people, creating the Jewish religion.

This holiday commemorates the giving of the Torah at Mount Sinai to Moses and then to the people. To honor this holiday, Jews all over the world study Torah all night long.

 It is also known as Yom HaBikurim, the Feast of Fruits, celebrating the beginning of the agricultural season. Yemenites call it "Night of Reading" due to Torah study throughout the night. Afghani Jews refer to Shavuot as the Feast of Roses, and roses are placed around the Torah scolls.

Later, the rabbis also associated Shavuot with the destruction of the Second Temple. It is one of three pilgrimage festivals, along with Pesach and Sukkot.

TRADITIONS AT THE TABLE

- Dairy foods are traditional. One of several legends has it that when G-d gave the Jewish people the new laws, they ate dairy foods to be safe while they were learning the laws of kashrut. So an oral tradition has been handed down from generation to generation of Jews all over the world to eat dairy food on this day.

- Another legend explains that the Israelites at Mount Sinai were too tired and hungry to wait for a meat meal, so they ate dairy.

- Dairy foods are appropriate also because white is a symbol of Shavuot.

Jewish women have always made creative dairy meals because of the laws requiring the separation of meat and milk. Dairy is more important in Judaism than perhaps in many other cultures.

Russian Ashkenazim created a soured milk product, *smetina* or sour cream, which is the key ingredient in many dairy dishes, such as cheese blintzes, cheesecakes, and borscht with sour cream.

Sephardim have pastries and cheese-filled phyllo-dough dishes.

MENUS

Recipes included in this book appear in **boldface.**

Dairy
Sara's Spinach Pie
Herbed Bread
Herbed Cucumber-Fennel Salad
Grilled vegetables brushed with balsamic vinegar or nonfat salad dressing
Sugarless Pineapple Cheesecake

Dairy
Grilled salmon
Cherry Dairy Kugel
Braised Carrots and Leeks
Italian Cheesecake or **Rosewater Angel Food Cake**

Dairy
Creamy Potato Chili Soup
Fish and Vegetable Platter
Cheesecake in Phyllo Pouches with **Raspberry Coulis**

TISHAH B'AV

Fast of the Ninth Av
9th of Av
July-August

The ninth day of the month of Av is a day of mourning and fasting as the Jewish people commemorate the destruction of both the First and Second Temples on that date. Several other calamities befell the Jewish people on that date. No food or drink is consumed from sunrise to sunset on Tishah b'Av.

The three weeks preceding Tishah b'Av is a period of semimourning, and this is intensified during the nine days immediately before Tishah b'Av. As a sign of mourning, observant Jews refrain from eating meat.

Here are some suggestions of meatless main dishes for dinners during the Nine Days:

Five-Vegetable Stew with Couscous
Polenta-Stuffed Peppers
Herb Baked Eggs
Stuffed Eggplant
Vegetarian Seneyeh with Apricot-Tomato Chutney
South African Malaysian Vegetable Curry
Sara's Spinach Pie
Austrian-Hungarian Eggplant Goulash
Syrian Mejadarra

Appetizers

MOROCCAN-STYLE BEET SALAD

PAREVE
SHABBAT

The combination of lemon, cumin, hot pepper sauce, and parsley gives this a Sephardic taste. This or a similar version is sometimes served Friday night for Shabbat dinner in the Moroccan and Algerian communities.

2 15-oz. cans low-sodium sliced beets, or 6 medium fresh cooked beets, sliced
¼ cup lemon juice or white vinegar
1 tbsp. orange-juice concentrate or sugar

1 tsp. olive oil
1 tsp. chopped garlic
½ tsp. ground cumin
¼ tsp. hot pepper sauce, or to taste
¼ cup chopped parsley
1 tbsp. toasted sesame seeds

Marinate the beets in the lemon juice, orange-juice concentrate, oil, garlic, cumin, and hot sauce 2 hours.

When ready to serve, toss the parsley with the beets and garnish with the toasted sesame seeds. Serves 8.

Calories—46; Saturated fat—0 g.; Total fat—1 g.; Carbohydrates—9 g.; Cholesterol—0 mg.; Sodium—47 mg.; Fiber—1 g.; Protein—1 g.

CHICKPEA SALAD

PAREVE

This colorful side salad can be served with almost any meal.

1½ cups cooked or canned chickpeas, drained
1 celery stalk, sliced
½ cup diced green bell pepper
½ cup diced red bell pepper

½ small red onion, minced
3 tbsp. low-fat mayonnaise
2 tbsp. lemon juice
Pinch cayenne pepper

Combine all ingredients in a salad bowl and marinate for 2-3 hours. Serve chilled. Serves 6.

Calories—109; Saturated fat—0 g.; Total fat—1 g.; Carbohydrates—20 g.; Cholesterol—0 mg.; Sodium—364 mg.; Fiber—2 g.; Protein—4 g.

RUSSIAN BEET SALAD

PAREVE
PASSOVER

This salad recipe was kindly given to me by Sofiya Sandler, at whose home I enjoyed tasting it on a Shabbat afternoon. Sofiya serves it as a side salad or even as an appetizer garnished with walnuts and cucumbers. This salad adds a splash of color as a garnish to any plate for holiday company. It's so quick to make, and it's the details that make a successful holiday table.

SALAD

2 cups drained, minced, cooked or low-sodium canned beets
½ cup low-fat or nonfat mayonnaise

1 tsp. horseradish
1 tsp. minced garlic
¼ cup minced parsley (optional)
Salt to taste

GARNISH

4 large green lettuce leaves of any variety

1 tbsp. walnuts, minced
½ cucumber, sliced

To cook fresh beets, clean them and remove the stems. Boil them in a saucepan with water 30 minutes until tender.

In a food processor, mince the beets. Do not puree.

Transfer to a bowl and stir in the mayonnaise, horseradish, and garlic. For color, I suggest adding the parsley. The seasonings are adjustable.

To serve as a side salad or appetizer, spoon it onto the lettuce leaves. Garnish by sprinkling the walnuts over the top of each serving, and arrange sliced cucumbers on the side. Serves 4 as a salad; 8 as a garnish.

Calories—59; Saturated fat—0 g.; Total fat—2 g.; Carbohydrates—9 g.; Cholesterol—0 mg.; Sodium—151 g.; Fiber—1 g.; Protein—1 g.

BLACK-EYED PEA SALAD

PAREVE

ROSH HASHANAH

*Black-eyed peas are popular as a hot side dish in North African communities.
They are also very popular in the American South as a cold or hot dish.
Here is a contemporary cold version.*

SALAD

2 15-oz. cans black-eyed peas,
   drained and rinsed
2 green onions, chopped
1 apple, cubed

1 stalk celery, sliced
1 medium red bell pepper,
   chopped

VINAIGRETTE

3 tbsp. lemon juice
2 tbsp. red-wine vinegar
2 tsp. yellow mustard
1 tsp. fresh thyme or
   ¼ tsp. dry thyme

1½ tsp. honey or
   brown-rice syrup
2 tsp. olive oil
⅛ tsp. black pepper

In a serving bowl, combine all the salad ingredients.
Whisk the vinaigrette ingredients together and toss with salad. Serves 6.

Variation: Use fresh black-eyed peas. Remove any stones from 1¼ cups raw peas
and rinse. Place in a medium saucepan with 3 cups water. Bring to a boil over
medium-high heat. Reduce heat and cover. Cook for 45 minutes. Drain the peas.
Chill. Combine the black-eyed peas with the remaining salad ingredients in a bowl.
Pour the vinaigrette over the salad and toss. Chill until serving time.

*Calories—118; Saturated fat—0 g.; Total fat—2 g.; Carbohydrates—21 g.;
Cholesterol—0 mg.; Sodium—156 mg.; Fiber—2 g.; Protein—3 g.*

GRILLED-PEPPER SALAD

PAREVE
SHABBAT
ROSH HASHANAH
PASSOVER

This salad is found in both Morocco and Tunisia, and probably originated in Spain. It's even found in South America. It's easy to prepare in advance and is great if you have a bumper crop of peppers. It works well around Rosh Hashanah, when peppers are plentiful. Normally, the salad has at least twice the amount of oil but I found the peppers are so delicious and moist when grilled that just a touch of olive oil for flavor is all that's needed.

3 lb. green, red, or yellow bell peppers
2-3 hot green peppers
6-7 garlic cloves, minced

2 tbsp. extravirgin olive oil
3 tbsp. lemon juice
½ tsp. salt
¼ tsp. white pepper

Grill or broil the peppers whole on all sides until the skin is somewhat charred (about 15 minutes). Place in a paper or plastic bag, and let sit for a few minutes to loosen the skin.

Peel the skin. (I do this over the sink, frequently rinsing my hands with water. You can also scrape the skin off with a paring knife.)

Remove the seeds, slice the peppers into 1-inch strips, and place in a bowl.

In a small bowl, whisk the garlic, olive oil, lemon juice, salt, and pepper, and stir gently into the peppers. Adjust the seasonings to taste. Serve at room temperature or chilled. Serves 8-10.

Calories—76; Saturated fat—0 g.; Total fat—3 g.; Carbohydrates—11 g.; Cholesterol—0 mg.; Sodium—121 mg.; Fiber—1 g.; Protein—2 g.

MOROCCAN CARROT SALAD

PAREVE
PASSOVER

*This is a little different from the Algerian style of carrot salad,
which is spicier due to the addition of a chili pepper. This is a common
Moroccan combination of paprika and cumin with lemon and garlic. In fact,
you could season chicken, fish, or vegetables with this combination, as well.*

1½ lb. carrots
3 garlic cloves, chopped
1½ tbsp. olive oil
3 tbsp. vinegar
2 tbsp. lemon juice
1 tsp. paprika

1 tsp. ground cumin
⅛ tsp. cayenne pepper
Salt and pepper to taste
½ cup water
¼ cup minced parsley or cilantro

Boil or steam the carrots until tender.

Meanwhile, in a nonstick skillet, sauté the garlic in the oil for a few minutes until lightly browned.

Drain the carrots. Rinse under cool water until cool enough to handle. Slice the carrots and add to the garlic along with the remaining ingredients, except the parsley. Simmer for 5 minutes. Chill. Garnish with parsley. Serves 8.

*Calories—69; Saturated fat—0 g.; Total fat—3 g.; Carbohydrates—10 g.;
Cholesterol—0 mg.; Sodium—32 mg.; Fiber—1 g.; Protein—1 g.*

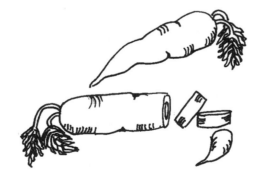

ISRAELI SALAD

PAREVE
PASSOVER
YOM HAATZMA'UT
LAG B'OMER

This has to be the most versatile vegetable salad. It goes with just about any meal. It illustrates how salads do not need lettuce to be complete.

VEGETABLE SALAD

2 tomatoes, diced

1 cucumber, peeled and diced

2 tbsp. chopped fresh chives

1 small dill pickle, chopped

2 radishes, chopped

½ stalk celery, chopped

VINAIGRETTE

3 tbsp. lemon juice or
   white vinegar

1 tsp. olive oil (optional)

2 tbsp. chopped parsley

2 tsp. snipped fresh dill,
   or to taste

Black pepper to taste

In a bowl, combine the salad vegetables.

In a cup, mix the lemon juice, oil, parsley, dill, and pepper. Pour over the vegetables and toss. Serves 4.

Serving suggestion: This is a traditional accompaniment to falafel and hummus. It can also be eaten in a pita alone with a little tahini.

Calories—63; Saturated fat—0 g.; Total fat—2 g.; Carbohydrates—10 g.; Cholesterol—0 mg.; Sodium—317 mg.; Fiber—2 g.; Protein—2 g.

TABBOULEH

PAREVE
YOM HAATZMA'UT
LAG B'OMER

Tabbouleh is actually a casual picnic salad. Mint is one of the signature ingredients in this famous grain salad. Since mint is not my family's favorite, I replaced it with more vegetables. You may omit the mint or add more to taste. This can be made the day before.

¾ cup cracked bulgur wheat
2 cups boiling water
2 cups diced tomatoes
1 small cucumber,
   peeled and diced
½ cup chopped carrots
½ cup chopped green pepper

1 cup minced parsley
1 tsp. toasted cumin seeds
2 tbsp. chopped mint (optional)
¼ cup lemon juice
1 tbsp. olive oil
½ cup minced scallions

Place the bulgur in a large bowl and pour the boiling water over it. Allow it to stand for 30 minutes or until the water is absorbed. Squeeze out any excess water.

Transfer to a serving bowl and add the tomatoes, cucumber, carrots, green peppers, parsley, cumin seeds, and mint.

Combine the lemon juice, oil, and scallions. Toss with the salad ingredients. Chill before serving. Serves 6.

Variation: Replace the bulgur wheat with 2½-3 cups cooked brown rice.

Calories—145; Saturated fat—0 g.; Total fat—3 g.; Carbohydrates—25 g.; Cholesterol—0 mg.; Sodium—23 mg.; Fiber—1 g.; Protein—4 g.

TURKISH SALAD (SALSA)

PAREVE

This is called a salad, but it is more like a salsa. There are many variations.
This one comes from my daughter Jennifer, who lives in Jerusalem.
Use it like salsa, as a dip, or—with less water—as a spread.
I use red onion for a milder flavor.

4 plum tomatoes
1 large green or red pepper
½ yellow or red onion
¼ cup minced parsley
2 tbsp. minced cilantro
1½ tsp. dry minced garlic

1 tsp. sugar
¾ tsp. salt
¼ tsp. mustard seed
6-oz. can tomato paste
¼ cup water

In a food processor, mince or pulse the tomatoes, pepper, and onion. Mix in the parsley, cilantro, garlic, sugar, salt, and mustard seed.

Stir in the tomato paste and water. Chill. This will keep for 2-3 days. Serves 6.

Variation: Add chopped chili peppers for a hotter flavor.

Calories—57; Saturated fat—0 g.; Total fat—1 g.; Carbohydrates—11 g.;
Cholesterol—0 mg.; Sodium—321 mg.; Fiber—1 g.; Protein—2 g.

HUMMUS WITH PEPPERS

PAREVE
SHABBAT
YOM HAATZMA'UT
LAG B'OMER

Hummus *is Hebrew and Arabic for chickpeas. Israelis have adopted this dish
as their own, usually flavored with olive oil, lemon juice, and tahini.
Here is a contemporary, spicy addition to the traditional ingredients,
and you won't miss the fat!*

⅓ cup green pepper
⅓ cup red pepper
1-2 tbsp. green chili pepper,
 or to taste, chopped
1½ cups cooked or
 canned chickpeas, drained

2 tbsp. tahini (optional)
½ tbsp. vinegar or lemon juice
2 tsp. chopped garlic
¼ tsp. salt
¼ tsp. cumin (optional)

Mince the green and red peppers. Transfer to a bowl, and add the chili peppers.
Process the chickpeas and tahini until smooth. Add the vinegar, garlic, salt, and
cumin. Pulse until the ingredients are mixed. Transfer to a bowl and stir in the pepper mixture. Serves 16.

Serving suggestion: Serve with a raw-veggie tray and Spice-of-Life Chips (see
index), fresh pita wedges, or crackers.

Variation: Try stirring in medium or hot Mexican salsa for a quick and tasty treat.

*Per 2 tbsp.: Calories—48; Saturated fat—0 g.; Total fat—1 g .; Carbohydrates—
8 g.; Cholesterol—0 mg.; Sodium—125 g.; Fiber—1 g.; Protein—2 g.*

CALIFORNIA HUMMUS

PAREVE
SUKKOT
YOM HAATZMA'UT
LAG B'OMER

To make this a California treat, use steamed artichoke leaves to scoop up the hummus. The tahini is just used to smooth out the hummus. If you like tahini, increase the amount to 2 tablespoons.

½ cup hot water
10 sun-dried tomatoes
1½ cups cooked or
   canned chickpeas
1 tbsp. lemon juice

2 tsp. tahini
1½ tsp. minced garlic
⅛ tsp. cumin
1 tsp. toasted sesame seeds

In a glass filled with the hot water, rehydrate the tomatoes for about 20 minutes. Set aside.

Combine the chickpeas, lemon juice, tahini, garlic, cumin and ¼ cup of the water from the sun-dried tomatoes in a food processor. Process until smooth.

Transfer to a serving bowl. Mince the tomatoes in the processor (no need to clean the food processor first), and stir into the hummus.

Stir the toasted sesame seeds into the hummus. Serves 16.

Serving suggestion: Besides artichoke leaves, provide raw veggies, crackers, or pita chips for dipping, or serve this hummus as a filling for pita bread.

Per 2 tbsp.: Calories—28; Saturated fat—0 g.; Total fat—1 g.; Carbohydrates—5 g.; Cholesterol—0 mg.; Sodium—56 mg.; Fiber—0 g.; Protein—1 g.

ROASTED PEPPER DIP

DAIRY
TU BISHEVAT

This is a contemporary dairy dip for crudités using a comomon Sephardic ingredient, roasted peppers. This is good for a dairy buffet.

8 oz. nonfat or
  low-fat cream cheese
¼ cup low-fat mayonnaise
1 large roasted red pepper,
  chopped

1½ tsp. ranch-style dressing
  seasoning mix
¼ tsp. dry dill or
  1 tsp. chopped fresh dill
Pinch garlic powder

In a food processor or mixer, blend the cream cheese and mayonnaise until smooth. Stir in the remaining ingredients. Chill. Makes 1 cup.

Per tbsp.: Calories—9; Saturated fat—0 g.; Total fat—0 g.; Carbohydrates—1 g.; Cholesterol—1 mg.; Sodium—40 mg.; Fiber—0 g.; Protein—1 g.

MOROCCAN EGGPLANT

PAREVE
PASSOVER
YOM HAATZMA'UT
LAG B'OMER

Normally, the eggplant is studded with garlic cloves and boiled, but I really like it baked. Try it both ways!

2 lb. eggplants
6-8 garlic cloves
2 tbsp. extravirgin olive oil
2 tsp. paprika

3 tbsp. vinegar or lemon juice
1½ tsp. cumin
¼ tsp. cayenne pepper

Make 3 long slits in the eggplants. Peel the garlic and slice in half if necessary to fit into the slits. Bake at 350 degrees for 40-45 minutes. Cool.

Peel the skin off the eggplants. Process with remaining ingredients to a coarse puree. Transfer to a serving dish. Serve at room temperature. Serves approximately 20.

Per 2 tbsp.: Calories—31; Saturated fat—0 g.; Total fat—2 g.; Carbohydrates—4 g.; Cholesterol—0 mg.; Sodium—2 mg.; Fiber—1 g.; Protein—1 g.

BABA GHANOUJ

PAREVE
SHABBAT
LAG B'OMER

*This Middle Eastern appetizer is increasing in popularity in the U.S.
Israelis have adopted baba ghanouj from neighboring Arab countries.
It is available everywhere. And if you want a high flavor impact,
grill the eggplant—it makes all the difference.*

2 lb. eggplants (about 2)
1/3 cup lemon juice
¼ cup tahini

½ tsp. salt (optional) or ¼ tsp.
crushed red pepper flakes
2 garlic cloves, minced

GARNISH

1 tbsp. chopped parsley

Grill the eggplants whole for 40-45 minutes, turning to char the skin on all sides.

Cool and peel the skin away in a colander and spoon out pulp. Squeeze out the liquid from the eggplant.

Process in a food processor for a smooth consistency, or mash in a bowl.

Add the remaining ingredients. Blend well. Garnish with parsley. Makes 1½ cups.

Serving suggestion: Serve with crackers, matzah, pita bread, or pita chips.

Variation: Pierce the eggplants several times with a fork and microwave for 12-14 minutes, or bake at 400 degrees for 30 minutes.

Per 2 tbsp.: Calories—57; Saturated fat—0 g.; Total fat—3 g.; Carbohydrates—6 g.; Cholesterol—0 mg.; Sodium—102 mg.; Fiber—1 g.; Protein—2 g.

ROMANIAN PUTLEJELA

PAREVE
SHABBAT
PASSOVER

This is a popular dish found in many regions with different names. Russians (who call this dish caviar—ikra) and Eastern Europeans use vinegar. Lemon juice is used by Jews farther south. Green peppers are not always used. This recipe is from Jeannette Male of Ft. Lauderdale. I have only slightly reduced the amount of oil from her original recipe.

2 lb. eggplants
4 green and/or red peppers
1 tsp. salt
¼ cup oil

2 tbsp. water or vegetable broth
3 tbsp. vinegar
1 tsp. sugar
4-5 garlic cloves

Preheat the oven to 350 degrees. Make several slits in the eggplants so that the steam escapes during baking or roasting. Bake along with the peppers for 45 minutes or until the eggplant is very soft.

Peel the eggplant skin away from the pulp. Scrape out and chop the eggplant. Transfer the eggplant, peppers, salt, oil, water or broth, vinegar, sugar, and garlic to a food processor and pulse until well blended. Serve chilled. Serves 10-12.

Variations:

- Jeannette's son Rich likes to peel the eggplant and bake it on a baking sheet.

- For a Mediterranean flavor, change the oil to extravirgin olive oil, replace the vinegar with lemon juice, and omit the sugar. Mix in ⅓-½ cup minced parsley or cilantro.

Calories—52; Saturated fat—0 g.; Total fat—2 g.; Carbohydrates—6 g.; Cholesterol—0 mg.; Sodium—192 mg.; Fiber—0 g.; Protein—0 g.

SMOKED EGGPLANT CAVIAR

PAREVE
SHABBAT
PASSOVER
YOM HAATZMA'UT
LAG B'OMER

This came from a Hungarian family in Israel. It has a great smoky flavor with very little seasoning added. Using the grill makes all the difference. It's just not the same under the broiler.

3 cloves garlic
1½ lb. eggplants, cut into
   1-inch slices
1 medium green pepper,
   quartered
1 onion, cut into 1-inch slices

3-oz. can tomato paste
1 tbsp. red-wine vinegar or
   lemon juice
1 tsp. olive oil
¼ tsp. salt (optional)

Roast the garlic cloves. Remove the peel.

Grill the eggplants, green pepper, and onion for 8-10 minutes on each side, or until lightly browned.

In food processor, pulse all ingredients to a coarse puree. This can be made 2 days in advance. Serves 6.

Serving suggestion: Serve as a warm side dish or as a cold appetizer. If a thinner consistency is desired, add a couple tablespoons water.

Variation: Omit the green pepper. Grill 2 onions and increase the garlic cloves to 6.

Calories—76; Saturated fat—0 g.; Total fat—1 g.; Carbohydrates—14 g.; Cholesterol—0 mg.; Sodium—113 mg.; Fiber—1 g.; Protein—2 g.

SMOKED-SALMON CREAM CHEESE

DAIRY

YOM KIPPUR BREAK-THE-FAST

A classic Ashkenazic spread for bagels, this is really better than the store-bought version. It is easy to make for company. Try serving this with minibagels for a portion-control snack.

**8 oz. nonfat or
light cream cheese
2 oz. smoked salmon**

**1 tbsp. fresh chopped chives or
1 tsp. dry chives or
1 tbsp. chopped fresh dill**

In a food processor, blend cream cheese and salmon together until the salmon is minced. Add chives or dill and pulse until well blended. Makes 7 2-tbsp. servings.

Serving suggestion: Serve this simple and delicious spread on bagels for brunch or break-the-fast.

With nonfat cream cheese: Calories—37; Saturated fat—0 g.; Total fat—0 g.; Carbohydrates—2 g.; Cholesterol—6 mg.; Sodium—358 mg.; Fiber—0 g.; Protein—6 g.

With light cream cheese: Calories—94; Saturated fat—5 g.; Total fat—8 g.; Carbohydrates—1 g.; Cholesterol—26 mg.; Sodium—291 mg.; Fiber—0 g.; Protein—5 g.

OLIVADA

PAREVE

This spread is a popular Mediterranean treat. It is prepared in many ways, with the main ingredient being olives. This recipe combines sun-dried tomatoes with olives to still get the taste of olives but with a delicious low-fat complement.

2 cups hot water
1 cup sun-dried tomatoes
 (not packed in oil)
¼ cup fresh parsley
Approximately 14 Kalamata
 olives, pitted

2 anchovy fillets or
 1 tbsp. olive oil
1 tsp. fresh oregano or ¼ tsp.
 dry oregano
1 tsp. fresh basil or ¼ tsp. basil

In a bowl filled with the hot water, rehydrate the tomatoes for 10-15 minutes or until plumped. Drain well.

Process the parsley until minced. Add the remainder of the ingredients and pulse several times to blend. Makes about 1 cup.

Serving suggestion: This is delicious as a spread on sandwiches, minibagels, crouton triangles, fresh pita bread, or Spice-of-Life Chips (see index).

Per 2 tbsp.: Calories—70; Saturated fat—0 g.; Total fat—4 g.; Carbohydrates— 5 g.; Cholesterol—10 mg.; Sodium—625 mg.; Fiber—1 g.; Protein—4 g.

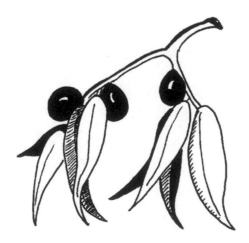

LENTIL PATE

This could be a substitute for chopped liver. If you want a little of the taste but not all the cholesterol, add two broiled livers to the lentils and process together.

2 tsp. oil
1 large onion, chopped
½ lb. mushrooms, chopped
1 carrot, chopped
1 bay leaf
2 tbsp. chopped garlic

½ tsp. dry basil
½ tsp. dry thyme
¼ tsp. black pepper
2 cups vegetable broth or water
½ cup dry red lentils

In a nonstick skillet, heat the oil over medium-high heat. Sauté the onion, mushrooms, carrot, bay leaf, garlic, basil, thyme, and black pepper for approximately 7 minutes or until the vegetables are soft and the onions are brown. Add the broth.

Rinse the lentils and add to the skillet. Bring to a boil; reduce heat to low. Cover partially and simmer, skimming any foam. Cook for 35-45 minutes until the lentils soften.

Discard the bay leaf. Transfer all to a food processor, and process until smooth. Transfer to a serving bowl and chill. Makes about 1¼ cups.

Serving suggestion: Serve with crackers, pumpernickel bread, or pita chips or use as a filler for pita bread.

Variation: Substitute 1 cup dry white wine for 1 cup of the water, or add a pinch of allspice and cinnamon.

Per ¼ cup serving: Calories—56; Saturated fat—0 g.; Total fat—1 g.; Carbohydrates—9 g.; Cholesterol—0 mg.; Sodium—5 mg.; Fiber—1 g.; Protein—3 g.

SPICE-OF-LIFE CHIPS

*Flavored pita chips are fun for buffets but also great for kids' snacks.
I try to flavor the chips according to the spices of different countries.
The measurements for the spice toppings are approximate.
Add more or less, according to taste.*

Easy preparation: Use kitchen shears to cut each pita into eighths. The double triangles easily pull apart. You will have 16 triangles from each pita. Spread the triangles out on a baking sheet, rough side up. Spray the tops with olive-oil cooking spray, sprinkle with your choice of topping, and bake at 350 degrees for 10-12 minutes. Try several different types of toppings on each cooking sheet.

TOPPINGS (PER 1 PITA)

American deli style: Combine 2 tsp. each dry dill and caraway seeds.

Israeli: Sprinkle 4 tsp. zataar (a blend of sesame seeds, thyme, sassafras, and other spices available at Middle Eastern food markets) or dry thyme and ¼ tsp. allspice.

Turkish: With pastry brush, brush lightly with lemon juice. Sprinkle 2 tsp. each dry parsley and dill.

Yemenite: Combine 2 tsp. garlic powder, 1 tsp. ground coriander, and ½ tsp. ground cardamom.

American Southwest: Brush the pita wedges lightly with lime juice. Sprinkle with 4 tsp. chili powder.

Armenian: Combine 1 tbsp. fennel seeds, 1 tbsp. sesame seeds, 1 tbsp. dry Parmesan cheese, and ½ tsp. garlic powder.

Italian: Combine 1 tsp. dry oregano, 1 tsp. dry basil, and ½ tsp. dry parsley or mixed Italian herbs with dry parsley.

Per chip without toppings: Calories—14; Saturated fat—0 g.; Total fat—0 g.; Carbohydrates—14 g.; Cholesterol—0 mg.; Sodium—13 mg.; Fiber—0 g.; Protein—0 g.

Note: Most toppings will not add significant calories or fat, the exceptions being Parmesan cheese and sesame seeds.

Salads

MIXED GREEN SALAD
WITH HONEY-MUSTARD DRESSING

PAREVE
SHABBAT
SIMCHAT TORAH
PURIM
PASSOVER

*This contemporary salad especially suits the springtime holidays.
It's appropriate for Purim because of the poppy seeds.
Add asparagus and you have a luscious salad for Passover.*

HONEY-MUSTARD DRESSING

½ cup low-fat mayonnaise
¼ cup white-wine vinegar
2 tsp. poppy seeds
1½ tsp. olive oil (optional)

4 tbsp. mustard or
  Passover mustard
3 tbsp. honey

SALAD

10 cups salad greens, such as
  spinach, watercress, arugula,
  and romaine lettuce
1 tbsp. chopped fresh dill
1 tbsp. chopped fresh mint
1 cup small cherry tomatoes,
  whole or halved

¼ cup sliced black olives
Approximately 12 oz. fresh thin
  asparagus spears, in season,
  ends snapped off, steamed

Whisk all dressing ingredients together. Refrigerate until ready to serve.
Combine the salad greens and herbs.
Either toss with the tomatoes, olives, and asparagus, or divide the lettuce among 8 plates and top with the vegetables.
Drizzle the dressing over the salad, or pass around. Serves 8.

*Calories—132; Saturated fat—0 g.; Total fat—5 g.; Carbohydrates—19 g.;
Cholesterol—0 mg.; Sodium—396 mg.; Fiber—1 g.; Protein—4 g.*

ZAHAVA'S MARINATED-VEGETABLE SALAD

PAREVE
SHABBAT
ANY HOLIDAY

Zahava Koll likes to make this for Shabbat. It's actually a healthy classic for any meal. Originally, the dressing had ½ cup sugar, 4 tbsp. mustard, 4 tbsp. fresh chopped tarragon, and 2 tbsp. oil. In reducing the sugar I also reduced the mustard and tarragon.

MARINADE

⅓ cup white-wine vinegar
¼ cup apple-juice concentrate
2 tbsp. water
2 tbsp. yellow mustard

2 tbsp. fresh tarragon
1 tbsp. oil
½ tsp. garlic powder

VEGETABLES

1 cup cauliflower florets
1 cup broccoli florets
1 cup green, red, and yellow
    bell pepper strips
1 cup mushrooms

1 cup sliced zucchini
1 cup cherry tomatoes
1 cup sliced celery
¼ cup sliced scallions

Mix all marinade ingredients and set aside.

Cut the vegetables in different shapes and sizes. Pour the marinade over the vegetables. Refrigerate overnight. Serves 16.

Calories—57; Saturated fat—0 g.; Total fat—2 g.; Carbohydrates—7 g.; Cholesterol—0 mg.; Sodium—76 mg.; Fiber—1 g.; Protein—76 g.

MEDITERRANEAN BROCCOLI SALAD

PAREVE

TU BISHEVAT

This contemporary salad is simple, refreshing, and delicious.

SALAD

1½ lb. small broccoli florets, steamed and cooled

1½ cups cooked or canned chickpeas or white beans

9-oz. pkg. frozen artichoke hearts, thawed and halved, or 1 can water-packed artichokes, drained and halved

12 cherry tomatoes, halved and seeded

½ cup red pepper, seeded and diced

¼ cup chopped red onion

2 tbsp. fresh chopped basil

Black pepper to taste

VINAIGRETTE

⅓ cup balsamic vinegar

1 tsp. honey

1 tsp. Dijon mustard

In a serving bowl, combine all the salad ingredients.

Combine all the vinaigrette ingredients and toss with salad. Serve chilled. Serves 6.

Variation: Omit the vinaigrette and toss the salad with the Tahini Dressing recipe.

Calories—154; Saturated fat—0 g.; Total fat—2 g.; Carbohydrates—25 g.; Cholesterol—0 mg.; Sodium—183 mg.; Fiber—3 g.; Protein—9 g.

CARROT-BEET SALAD "BI TAHINI"

PAREVE
SHABBAT
ROSH HASHANAH

This holiday salad can be doubled or tripled for a crowd.
The dressing can easily go with a lettuce salad as well.

2 cups spinach leaves, washed
3 carrots, grated
2 beets, scrubbed, trimmed,
   and grated

1 cucumber, peeled, seeded,
   and diced
2 stalks celery, sliced
2-3 scallions, thinly sliced

TAHINI DRESSING

3 tbsp. tahini
4 tbsp. low-fat mayonnaise
3 tbsp. lemon juice
2 tbsp. water

1 garlic clove, crushed
1 tbsp. chopped parsley
¼ tsp. paprika
¼ tsp. salt

Either on a platter or on individual plates, lay out the spinach leaves. Arrange the carrots, beets and cucumber side by side on the spinach.

Sprinkle the celery and scallions on top.

In a bowl, stir all the dressing ingredients together until well mixed.

Pass around the dressing or spoon it over the salad on a platter. Serves 4-6.

Calories—197; Saturated fat—1 g.; Total fat—6 g.; Carbohydrates—29 g.; Cholesterol—0 mg.; Sodium—479 mg.; Fiber—4 g.; Protein—6 g.

GREEK SALAD

DAIRY/PAREVE
SUKKOT
TU BISHEVAT
PASSOVER

This is normally a very high calorie salad. It is just as good without the feta cheese—and then it goes with any dairy or meat meal.

1 large cucumber, peeled, halved, seeded, and diced
5 small plum tomatoes, diced, or 2 cups cherry tomatoes
2 yellow peppers or 1 yellow and 1 green pepper, thinly sliced
2 cups thinly sliced green cabbage leaves

¼ cup chopped red onion
4 Kalamata olives, thinly sliced
⅓ cup crumbled feta cheese (optional)
2 tbsp. chopped parsley
Olive-oil spray or 1 tsp. extravirgin olive oil

VINAIGRETTE

¼ cup red-wine vinegar
1 tbsp. lemon juice
1½ tsp. dry oregano

½ tsp. basil
½ tsp. thyme

In a bowl, combine the cucumber, tomatoes, peppers, cabbage, red onions, olives, cheese, and parsley. Spray the salad with olive-oil spray to coat the vegetables lightly. Toss and spray again briefly.

Whisk the vinaigrette ingredients and pour over the vegetables. Marinate a couple of hours to blend the flavors. Serves 4.

Variation: For extra nutrition, extend the feta by mashing it with ⅓ cup light tofu and adding it to the vinaigrette.

With feta cheese: Calories—98; Saturated fat—1 g.; Total fat—4 g. (34 percent of calories); Carbohydrates—11 g.; Cholesterol—13 mg.; Sodium—289 mg.; Fiber—1g.; Protein—4 g.

Without feta cheese: Calories—65; Saturated fat—0 g.; Total fat—2 g.; Carbohydrates—10 g.; Cholesterol—0 mg.; Sodium—132 mg.; Fiber—1 g.; Protein—2 g.

RUSSIAN SWEET AND SOUR ZUCCHINI SALAD

PAREVE
SHABBAT
PASSOVER
YOM HAATZMA'UT
LAG B'OMER

This light-tasting salad is good for a summer side dish.
It's sweet and sour, but there's no sugar in it.

1 sweet Walla Walla or
  Vidalia onion, chopped
Cooking spray
2 large zucchinis (about 2 lb.),
  sliced ½-inch thick
4 tbsp. frozen apple-juice
  concentrate

1 green or red pepper,
  cut into strips
2 medium tomatoes, cut into
  thin wedges
1 tbsp. finely snipped fresh dill
3 tbsp. cider vinegar
½ tsp. salt

In a nonstick skillet, sauté the onions with cooking spray over medim-high heat until lightly golden, 4-5 minutes. Add the zucchini. Cover and steam with 3 tbsp. of the apple-juice concentrate until the zucchini is tender (about 15 minutes), stirring occasionally.

Add the peppers. Steam for another 5 minutes.

Add tomatoes. Steam for approximately 5 minutes. Add the dill, vinegar, salt, and remaining 1 tbsp. apple-juice concentrate.

Transfer to a serving dish and chill before serving, Makes approximately 4 cups.

Calories—47; Saturated fat—0 g.; Total fat—0 g.; Carbohydrates—9 g.; Cholesterol—0 mg.; Sodium—204 mg.; Fiber—1 g.; Protein—2 g.

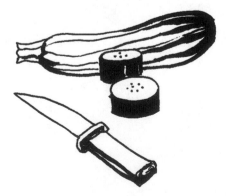

PICNIC POTATO SALAD

PAREVE
SHABBAT
LAG B'OMER

*Potato salad has always been a staple in Jewish cuisine—both Ashkenazic
and Sephardic—because it is an easy, cold dish to serve over Shabbat
when no cooking is allowed.*

6 cups red potatoes, boiled,
   peeled, and cubed
1 celery stalk, sliced
¼ cup nonfat or low-fat Italian
   salad dressing
¼ cup marinated artichokes
⅓ cup low-fat mayonnaise

2 tbsp. white-wine vinegar
¼ cup minced red onions
¼ cup chopped pimientos or
   red bell peppers
1 tbsp. yellow mustard or Dijon
¼ tsp. paprika
¼ tsp. black or white pepper

In a large bowl combine all of the ingredients and stir to mix. Chill overnight.
This will marinate the potatoes and intensify the flavors. Serves 8.

*Calories—168; Saturated fat—0 g.; Total fat—2 g.; Carbohydrates—35 g.;
Cholesterol—0 mg.; Sodium—348 mg.; Fiber—2 g.; Protein—4 g.*

HERBED CUCUMBER-FENNEL SALAD

DAIRY
SHABBAT
YOM KIPPUR BREAK-THE-FAST
PASSOVER
SHAVUOT

*Cucumber salads are especially common with Ashkenazim.
Here's a contemporary twist on a familiar salad.
Fennel is added for extra flavor and texture.*

2 cucumbers, seeded and cubed
8 oz. fennel, cored and chopped
½ cup nonfat plain yogurt or
   low-fat sour cream
Juice of 1 lemon
2 tbsp. fresh dill

2 tbsp. chopped fresh chives
1 tbsp. chopped fresh parsley or
   cilantro
1 tbsp. chopped fresh mint
   (optional)
⅛ tsp. white pepper

Combine the cucumber with remaining ingredients. Cover and chill before serving. Serves 4.

Calories—43; Saturated fat—0 g.; Total fat—0 g.; Carbohydrates—7 g.; Cholesterol—1 mg.; Sodium—75 mg.; Fiber—1 g.; Protein—3 g.

ROMANIAN COLESLAW

PAREVE
*SHABBAT
PURIM
PASSOVER
YOM HAATZMA'UT
LAG B'OMER*

The telltale technique that makes this slaw Romanian is pouring the hot vinegar dressing over the salad and leaving it to marinate. This has been lightened and updated a bit, but it's just as delightful as the traditional version.

1 cup thinly sliced red cabbage
1 cup thinly sliced green cabbage
½ green pepper, cut in strips
½ red pepper, cut in strips

1 medium carrot, grated
1 stalk celery, sliced
½ small onion, thinly sliced

MARINADE

⅓ cup water
½ cup raspberry vinegar or red-wine vinegar
1 tbsp. oil

1 bay leaf
3 peppercorns
2 tbsp. sugar
¾ tsp. salt

In a glass dish, layer the vegetables in order.

In a saucepan, combine marinade ingredients and bring just to a boil. Remove from heat and pour over vegetables. Cover and refrigerate overnight. Mix slaw before serving. Makes about 6 cups.

Variation: In a bowl, combine 4 cups thinly sliced red cabbage; ½ small onion, thinly sliced; 2 medium carrots, grated; and 3 tbsp. minced parsley. Pour the warm marinade over the vegetables and refrigerate, covered, overnight.

Calories—68; Saturated fat—0 g.; Total fat—2 g.; Carbohydrates—11 g.; Cholesterol—0 mg.; Sodium—327 mg.; Fiber—1 g.; Protein—1 g.

COLESLAW WITH LIME AND CILANTRO

DAIRY
CHANUKAH
PURIM
PASSOVER
YOM HAATZMA'UT

Some people don't like the sweet and sour combination that is common in Jewish coleslaws. This unique slaw has no sugar and no oil and is very refreshing . . . a contemporary combination!

1 cup thinly sliced fennel (washed and tough leaves removed) (optional)

2 cups coarsely grated cabbage

1 cup grated carrots

¼ cup lime juice

2 green onions, sliced

1-2 tbsp. minced cilantro

1 tsp. chopped fresh mint or ¼ tsp. dry mint

⅓ cup low-fat mayonnaise

3 tbsp. nonfat plain yogurt

In a bowl, mix all ingredients thoroughly. Serves 4.

Variations:

- Omit the fennel and add another cup of grated cabbage.

- To make this even easier, use 4 cups prepared mixed cabbage or broccoli slaw in a bag. For a different taste, omit the cilantro and add 2 tbsp. minced parsley or any fresh herb.

Calories—68; Saturated fat—0 g.; Total fat—2 g.; Carbohydrates—12 g.; Cholesterol—0 mg.; Sodium—184 mg.; Fiber—1 g.; Protein—1 g.

FRUIT 'N' CARROT SALAD

PAREVE
SIMCHAT TORAH
PASSOVER
SHAVUOT

Carrot salads are popular in North Africa and Israel. This is a contemporary salad using dried cranberries as a departure from the more typical raisins.

1 lb. carrots, grated
½ cup dried cranberries
½ tsp. cumin seeds, or more
   to taste
¼ cup orange juice

1 apple, peeled and grated
2 tbsp. red-wine vinegar
2 tbsp. parsley
Dash cinnamon (optional)

Place the carrots, cranberries, cumin seeds, and orange juice in a pot. Bring to a boil. Reduce heat to medium and simmer for 3 minutes. Remove from heat and add the apple, red-wine vinegar, parsley, and cinnamon. Chill. Serves 4.

Calories—71; Saturated fat—0 g.; Total fat—0 g.; Carbohydrates—15 g.; Cholesterol—0 mg.; Sodium—44 mg.; Fiber—1 g.; Protein—2 g.

AVOCADO-GRAPEFRUIT SALAD

PAREVE
ROSH HASHANAH
SUKKOT

This salad features fruits popular in Israel. In the fall, Florida avocados are on the market. They contain 50 percent less fat than their California cousins. Their season is September to October, just in time for the holidays. Pomegranates are also in season at that time.

6 cups torn red-leaf lettuce or
   baby spinach leaves
2 large grapefruits, peeled,
   sectioned, membranes
   removed, and sliced in half
1½ cups mandarin orange
   sections, drained

1 large avocado, peeled, pitted,
   and diced
1 pomegranate, sliced in half,
   seeds removed, and seeds and
   juice reserved

DRESSING

¼ cup pomegranate juice,
   or add enough orange juice
   to equal ¼ cup
3 tbsp. lime juice

1 tbsp. honey
2 tsp. canola or extravirgin
   olive oil

Gently mix the lettuce leaves, grapefruits, oranges, and avocado on individual plates.

Combine the dressing ingredients and drizzle over the salads. Sprinkle with pomegranate seeds. Serves 6.

Calories—192; Saturated fat—1 g.; Total fat—4 g.; Carbohydrates—30 g.; Cholesterol—0 mg.; Sodium—15 mg.; Fiber—2 g.; Protein—2 g.

LEMON WALDORF SALAD

DAIRY
TU BISHEVAT
PASSOVER

*This is an old American salad. Some of the ingredients have been changed,
but only for the healthier. Waldorf salad never made it into my family
when I was growing up, but many families have adopted it,
and I thought it would be a great lunch or snack for kids.*

3 heaping cups mixed tart red
   and green apples, peeled
   and diced
1 cup halved red seedless grapes
2 stalks celery, sliced
1 cup finely grated red cabbage

¼ cup raisins
2 tbsp. toasted sliced almonds
1 tbsp. minced fresh ginger or
   ¼ tsp. dry ginger
1 cup nonfat lemon yogurt

In a bowl, mix all the ingredients, stirring in the yogurt at the end. Refrigerate, covered, for approximately 1 hour before serving. Serves. 6.

Variations:

- Omit 1 cup of apple, and add 1 cup seasonal fruit such as cantaloupe, mango, or watermelon.
- Add 2 tbsp. lemon juice and 2 tsp. honey to nonfat plain yogurt.

Calories—94; Saturated fat—0 g.; Total fat—2 g.; Carbohydrates—17 g.; Cholesterol—0 mg.; Sodium—34 mg.; Fiber—1 g.; Protein—2 g.

VEGETABLE-STUFFED TOMATOES

This was inspired by a Moroccan salad, for which the tomatoes were actually made into little baskets. If you have the time or artistic desire, making baskets out of the tomatoes would make these extraspecial, but they are also attractive and delicious served as instructed here. The best part of all is that this is really easy and doesn't need measuring of seasonings.

8 very small salad tomatoes
8 oz. cooked fresh or
   low-sodium canned diced beets
1 cup diced baby carrots
½ cup peeled and diced jicama

½ cup sliced green olives
Dash lemon juice
Dash cinnamon
Dash cumin
8 sprigs parsley

Cut open a circle on the top of each tomato and lift off. Scoop out the insides of the tomatoes to leave shells.

In a bowl, mix the remaining ingredients except the parsley, adding the seasonings to your taste.

Spoon the mixture into the tomatoes.

Garnish each tomato with a parsley sprig standing up in the salad—either in the middle or to the side of the salad. Serves 8.

Serving suggestion: This is a colorful, decorative accompaniment to gefilte fish as an appetizer, or can be served as a side dish.

Calories—49; Saturated fat—0 g.; Total fat—1 g.; Carbohydrates—8 g.; Cholesterol—0 mg.; Sodium—228 mg.; Fiber—1 g.; Protein—1 g.

BARRIA BRUSCA

PAREVE
SHABBAT
SUKKOT

This is delightful for a buffet. It is, Alisa Benabu says, a purely Italian recipe,
with anchovies in it. Alisa did not tell me how much oregano to add—
I'm sure it's to taste. I have added sweet basil at times,
and it's equally delicious! This is also good for Shabbat afternoon lunch.

1 lb. pasta or 2 cups cooked
    white rice
Olive-oil cooking spray
2 onions, chopped
4 garlic cloves, chopped
2 celery stalks, chopped
2 anchovy slices

28-oz. can crushed no-salt-added
    tomatoes
Water to fill the can
Salt and pepper to taste
8-10 leaves chopped fresh
    oregano, or to taste

Cook the pasta according to package directions.

Transfer to a bowl. Spray briefly with olive-oil spray to prevent stickiness. Chill.

Meanwhile, coat a nonstick skillet with cooking spray and sauté onions, garlic, and celery until the onion becomes transparent (about 5 minutes). Add the anchovies and stir with a wooden spoon until the anchovies dissolve.

Add the tomatoes, water, salt, pepper, and oregano. Simmer over low heat for 30 minutes. Cool.

Transfer sauce to a blender or food processor and puree. Serve sauce with the chilled pasta—the Italian way. Serves 8.

Calories—273; Saturated fat—1 g.; Total fat—3 g.; Carbohydrates—48 g.; Cholesterol—51 mg.; Sodium—640 mg.; Fiber—3 g.; Protein—13 g.

ITALIAN PESTO SAUCE WITH PASTA

DAIRY
SHABBAT
PASSOVER

This is so easy and tasty that you don't miss all of the oil, and you could even omit the pine nuts. This would be a very nice vegetarian Shabbat dish. For Passover you can serve this over steamed spaghetti squash.

12 oz. fusilli pasta
1 medium tomato, coarsely chopped
1 small red onion, coarsely chopped
2 tsp. chopped garlic
1 cup fresh basil leaves

1 cup spinach leaves
¼ cup Parmesan cheese
1 tbsp. olive oil
2 tbsp. water
¼ tsp. salt
¼ tsp. black pepper
2½ tbsp. toasted pine nuts

In a pot of boiling water, cook the pasta according to package directions.

Meanwhile, place the tomato, onion, and garlic in a food processor or blender and process until minced. Add the basil and spinach leaves, Parmesan cheese, olive oil, water, salt, pepper, and pine nuts. Pulse until smooth.

Toss with the pasta, or spoon over hot pasta. Serves 6.

Calories—282; Saturated fat—1 g.; Total fat—6 g.; Carbohydrates—46 g.; Cholesterol—3 mg.; Sodium—274 mg.; Fiber—1 g.; Protein—10 g.

PASTA SALAD COL D'VAR

DAIRY
SHABBAT
YOM KIPPUR BREAK-THE-FAST
TU BISHEVAT
SHAVUOT

Col d'var is Hebrew for "everything." This pasta salad is gentle on the stomach for breaking the Yom Kippur fast. Add tofu or seitan for a complete meal. (Seitan is a meatlike texturized soy product made in blocks like tofu. It comes in plain, beef, or chicken flavors and is available at whole-foods grocery stores.)

SALAD

3 cups corkscrew pasta
1 cup peeled, sliced jicama or water chestnuts
2 oranges, peeled and sectioned
1 cup mango, papaya, or pineapple chunks, peeled and seeded

1 medium red bell pepper, seeded and thinly sliced
½ cup chopped red onion
4 cups baby spinach or mixed greens, loosely packed
1 cup firm tofu or chicken-flavored seitan cubes (optional)

DRESSING

6-oz. can frozen orange-juice concentrate, thawed

¼ cup low-fat mayonnaise
½ cup nonfat plain yogurt

Bring a large pot of water to a boil over high heat. Cook the pasta according to package directions until the pasta is tender.

Drain the pasta and rinse in cool water. Transfer to a large bowl and stir in the jicama, fruit, red bell pepper, onion, spinach leaves, and tofu or seitan, if desired.

Mix dressing ingredients well and toss with pasta salad. Serves 10 as a side dish, 5 as an entree salad.

As a side dish: Calories—186; Saturated fat—0 g.; Total fat—1 g.; Carbohydrates—38 g.; Cholesterol—0 mg.; Sodium—75 mg.; Fiber—1 g.; Protein—6 g.

As an entree: Calories—373; Saturated fat—0 g.; Total fat—2 g.; Carbohydrates—76 g.; Cholesterol—0 mg.; Sodium—150 mg.; Fiber—1 g.; Protein—12 g.

TUNISIAN PASTA WITH TUNA

PAREVE
TU BISHEVAT

Unlike Americans, Israelis eat their lunches as they walk.
Readymade Tunisian tuna sandwiches are on virtually every corner in Israel.
Here is a pasta salad similar in flavor to this Tunisian specialty
for people who like to sit while they eat.

10 oz. pasta shells or penne
2 6½-oz. cans water-packed tuna,
  drained
12 oz. cherry tomatoes, halved
½ cup diced jarred roasted
  peppers
¾ tsp. cumin or coriander
  (optional)
¼ cup capers, rinsed and drained

1 garlic clove, minced
3 tbsp. lemon juice or
  red-wine vinegar
1 tsp. hot sauce, or to taste
1 tsp. olive oil
2 tbsp. cilantro (optional)
⅓ cup chopped scallions or
  red onions

In a pot, boil the noodles according to package directions until tender.
Meanwhile, in a bowl, combine the remaining ingredients.
Drain the pasta. Run cold water over it to cool. Drain again, well.
Transfer to a serving bowl and toss with the tuna mixture to coat pasta. This is best served at room temperature. Serves 5-6.

Calories—275; Saturated fat—0 g.; Total fat—2 g.; Carbohydrates—40 g.;
Cholesterol—10 mg.; Sodium—180 mg.; Fiber—1 g.; Protein—24 g.

SESAME NOODLES

MEAT/PAREVE
SHABBAT

Although there is no Asian influence on Jewish cuisine, Ashkenazic Jews have
an affinity for Chinese and other Asian food. These noodles are easy to make
on a Friday afternoon for Shabbat lunch the next day or shalosh seudot,
as they are served cold or at room temperature.

Water
2 tbsp. sesame seeds
Cooking spray (Oriental flavored
   is nice)
2 tsp. chopped garlic
1½ cups thinly sliced napa
   cabbage
2½ tbsp. reduced-fat
   peanut butter
4 tsp. hot pepper sauce or
   ½ tsp. crushed red pepper

½ cup chicken broth or chicken-
   flavored pareve bouillon
¼ cup sodium-reduced soy sauce
¼ cup brown-rice vinegar or
   rice-wine vinegar
12 oz. thin yolk-free egg noodles
   or Oriental noodles
1½ cups bean sprouts
½ cup chopped scallions,
   green and white parts
¼ cup chopped cilantro

Boil water for the noodles.

Meanwhile, toast the sesame seeds in a dry nonstick skillet until lightly browned. Remove and set aside.

Coat the same skillet with the cooking spray and sauté the garlic for 2 minutes.

Add the cabbage slices and cook another 30 seconds. Remove from the heat and add the peanut butter, hot sauce, broth, soy sauce, and vinegar.

Add the noodles to the water and cook them according to package directions.

Drain the cooked noodles and place them in a serving bowl. Stir in the cabbage mixture. Toss with the bean sprouts and sesame seeds. Top each serving with both scallions and cilantro. Serves 8.

Variation: For added protein, add 1 lb. sautéed boneless chicken-breast strips or cubed tofu.

Calories—204; Saturated fat—1 g.; Total fat—4 g.; Carbohydrates—34 g.; Cholesterol—40 mg.; Sodium—310 mg.; Fiber—1 g.; Protein—8 g.

ORZO SALAD

DAIRY
PURIM

Orzo is a rice-shaped pasta. Here is a way of serving it cold in a salad.

VINAIGRETTE

¼ cup red-wine vinegar or
   balsamic vinegar
1 tbsp. lemon juice

1 tbsp. olive oil (optional)
1 garlic clove, crushed, or
   ½ tsp. garlic powder

SALAD

1 cup uncooked orzo
1 cup diced tomato
⅓ cup finely diced red onion
½ cup diced yellow bell pepper

3 tbsp. minced parsley
¼ cup minced fresh basil
⅓ cup crumbled feta cheese

In a bowl, whisk all vinaigrette ingredients together. Set aside.

In a saucepan, cook the orzo in boiling water for 8-10 minutes just until tender. Drain and rinse under cool water.

Transfer the orzo to a serving bowl and toss with remaining salad ingredients. Stir in the vinaigrette. Cover and chill before serving, although it is just as tasty at room temperature. Serves 6-8.

Variations:

- Substitute bottled fat-free or reduced-fat Italian dressing for the vinaigrette.

- Omit the bell peppers and add steamed and cooled broccoli florets.

Calories—138; Saturated fat—1g.; Total fat—3 g.; Carbohydrates—22 g.; Cholesterol—5 mg.; Sodium—70 mg.; Fiber—0 g.; Protein—4 g.

Breads

ETTA CHAYA'S BACK-TO-NATURE
EGGLESS CHALLAH

PAREVE
SHABBAT
ROSH HASHANAH
SUKKOT
TU BISHEVAT
SHAVUOT

This is not your bubbe's challah, but it's very tasty. Etta Chaya says:
no substitutes for the millet. It really makes the challah. Here's a hint.
To keep the crust crispy, cool the challah on a wire rack for 10-15 minutes,
then wrap it in a towel until it is completely cool. If a softer crust is desired,
let it cool on a wire rack without a covering.

YEAST MIXTURE

2 pkg. active dry yeast
½ cup medium-warm water
   (110-15 degrees)

Pinch of sugar

BREAD

7 cups flour
1 cup oatmeal
½ cup finely ground millet
1 cup unsweetened applesauce
¼ cup wheat germ

¼ cup oil
¾ cup honey (or brown-rice
   syrup)
2 tsp. salt
2 tbsp. wheat gluten (optional)

TOPPING

1 tbsp. water
1½ tbsp. honey

Sesame seeds
Poppy seeds

In a bowl, add the yeast to the warm water. Mix in the sugar and stir to blend.
When the yeast becomes frothy, it will be ready.

In a bowl, combine all the bread ingredients. Blend in the yeast mixture and
knead together until it forms a smooth dough.

Punch down, cover, and let it rise in a draft-free place for approximately 1 hour
or until the dough doubles in volume.

Punch down several times and break the dough into 2 halves to make 2 medium
loaves (or 4 smaller loaves). Divide each half into 3 parts.

Make 3 thick ropes for each loaf, about 18 inches long. Pinch the ends together on one end, and braid, tucking the finished end under. Place on a greased baking sheet.

Let the loaves rise again, covered, in a draft-free place for 20 minutes.

Mix the water and honey. Drizzle or brush over the challahs, and sprinkle sesame or poppy seeds on top.

Bake at 350 degrees on the center oven rack for approximately 35-45 minutes or until the bread is golden brown and the bottom sounds hollow when thumped. Makes 2 loaves, 20 slices each.

Variations:

- For a different twist, bake the challah loaves on top of a single layer of raw Spanish-onion slices on the greased baking sheet. It's really delicious.
- Replace 2 cups of the flour with whole-wheat pastry flour.
- Omit ¼ cup white flour and replace with barley flour or flaxseed meal.

Calories—140; Saturated fat—0 g.; Total fat—2 g.; Carbohydrates—27 g.; Cholesterol—0 mg.; Sodium—119 mg.; Fiber—0 g.; Protein—3 g.

BAKED EGGLESS FRENCH TOAST COCHIN STYLE

DAIRY

This rich-tasting dish has very humble beginnings in India. It is referred to as Poor Man's Cake by cookbook author Lilian Cornfeld. Eggs and sugar weren't included because they used to be expensive ingredients saved for special occasions. This is a delicious choice for people with egg intolerance. If you're using homemade challah, you might want thinner slices for better absorption.

3 tbsp. sugar or reduced-calorie maple syrup	**Butter-flavor cooking spray**
1 cup skim milk	**16 slices stale challah, French, or sourdough bread**
1 tsp. cinnamon	**More cinnamon for garnish**

Mix the sugar (or syrup), milk, and cinnamon.

Spray one or two casserole dishes with the butter-flavor cooking spray. Place the bread in a single layer in the casserole(s) and spray the bread with the cooking spray. Pour the liquid mixture over the bread. Sprinkle extra cinnamon on top. Refrigerate for 1 hour.

Bake at 400 degrees for 10 minutes. Turn the slices and bake for 10 more minutes. Serve as you would French toast, with powdered sugar, syrup, or fruit topping. Serves 8.

Calories—175; Saturated fat—0 g.; Total fat—2 g.; Carbohydrates—34 g.; Cholesterol—2 mg.; Sodium—306 mg.; Fiber—0 g.; Protein—6 g.

RUSSIAN RYE CROUTONS

PAREVE OR DAIRY

*Rye flour is a popular basis for Russian and Eastern European bread.
Rye-flavored croutons are easy to make with leftover rye bread.
They're great for salads and soups.*

4 slices rye bread, cut into cubes
Butter-flavor or olive-oil spray

Dry minced garlic
Seasoned salt

Spread the bread cubes on a baking sheet. Spray with butter-flavor or olive-oil spray. Sprinkle on the minced garlic and seasoned salt.

Bake at 375 degrees until lightly toasted (5-8 minutes). Use for salad croutons or with soup. Serves 4.

Variations:

- For Crouton Wedges, quarter the slices into 4 pieces. Follow instructions above.

- For French Croutons, use 4 French bread slices, cut into cubes. Place them on a large baking sheet and coat all sides with any flavored cooking spray. Sprinkle with onion powder, garlic powder, and paprika. Bake at 350 degrees until lightly toasted.

Calories—72; Saturated fat—0 g.; Total fat—1 g.; Carbohydrates—12 g.; Cholesterol—0 mg.; Sodium—315 mg.; Fiber—0 g.; Protein—3 g.

HERBED BREAD

DAIRY/PAREVE
SUKKOT
SHAVUOT

*This is a recipe that I submitted to our local daily newspaper back in 1985.
I had trouble adjusting yeast recipes to our high altitude, so using the frozen bread dough really helped me. This is a good accompaniment to Barria Brusca.*

1 lb. frozen white bread dough
Garlic-flavored cooking spray
¼ cup minced parsley
3 tbsp. chopped dill
3 tbsp. mixture of basil and
oregano

1 garlic clove, minced
2 tbsp. grated Parmesan cheese
(optional)
3 tbsp. reduced-fat feta cheese
(optional)

TOPPING

1 egg white

2 tsp. sesame seeds

Thaw the bread dough according to package instructions. Coat a 9-by-5-inch bread-loaf pan with the garlic cooking spray.

Punch down the dough. Mix all the herbs, garlic, and cheeses on a board, and knead the dough into this mixture until the herbs, garlic, and cheeses are worked into the dough. Form the dough into a ball and place in the loaf pan.

Cover and let rise until double in size or about 45 minutes.

Preheat the oven to 375 degrees. Brush the outside of the bread with the egg white and sprinkle with the sesame seeds. Bake for 30 minutes or until the bread is golden and sounds hollow when tapped. Serves 8-9.

With cheeses: Calories—46; Saturated fat—1 g.; Total fat—2 g.; Carbohydrates—4 g.; Cholesterol—3 mg.; Sodium—105 mg.; Fiber—1 g.; Protein—3 g.

Without cheeses: Calories—32; Saturated fat—0 g.; Total fat— 1 g.; Carbohydrates—4 g.; Cholesterol—0 mg.; Sodium—39 mg.; Fiber—1 g.; Protein—3 g.

VEGETABLE BROTH

PAREVE
ROSH HASHANAH
SUKKOT
PASSOVER

If salt needs to be reduced in your diet, or you are interested in making a better-tasting broth than is found in cans, this will definitely elevate the quality of recipes calling for vegetable broth. This can be frozen in 1-cup increments in freezer bags, layered flat on a tray in your freezer, then stacked. Keep the same measurement in each bag so you always know how much you have.

1 large onion, quartered	**1 tsp. peppercorns**
3 celery stalks, thickly sliced, tops included	**½ bunch parsley**
	1 tsp. dry dill
3 large carrots, thickly sliced	**1 tsp. dry thyme**
1 large red bell pepper, quartered and seeded	**1 bay leaf**
	2 qt. (8 cups) water
2 garlic cloves	

Roughly chop all the vegetables and place in a soup pot. Add the remaining ingredients. Bring to a boil over high heat. Reduce heat to medium low and slowly simmer for 1 hour.

Strain, and adjust the seasonings if desired. Makes 7-8 cups.

Per cup: Calories—23; Saturated fat—0 g.; Total fat—1 g.; Carbohydrates—5 g.; Cholesterol—0 mg.; Sodium—150 mg.; Fiber—1 g.; Protein—1 g.

CHICKEN KASHA SOUP

MEAT/PAREVE
SHABBAT
YOM KIPPUR
CHANUKAH

6 cups defatted chicken broth
3 cups water
½ cup barley
1 small onion, chopped
8 oz. skinless, boneless chicken breast, cut into bite-size pieces
2 carrots, sliced

2 stalks celery, sliced
1 tomato, chopped
½ cup medium-grain kasha
1 cup frozen peas
2 tbsp. chopped fresh parsley or cilantro
Salt and black pepper to taste

In a pot over medium-high heat, bring the broth and water to a boil.

Add the barley and onion. Reduce heat to medium low, cover, and simmer for 30 minutes.

Add the chicken, carrots, celery, tomato, and kasha. Cook, covered, for approximately 30 minutes, or until the vegetables reach desired tenderness.

Add the peas and parsley, and continue to cook, covered, for approximately 4 minutes or until the peas are heated through. Season to taste. Serves 6.

Variations:

- Omit the kasha and add 1 cup cooked chickpeas or 2 cups cubed butternut squash with 3 chopped garlic cloves.

- For a vegetarian soup, substitute vegetable broth for the chicken broth and water, and substitute chicken-flavored seitan cubes for the chicken.

With chicken: Calories—287; Saturated fat—0 g.; Total fat—2 g.; Carbohydrates—50 g.; Cholesterol—22 mg.; Sodium—336 mg.; Fiber—7 g.; Protein—18 g.

FESTIVALS OF LITE

SPRINGTIME CHICKEN SOUP

This is a very flavorful version of chicken soup.

3 lb. bone-in chicken breast
9 cups water
2 stalks celery, sliced
1 large onion, peeled
1 small bunch parsley
4 dill sprigs
½ lb. baby carrots, sliced
   in half lengthwise

2 parsnips, sliced
8-10 slender stalks asparagus,
   ends snapped off and
   stalks sliced
2 medium zucchinis, sliced
¼ cup minced fresh dill
¼ cup sliced green onions

In a soup pot, combine chicken, water, celery, and whole peeled onion. Bring to a boil over high heat and skim the surface when needed. When it no longer needs to be skimmed, add the parsley and dill sprigs. Cover, reduce heat to medium low, and simmer for approximately 2 hours.

Strain the soup, discarding the vegetables and herbs but reserving the chicken. Add the carrots, parsnips, asparagus, zucchinis, fresh dill, and green onions. Simmer for 30 minutes or until the vegetables are tender. Meanwhile, remove chicken from bones, cut up meat into bite-size pieces, and add back to soup. Simmer 5 minutes to rewarm chicken. Serves 8.

Soup with chicken: Calories—278; Saturated fat—1 g.; Total fat—3 g.; Carbohydrates—21 g.; Cholesterol—99 mg.; Sodium—324 mg.; Fiber—3 g.; Protein—43 g.

MOROCCAN COUSCOUS
(Chicken Vegetable Soup)

This soup is for festive times, according to Yaffa Hanouna, who makes it the same way her grandmother did. It is made for such occasions as moving into a new home. This celebrated dish symbolizes richness, as if to say, "May your house always be rich with food. May you have a rich and healthy and happy life in this home." Yaffa says that mezzas (appetizers and salads) are usually served with this meal. This is an example of an age-old recipe but it is really easy to make. The vegetables are just cleaned and placed in the pot until they are soft enough to slice.

3 large onions, chopped
2 tsp. canola oil
4 ripe medium tomatoes
2 lb. chicken breast, skinned
10-15 cups water to cover
   ingredients
1 lb. chickpeas, soaked overnight
5 large carrots, scrubbed and
   sliced in half
1½ lb. small pumpkin or butternut squash, well scrubbed

3 zucchinis, scrubbed
5 medium potatoes, scrubbed
½ bunch celery, sliced in thirds
5 garlic cloves, peeled
1 bunch parsley, chopped
1 bunch cilantro, chopped
4 cubes chicken bouillon
½ tsp. salt
Cooked couscous to serve 15

In a 12-qt. pot, sauté the onions in the oil over medium-high heat until they start to turn golden, about 10 minutes.

Hold a hand grater across the top of the pot, grate 1 tomato into the onions, and mix in. Repeat with the 3 remaining tomatoes. Reduce heat to low and simmer for 10-15 minutes until the mixture looks like a tomato jelly.

Over medium heat, add the chicken and sauté for approximately 10 minutes, stirring often.

Add approximately 2 qt. water or until the pot is quarter-filled. Bring to a boil and let it boil for 3-5 minutes.

Add the chickpeas, halved carrots, the whole pumpkin or squash, zucchinis, potatoes, and celery. Add the garlic, parsley, cilantro, chicken bouillon cubes, and salt. Add the remaining water up to 1-2 inches from the top. Bring the water to a boil. Reduce heat to low, cover, and simmer for 4-6 hours.

Two hours or so into the cooking process, remove the pumpkin or squash and slice in half. Discard the seeds and return to the pot.

When the soup is ready, the vegetables can be sliced. Drain the vegetables, reserving the broth and chicken. Slice the squash into quarters, then slice remaining vegetables into serving-size pieces. Spoon couscous onto a platter and arrange the vegetables attractively around it. To serve, place couscous in individual bowls and top with the vegetables. Ladle the broth and chicken into each bowl. Serves 15.

Calories—523; Saturated fat—1 g.; Total fat—4 g.; Carbohydrates—91 g.; Cholesterol—35 mg.; Sodium—243 mg.; Fiber—4 g.; Protein—31 g.

GOURMET MATZAH BALLS

PAREVE
SHABBAT
ROSH HASHANAH
SUKKOT
PASSOVER

*A staple and tradition in Ashkenazic cuisine, matzah balls today are made
with a variety of flavors added to the matzah meal batter.
This slight twist includes garlic, shallots, and a flavored broth.*

MATZAH BALLS

Olive-oil cooking spray
1½ tsp. minced garlic
1 tbsp. minced shallots
1 egg
4 egg whites

2 tbsp. lemon-lime soda or
   seltzer
¼ cup matzah meal
½ tsp. salt
3 tbsp. minced parsley

FLAVORED BROTH

½ tsp. saffron or turmeric
4 qt. water

1 bay leaf
1 tsp. thyme

In a nonstick skillet sprayed with olive-oil cooking spray, sauté the garlic and shallots over medium-high heat for approximately 2 minutes. Set aside.

In a bowl, combine remaining matzah ball ingredients in the order listed, including the cooked garlic and shallots. Cover and chill in refrigerator for 1 hour.

Dissolve the saffron or turmeric in 4 qt. water; add bay leaf and thyme. Bring to a boil.

With wet hands, shape the matzah mixture into 10 small balls and drop matzah balls into water. Cover and simmer on medium low for 30 minutes. Discard the broth. Makes 10 matzah balls.

Variation: Omit the garlic and shallots. Add 2 tbsp. fresh chopped dill or 2 tsp. dry dill. Omit the seasonings in the broth.

*Calories—57; Saturated fat—0 g.; Total fat—1 g.; Carbohydrates—8 g.;
Cholesterol—13 mg.; Sodium—144 mg.; Fiber—0 g.; Protein—2 g.*

SOUPE A LA GRECQUE

MEAT/PAREVE

This is a simple soup that crosses the borders, being found in both Turkish and Romanian homes, but originated in Greece. It can be a vegetarian or meat soup. Good low-fat choices are 1 lb. boneless chicken-breast pieces or low-fat meatballs. My gracious friend Felicia Herscovici introduced this soup to me.

MEATBALLS

½ lb. extralean ground chicken, turkey, or beef

Thyme
1 egg white

SOUP

Cooking spray
2 parsnips, sliced (optional)
2-3 carrots, grated
1 green pepper, diced
1 red pepper, diced
½ cup minced onion
½ cup raw white rice

Black pepper to taste
7 cups water
Juice of 1 large lemon or
 ¼ cup lemon juice
¼ cup minced parsley
3 dill sprigs
Salt to taste

Mix the meat, thyme, and egg white. Form into 1-inch meatballs. Set aside.

In a large pot that has been coated with the cooking spray, add the meatballs, parsnips and carrots. Sauté over medium heat for approximately 3 minutes until the vegetables are soft. Add the green pepper, red pepper, and onion, and continue to sauté for another 3-5 minutes.

Add rice, pepper, and water to cover. Cover and simmer over medium-low heat until vegetables are tender and rice is cooked, about 20 minutes.

Before serving, add the lemon juice, parsley, dill, and salt. Adjust seasonings to taste. Serves 6-8.

With chicken meatballs: Calories—134; Saturated fat—0 g.; Total fat—1 g.; Carbohydrates—22 g.; Cholesterol—21 mg.; Sodium—46 mg.; Fiber—1 g.; Protein—9 g.

Without meatballs: Calories—94; Saturated fat—0 g.; Total fat—0 g.; Carbohydrates—21 g.; Cholesterol—0 mg.; Sodium—14 mg.; Fiber—1 g.; Protein—2 g.

ASHKENAZIC SPLIT-PEA SOUP

PAREVE
SUKKOT
CHANUKAH

This soup is very popular at Israeli lunch stops. It's economical and pareve. While I was in Jerusalem on a cool December day, I came across a small vegetarian soup and salad restaurant. The pea soup was very comforting and warming. The serving size here is for a first course; for a main dish serving 6-8, double the recipe.

Cooking spray
1 large onion, chopped
1 tsp. chopped garlic
1 carrot, diced
2 stalks celery, diced

2 small potatoes, diced
3 tbsp. barley
1 cup (8 oz.) dried split peas
6½ cups water
½ tsp. salt

Coat the bottom of a soup pot with the cooking spray. Over medium heat, cook the onions, garlic, carrot, and celery for 6-7 minutes, stirring often. Add the remaining ingredients. Cover and simmer over low heat for approximately 1½ hours or until all ingredients are tender.

Transfer the soup to a blender or food processor, and puree. Return to the pot. Adjust the salt if desired. Serves 6.

Variation: For a Sephardic taste in an Ashkenazic soup, add ½ tsp. cumin and a pinch of cinnamon.

Calories—233; Saturated fat—0 g.; Total fat—1 g.; Carbohydrates—44 g.; Cholesterol—0 mg.; Sodium—471 mg.; Fiber—4 g.; Protein—12 g

ALGERIAN SPLIT-PEA SOUP

PAREVE
SUKKOT
CHANUKAH

The surprise ingredient here is the cabbage. I had never had it this way before, but I really liked it. My sister-in-law Joelle says the noodles are a must to make this Algerian style. Actually, it is quite common for cooked fine noodles to be added to Sephardic soups.

Cooking spray
1 large onion, chopped
1 cup (8 oz.) dried split peas
¾-1 tsp. salt
¼ tsp. white pepper
½ small head of cabbage,
   shredded (about 2 cups)

6 cups water
Heaping cup fine noodles,
   such as tagliatelle, fideo
   cortado, or vermicelli

Coat the bottom of a soup pot with cooking spray. Add the onions and sauté over medium-high heat for approximately 5-6 minutes.

Add the remaining ingredients except the noodles. Cover and cook on medium low about 1½ hours until all ingredients are tender. When almost done, boil the noodles in a separate pot until tender and drain.

In a food processor, puree about ¾ of the soup, then return it to the pot, add the noodles, and heat through. Serves 5.

Calories—196; Saturated fat—0 g.; Total fat—1 g.; Carbohydrates—36 g.; Cholesterol—0 mg.; Sodium—386 g.; Fiber—2 g.; Protein—12 g.

ALGERIAN LENTIL VEGETABLE SOUP

PAREVE
SHABBAT
CHANUKAH

Lentil soup is found throughout the Mediterranean region. Use red lentils, available in natural-food stores or Middle Eastern food markets, since they are common in North African cuisine. Red lentils are thinner than the brown variety and cook a lot faster.

Cooking spray
1 onion, chopped
2 celery stalks, sliced
2 medium carrots, shredded
6 cups water
1 cup red lentils, rinsed
1½ cups sliced mushrooms (4 oz.)

2 Roma tomatoes, chopped, or
   8-oz. can tomato sauce
¼ cup chopped parsley
1 tsp. paprika
1 tsp. turmeric
Salt to taste

Coat a 6-qt. saucepan or soup pot with the cooking spray. Over medium-high heat, sauté the onion, celery, and carrots for 3-5 minutes.

Add the remaining ingredients and bring to a boil. Reduce heat. Cover and simmer on low for approximately 40 minutes. Serves 6.

Variations:

- Italian flavor—omit the paprika and turmeric.

- Brown Lentil Soup—sauté the onion, celery, and carrots as directed. Add 6 cups water and 1 cup brown lentils. Simmer the brown lentils in water for 1 hour. Add the remaining ingredients. Bring to a boil, reduce heat, cover, and simmer for 20-25 minutes.

Calories—251; Saturated fat—0 g.; Total fat—1 g.; Carbohydrates—44 g.; Cholesterol—0 mg.; Sodium—336 mg.; Fiber—6 g.; Protein—15 g.

VEGETARIAN MOROCCAN HARIRA SOUP

PAREVE
SHABBAT
SUKKOT

My dear Moroccan friend Marcelle Morgan introduced this new taste to me. I had to watch her make the soup and try to measure her ingredients before they went into the pot. It was worth it. This is a low-fat version.

1 cup lentils
1 large onion, chopped
1½ tsp. olive oil
6 cups water
1½ cups canned chickpeas, drained, or ½ cup dried chickpeas soaked overnight
3 tbsp. rice or 2 oz. vermicelli noodles

15-oz. can diced tomatoes
1 tsp. turmeric
1 tsp. paprika
½ tsp. salt
¼ tsp. black pepper
⅓ cup loosely packed cilantro or parsley
Juice of 1 whole lemon or ¼ cup lemon juice

Rinse the lentils with cold water. Drain.

In a soup pot over medium-high heat, sauté the onion in olive oil 4-5 minutes or until translucent. Add the lentils and water. Cover and simmer over medium low for approximately 45 minutes.

Add the chickpeas, rice or noodles, tomatoes, turmeric, paprika, salt, and pepper.

Cover and simmer for 45 minutes.

In a food processor, coarsely puree the soup with the cilantro and return to pot. Add the lemon juice. Simmer, covered, about 10 minutes more. Adjust seasonings if desired. Serves 4-6.

Variation: Add 2 sliced carrots to the sautéing onion.

Calories—303; Saturated fat—0 g.; Total fat—3 g.; Carbohydrates—52 g.; Cholesterol—0 mg.; Sodium—490 mg.; Fiber—4 g.; Protein—17 g.

Note: To use raw chickpeas, soak ½ cup overnight. After sautéing the onion, add the chickpeas with water first and simmer for 2 hours. Add the rinsed lentils and continue as directed.

BRAZILIAN BLACK BEAN SOUP

PAREVE
SHABBAT
YOM KIPPUR BEFORE THE FAST
SUKKOT
SIMCHAT TORAH

The cuisine of the Jews of Brazil has been influenced, like that of Jews in other countries, by the native cuisine. Try this or a Balkan version of this soup, as suggested in the variation.

1½ tsp. oil
1 medium yellow onion, chopped
2 tsp. chopped garlic
3 cups cooked or canned black
   beans, drained
4 cups water with ½ Telma
   mushroom-soup cube
15-oz. can chopped tomatoes,
   or 2 large fresh tomatoes,
   chopped

2 tsp. fresh thyme or
   ½ tsp. dried thyme
¼ tsp. salt
¼ tsp. pepper
½ tsp. cumin
½ tsp. liquid smoke (optional)
Parsley for garnish

In a pot, heat the oil over medium-high heat and brown the onions and garlic a few minutes.

Mash the beans with a potato masher and add the remaining ingredients. Simmer on low 20-25 minutes. Serves 6.

Variation: For Sephardic Black Bean Soup with more of a kick, do as the Jews of the Balkan countries do. Add 1 bay leaf; a few peppercorns; ½ small red chili pepper, seeded and chopped; and ½ red bell pepper, chopped, to the simmering process.

Calories—138; Saturated fat—0 g.; Total fat—1 g.; Carbohydrates—24 g.; Cholesterol—0 mg.; Sodium—303 mg.; Fiber—2 g.; Protein—8 g.

VEGETABLE RICE SOUP

PAREVE
SHABBAT
ROSH HASHANAH
YOM KIPPUR BREAK-THE-FAST
SUKKOT

The Mexican Jewish community is known to be close-knit, with a mixture of Ashkenazic and Syrian Jews. Many of the children attend Jewish day school, where both Hebrew and Yiddish are taught. This is similar to a vegetarian Mexican tortilla soup. It would be good with a side of Spice-of-Life Chips.

1 cup uncooked white rice
Cooking spray
¼ cup sliced green onions
1 tsp. chopped garlic
6 cups Vegetable Broth recipe
1 carrot, sliced
1 celery stalk, sliced
1 cup diced tomato
1 zucchini, sliced into half-moons

1 cup cut-up sugar snap peas or green beans
2 tbsp. chopped parsley
1½ tbsp. minced, seeded green chili pepper or to taste
Salt and pepper to taste
¼ tsp. cumin
Juice of 1 lime (optional)

Cook the rice according to directions until tender. Set aside.

Meanwhile, in a medium soup pot coated with cooking spray, sauté the onions and garlic on medium-high heat for 2-3 minutes. Add the broth, carrot, and celery. Cook for 10 minutes.

Add the tomato, zucchini, sugar snap peas, parsley, chili pepper, salt, pepper, cumin, and cooked rice. Simmer on low for 10 minutes.

Squeeze the lime juice into the soup and serve. Serves 6.

Calories—239; Saturated fat—0 g.; Total fat—1 g.; Carbohydrates—50 g.; Cholesterol—0 mg.; Sodium—315 mg.; Fiber—4 g.; Protein—7 g.

ISRAELI TOMATO NOODLE SOUP

MEAT/PAREVE

*My daughter Jennifer, who lives in Israel, introduced me to this easy
and economical soup. She needed recipes like this for her student lifestyle.
This turns out best with a nonstick soup pot. Otherwise, use a nonstick skillet
to sauté the onions and noodles, and transfer to a soup pot.
It is best also with a garden-fresh tomato in the summer.*

**1½ tsp. olive oil
1 onion, minced
1 tsp. chopped garlic
½ cup vermicelli noodles,
   broken into very small pieces
   or crushed**

**1 large tomato, cut into thin
   wedges
3 cups chicken or vegetable broth
½ cup dry white wine (optional)**

In a soup pot, heat the olive oil over medium heat. When the oil is hot, sauté the onions and garlic for 5 minutes. Add the noodles, and continue to sauté for 3-4 minutes more or until the noodles begin to turn a golden brown.

Add the tomato wedges and broth. Bring to a boil over high heat. Reduce heat to low, cover, and simmer for 10 minutes. If using wine, add it now and simmer for another 2 minutes. Serves 4-6.

Variation: For a spicier taste, add a tiny amount of harissa or Harissa Seasoning recipe (see index) to taste.

*Calories—111; Saturated fat—0 g.; Total fat—2 g.; Carbohydrates—19 g.;
Cholesterol—0 mg.; Sodium—39 mg.; Fiber—1 g.; Protein—4 g.*

LUCIE PRENZLAU'S VEGETABLE SOUP

PAREVE
SHABBAT
SUKKOT

Lucie Prenzlau, well known in the Denver Jewish community as a wonderful cook, was born in Hungary. She was kind enough to share her delicious vegetable soup recipe. She says she always receives compliments with this soup. When you taste it, you will see why. The twist to this soup is the addition of oatmeal, which is actually Scottish in origin. I thought I would never see this again, until I became a judge in a chicken soup cook-off at our Jewish Community Center, and one of the contestants had a recipe from her Lithuanian grandmother who added oatmeal to her chicken soup. The seasonings of this soup, basil, dill, and cumin, are all to taste.

1 large onion, diced
2 tsp. olive oil
3 medium carrots, diced
3 stalks celery, diced
1 parsnip, diced
⅓ cup oatmeal
1 tbsp. flour
2 qt. water

1 small potato, diced
½ tsp. basil
¼ tsp. dry dill
¼ tsp. cumin
Salt and black pepper to taste
2½ tbsp. chicken-flavored
 pareve bouillon granules
2 cups frozen peas

In a food processor, chop onion. In a large soup pot, sauté onion in olive oil over medium-high heat for 5 minutes until soft. Add remaining vegetables. Stir in oatmeal and flour.

Add water, potato, spices, and bouillon. Bring to a boil over high heat. Reduce heat to low, cover, and simmer for 30 minutes or until the potatoes are fork tender. Adjust the seasonings if desired.

At the very end, add peas. The soup will heat them through in 1-2 minutes. Serves 4-6.

Variation: Mrs. Prenzlau suggests, as a variation, omitting the carrots and adding 1 small head cauliflower, broken into florets.

Calories—243; Saturated fat—0 g.; Total fat—2 g.; Carbohydrates—47 g.; Cholesterol—0 mg.; Sodium—641 mg.; Fiber—7 g.; Protein—10 g.

VEGETARIAN MUSHROOM BARLEY SOUP

PAREVE/MEAT
SHABBAT
YOM KIPPUR BEFORE THE FAST
SUKKOT
CHANUKAH

*This is a classic Ashkenazic soup. The original version was usually made
with beef stew meat. This is a meatless version.
We always have this around Chanukah with latkes on the side.*

Cooking spray
1 large onion, chopped
2 celery stalks, chopped
3 medium carrots, grated
2½ qt. (10 cups) water
2 pareve mushroom-flavored or
  beef bouillon cubes
1 cup barley

8 oz. sliced mushrooms or
  ¾ cup dried mushrooms
2 tomatoes, chopped, or
  14½-oz. can chopped tomatoes
½ tsp. salt
¼ tsp. thyme
¼ tsp. marjoram
¼ tsp. black pepper

In a soup pot coated with cooking spray, over medium-high heat, sauté the
onions, celery, and carrots for 4-5 minutes. Add the remaining ingredients. Bring
to a boil.

Reduce heat to low and simmer covered for 1 hour and 15 minutes. Serve with
crusty rye or pumpernickel bread. This is really best when made the day before
serving. Serves 6.

*Calories—249; Saturated fat—0 g.; Total fat—1 g.; Carbohydrates—51 g.;
Cholesterol—0 mg.; Sodium—313 mg.; Fiber—4 g.; Protein—7 g.*

SEPHARDIC PORTUGUESE ZUCCHINI SOUP

PAREVE/DAIRY
SHABBAT
PASSOVER

This recipe was handed down to an Italian-Israeli cooking expert, Alisa Benabu, from her mother-in-law, the late Sete Benabu, originally from Gibraltar. This can be a very elegant first course. It is suggested that this be made in advance for company so that the mellow flavors have a chance to meld. The Italian variation below comes from Alisa's Italian background.

2 tsp. olive oil
1 large Spanish onion, chopped
2 romaine lettuce leaves
4-5 cups (approximately 1½ lb.) diced zucchini
1 tsp. salt

¼ tsp. black pepper, or to taste
1-2 garlic cloves
½ tsp. cumin, or to taste
2 tbsp. pareve chicken-flavored bouillon granules
8 cups water

In a soup pot, heat the olive oil over medium-low heat. Add the onion and romaine lettuce and cook, covered, over medium heat for approximately 15 minutes. Do not brown.

Add the zucchini, and continue to cook slowly, uncovered, for 15-20 minutes, stirring frequently.

Add the salt, pepper, garlic and cumin. Add the bouillon and water. Cover and bring to a boil over high heat.

Reduce heat to low and simmer for 15 minutes.

With a slotted spoon, scoop out about ⅔ of the diced zucchini, transfer to a blender or food processor, and puree until smooth. Return the puree to the pot.

This soup is to be served hot, but it is best to make it a day in advance. It's delicious chilled as well. Serves 8.

Variation: For a "very Italian" creamy soup, add a cup of skim milk when processing the zucchini, and serve cold. Add a French Crouton Wedge to each bowl and top with 2 tsp. freshly grated Parmesan cheese.

Pareve version: Calories—49; Saturated fat—0 g.; Total fat—1 g.; Carbohydrates—7 g.; Cholesterol—0 mg.; Sodium—257 mg.; Fiber—1 g.; Protein—2 g.

Dairy version: Calories—55; Saturated fat—0 g.; Total fat—1 g.; Carbohydrates—8 g.; Cholesterol—1 mg.; Sodium—275 mg.; Fiber—1 g.; Protein—3 g.

CREAMY POTATO CHILI SOUP

PAREVE/MEAT
PASSOVER
SHAVUOT
ANY HOLIDAY

*Potato soup is popular in Polish cuisine—usually flavored with a little dill
or parsley. This soup has more of a kick to it. The combination
of chili peppers and tomatoes makes this more of a Mexican-style soup.*

1 tsp. oil
1 tbsp. minced garlic
2 tbsp. chopped mild chili
   peppers
5 cups water
4 tsp. pareve chicken-flavored
   bouillon granules
2 lb. white potatoes, peeled and
   cut into 1-inch cubes

15-oz. can chopped tomatoes,
   drained and juice reserved
½ tsp. dry basil
⅛ tsp. white pepper
1 tbsp. chopped cilantro or
   parsley

In a 6-qt. soup pot, heat the oil over medium-high heat, and sauté the garlic and
chili peppers for 1 minute. Add the water, bouillon, potatoes, tomatoes, basil, and
white pepper, and bring to a boil over high heat. Reduce heat to low/medium low
and simmer for 30 minutes or until the potatoes are tender.

Remove approximately 1½ cups of the potatoes, process or mash until smooth,
and return to the pot, stirring to thicken the soup. Sprinkle in the cilantro and
serve. Serves 6.

Variation: Omit pareve chicken-flavored bouillon granules. Replace 5 cups of
water with 5 cups of chicken broth.

*Calories—188; Saturated fat—0 g.; Total fat—1 g.; Carbohydrates—40 g.;
Cholesterol—0 mg.; Sodium—48 mg.; Fiber—21 g.; Protein—4 g.*

CREAM OF ARTICHOKE SOUP

Artichokes are very popular in Israel. Cream soups are not common in Jewish cuisine, but this is the South American influence that I have found while visiting Israel. This mellow yet rich-tasting soup is delightfully different; cornmeal is the thickening agent. It has a touch of two cuisines: Brazilian and Italian. (Brazil has a large Italian population.) Russian Rye Croutons are suggested to accompany this delicious treat.

2 pkg. (or approximately 12) frozen artichoke hearts, thawed and cut into smaller pieces

3½ cups water or Vegetable Broth

½ cup chopped onion

⅛ tsp. white pepper

1 cup skim milk

2 tbsp. fine cornmeal (grind in coffee grinder a few seconds)

1 tbsp. butter-flavored granules

1½ tbsp. lemon juice

¼ cup grated Parmesan or Gruyere cheese, or a combination

1 tbsp. chopped fresh parsley or chives for garnish

In a pot, place the artichoke hearts in the broth with the onion. Bring to a boil. Reduce heat and simmer for 5 minutes or until the artichokes are tender.

Using a slotted spoon, transfer half the artichokes to a blender. Add the pepper, milk, cornmeal, butter-flavored granules, lemon juice, and cheese to the blender. Blend to a smooth texture.

Return to pot and stir well. Heat through over medium heat for a few minutes until the soup begins to thicken and boil. Add a little more milk if desired for a thinner consistency. Serve hot with parsley and croutons. Serves 4.

Calories—133; Saturated fat—1 g.; Total fat—2 g.; Carbohydrates—22 g.; Cholesterol—5 mg.; Sodium—152 mg.; Fiber—1 g.; Protein—7 g.

COLD APPLE-BEET BORSCHT

PAREVE
SHABBAT
PASSOVER

*Borscht originated in the Ukraine. In fact, borscht is an old Slavic word
meaning beets. There are as many different borscht recipes, old and new,
hot and cold, as there are people who enjoy them. My grandfather
coming from Byelorussia, liked his borscht hot with lots of meat,
and would never eat it with lemon juice—only sour salt (citric acid).
That's a true Russian borscht. The fruit in the borscht recipe that follows
comes from the Scandinavian influence on Russian cuisine.
Originally, this recipe had ½ cup dried fruit. I've substituted fresh apples,
while still playing on the sweet and sour taste for which borscht is famous.*

1 lb. beets, cleaned, stemmed,
and trimmed
5 cups water
1 cup chopped red onion
2 cups peeled chopped
tart green apples
4 tsp. white vinegar

½ tsp. horseradish
1½ tsp. sugar
¼ tsp. salt
⅛ tsp. black pepper
Nonfat plain yogurt or
nonfat sour cream for garnish

Grate the beets. While grating, heat the water to boiling.

Add the beets. Bring back to a boil. Reduce heat. Cover and simmer on medium
low for approximately 20 minutes.

Add the onions and apples and continue to simmer, covered, for another 10-15
minutes.

Scoop out approximately 2 cups of the beet-apple mixture and process until
smooth. Return to the soup. Add the vinegar, horseradish, sugar, salt and pepper.
Adjust the seasonings if desired. Russians like a lot of vinegar in their borscht. Chill.

Serve in shallow bowls with dollops of nonfat plain yogurt or nonfat sour cream.
Serves 4.

*Calories—106; Saturated fat—0 g.; Total fat—0 g.; Carbohydrates—23 g.;
Cholesterol—0 mg.; Sodium—240 mg.; Fiber—1 g.; Protein—3 g.*

CHILLED APPLE SOUP

DAIRY
ROSH HASHANAH
CHANUKAH
PURIM
PASSOVER

Cold soups are common in the Baltic region and Poland. This is an old Polish soup that could be served as a delicious, healthy dessert.

3 lb. apples, peeled, cored, and sliced	1 cup Zinfandel wine
2 cups water	1 cinnamon stick
2 cups orange juice	1 tsp. ground cloves
¼ cup lemon juice	½ cup low-fat sour cream or nonfat plain yogurt

In a medium soup pot, combine the apples, water, juices, wine, cinnamon stick, and cloves. Bring to a boil. Cover and simmer over medium-low heat for 15-20 minutes until the apples are tender.

Remove the apples from the pot and puree in a blender.

Return the pureed apples to the soup. Discard the cinnamon stick, and chill the soup.

Serve with a spoonful of low-fat sour cream in each bowl, or mix the sour cream into the soup before serving. Of course, this is delicious pareve, without the sour cream, as well. Serves 6.

Variation: When you heat wine, the alcohol cooks away. If you like the taste of wine, add it to the soup after the simmering process. The calorie count will be higher, though.

Calories—217; Saturated fat—1 g.; Total fat—2 g.; Carbohydrates—47 g.; Cholesterol—3 mg.; Sodium—24 mg.; Fiber—2 g.; Protein—2 g.

PEACH SOUP

DAIRY
PASSOVER
LAG B'OMER
SHAVUOT

*Cold fruit soups reflect a Scandinavian influence in Russian cuisine.
This is a contemporary version that becomes a very appealing summer soup.
This is just as delicious made several days in advance.*

1½ lb. peaches, peeled and
  cut into chunks
6-oz. can orange-juice
  concentrate
1 cup pineapple juice

1 banana, cut into chunks
  (optional)
1½ cups plain nonfat yogurt
2 tbsp. honey (optional)
1 tsp. vanilla

In a food processor or blender, combine the peaches and orange-juice concentrate and puree. Add the pineapple juice and banana and puree.

Combine the yogurt, honey, and vanilla and blend into the peach mixture. Chill for at least 1 hour before serving. The soup can be kept several days. Serves 6.

Serving suggestion: For a fancy presentation, omit the honey. Heat 6 tsp. raspberry preserves just to melt, and drizzle on top of the soup in each bowl. With a knife, lightly swirl the preserves. Sprinkle a few fresh raspberries onto the center.

Variation: Use only half a banana or omit it.

*Calories—199; Saturated fat—0 g.; Total fat—0 g.; Carbohydrates—44 g.;
Cholesterol—1 mg.; Sodium—45 mg.; Fiber—1 g.; Protein—5 g.*

Fish

SOUTH AFRICAN GEFILTE FISH

PAREVE
SHABBAT
ROSH HASHANAH
YOM KIPPUR BREAK-THE-FAST
PASSOVER

Bernice Tarley shared with me some of her South African Jewish cookbooks. This is a fairly typical recipe from the King David Day School Cookbook *for South African gefilte fish. I modified it slightly to reduce the fat. This fish broth is very flavorful, with a combination of vegetables and herbs.*

COURTBOUILLON

2 qt. water
1 tsp. salt
1 tsp. sugar
¼ tsp. black or white pepper
1 bay leaf
3 carrots

1 parsnip
1 stalk celery, leaves discarded
1-2 sprigs thyme
1-2 sprigs parsley
1 small onion, sliced

GEFILTE FISH

3 lb. mixed fish fillets, such as
  cod, salmon, and whitefish
Cooking spray
1 tsp. oil
1 large onion, chopped
2 tsp. sugar
1½ tsp. salt

¼ tsp. white pepper
½ cup egg substitute
3 tbsp. matzah meal
1 carrot, minced
1 tbsp. ground almonds
  (optional)

Combine all the courtbouillon ingredients in a soup pot and bring to a slow boil to give you time to prepare the gefilte fish.

In a food processor or grinder, process the fish. Transfer to a large bowl. Set aside. Over medium-high heat in a nonstick skillet coated with cooking spray and oil, brown the onion (4-5 minutes). Add to the fish and stir in the remaining ingredients.

With wet hands, form the fish into approximately 25 oval patties. Place carefully into boiling courtbouillon. Reduce heat to medium low. Cover and simmer for approximately 1½ hours. Serve the patties as an appetizer, perhaps garnished with colorful vegetables such as carrots, bell peppers, and pickles. Makes 25 patties.

Calories—54; Saturated fat—0 g.; Total fat—0 g.; Carbohydrates—23 g.; Cholesterol—23 mg.; Sodium—179 mg.; Fiber—0 g.; Protein—10 g.

BAKED SALMON GEFILTE FISH

PAREVE/ DAIRY
SHABBAT
ROSH HASHANAH
PASSOVER

An updated gefilte fish, this is as elegant as they come for an Ashkenazic appetizer. The garnish is already in the loaf. With each slice, three carrot coins are revealed, which are fitting for Rosh Hashanah. Carrot coins symbolize our wishes for a prosperous new year.

3 large carrots, approximately
    9 inches long, peeled
1 small zucchini, coarsely
    chopped
1 small onion, coarsely chopped
3 egg whites
2 tbsp. white horseradish
2½ tsp. dry dill or
    ¼ cup fresh dill

⅛ tsp. black pepper
1¼ lb. fresh salmon fillet chunks
    or 16-oz. can salmon, bones
    and skin removed
1 cup soft bread crumbs or ½
    cup matzah meal (for Passover)
1 cup vegetable broth
Cooking spray

Boil or steam the carrots 15-20 minutes or until tender.

Meanwhile, in a food processor, mince the zucchini and onion. Add the egg whites, horseradish, dill, and pepper, and process until just combined.

Add the salmon, bread crumbs, and vegetable broth, and process until the ingredients are well mixed.

Spray a 9-by-5-inch loaf pan with the cooking spray. Place half of the salmon mixture into the pan. Place the 3 carrots across the top, and top with the remaining salmon mixture.

Bake at 375 degrees for 45 minutes or until the loaf is firm to the touch. Cool.

Turn out onto a platter. Slice and garnish with lemon wedges and parsley sprigs, if desired. Serve with horseradish or Dairy Horseradish Sauce. Serves 12 as an appetizer and 6 as a main course.

Calories—135; Saturated fat—1 g.; Total fat—5 g.; Carbohydrates—10 g.; Cholesterol—32 mg.; Sodium—100 mg.; Fiber—0 g.; Protein—12 g.

Note: This freezes well.

FESTIVALS OF LITE

SALMON IN PHYLLO

DAIRY/PAREVE
CHANUKAH

French inspired from my sister-in-law Joelle Hankin,
this is great for entertaining. It can be easily doubled.

¾-1 cup white wine
2 sprigs fresh rosemary
2 sprigs fresh tarragon
2 sprigs fresh parsley
Pinch salt

Black pepper to taste
2 lemon slices
1 lb. salmon fillets
5 sheets phyllo dough
1 egg

MUSHROOM WHITE SAUCE (OPTIONAL)

½ lb. mushrooms
Olive-oil cooking spray
1 tbsp. margarine (optional)
1½ tbsp. flour

¾ cup milk or soy or rice milk
Salt and pepper
Parsley for garnish (optional)

The night before, or before work, combine the wine, rosemary, tarragon, parsley, salt, black pepper, and lemon slices, and pour them over the salmon. Cover with plastic wrap and refrigerate for at least 4 hours.

Cut the salmon fillets into 10 pieces.

Remove a sheet of phyllo dough. Place a large piece of plastic wrap on top of the remaining phyllo dough. Tear or cut the phyllo sheet in half crosswise. Place one salmon piece on the edge nearest you. Roll the phyllo over the salmon once, fold both sides toward the middle, and continue to roll over blintz style.

Repeat until you use all the salmon.

With a fork, beat the egg and brush the tops of the salmon bundles. Bake at 350 degrees for approximately 25 minutes or until the phyllo turns a light golden brown.

Meanwhile, prepare the sauce. In a food processor, mince the mushrooms.

In a nonstick skillet coated with the cooking spray, sauté the mushrooms over medium-high heat for 8-10 minutes or until much of the moisture has evaporated. Add the margarine and melt. Add the flour and stir until the sauce thickens. Slowly add the milk and stir until the sauce thickens. Add salt and pepper to taste.

To serve, spoon 1 tbsp. of sauce over each salmon bundle. For company, garnish with parsley. Makes 10 appetizers.

Variation: You can serve this with Dairy Horseradish Sauce.

Calories—152; Saturated fat—1 g.; Total fat—6 g.; Carbohydrates—10 g.; Cholesterol—52 mg.; Sodium—88 mg.; Fiber—0 g.; Protein—11 g.

SALMON PIE IN A POTATO SHELL

DAIRY
CHANUKAH
PASSOVER
SHAVUOT

This is a contemporary, American-style quiche.

14¾-oz. can salmon, bones and
    skin removed
1 cup nonfat sour cream or
    yogurt cheese, drained,
    or light tofu, pureed
½ cup grated low-fat cheese,
    such as cheddar, Swiss,
    Muenster, Gruyere, or mixed
½ cup minced onion
⅓ cup skim milk

2 egg whites
2 tbsp. flour
2 tbsp. minced parsley
1 tbsp. lemon juice
2 tsp. dried dill
1 tsp. Worcestershire sauce
1 tsp. mustard
½ tsp. minced garlic
1 recipe Potato Shell

In a food processor or with a potato masher, blend the salmon and sour cream, yogurt cheese, or tofu. Stir in the remaining ingredients, except the Potato Shell, until well blended. Turn into the baked Potato Shell.

Bake at 350 degrees for 40 minutes or until a knife comes out clean when inserted in the center. Serves 8.

Variation: For Passover, substitute matzah cake meal for the flour. Replace the Worcestershire sauce with Passover mustard.

Calories—156; Saturated fat—2 g.; Total fat—6 g.; Carbohydrates—9 g.; Cholesterol—37 mg.; Sodium—398 mg.; Fiber—0 g.; Protein—16 g.

POTATO SHELL

PAREVE
SUKKOT
CHANUKAH
PASSOVER

This is an all-purpose shell for a quiche or any vegetable pie.
Serve a baked filled Potato Shell in place of latkes one night of Chanukah.

Cooking spray
2 cups (1 lb.) grated russet
　potatoes, drained

2 egg whites
5 tbsp. grated onion
½ tsp. salt

Preheat the oven to 400 degrees. Coat the bottom and sides of an 8- or 9-inch square baking dish with cooking spray. Before combining the ingredients, squeeze as much liquid as you can out of the potatoes with your hands.

Mix all the ingredients and press the mixture into the baking dish, building up the sides as well.

Place on the bottom rack of the oven and bake for 20 minutes.

Coat the potato shell with cooking spray. Bake for approximately 20 minutes more. Fill with Salmon Pie filling or filling of your choice. Serves 8.

Calories—31; Saturated fat—0 g.; Total fat—0 g.; Carbohydrates—6 g.; Cholesterol—0 mg.; Sodium—163 mg.; Fiber—1 g.; Protein—2 g.

POACHED HERB SALMON

PAREVE
ANY HOLIDAY

Poaching is really good because it keeps the moisture in. Cooked salmon freezes well, so if there's a good sale and you want it for a holiday or Shabbat instead of gefilte fish, this is easily made in advance. This has a higher percentage of fat because it's salmon. This is beneficial fat, so don't worry . . . enjoy!

2 cups water
1 cup dry white wine
½ cup fresh herbs, combination
　of your choice: basil, parsley,
　dill, tarragon

1 bay leaf
6 peppercorns
1½-2 lb. salmon (4-5 oz. for each
　guest), or halibut, sea bass,
　or tuna

In a deep skillet, combine the water, wine, herbs, bay leaf, and peppercorns. Bring to a boil on medium high. Cook for 5 minutes.

Gently lower salmon, skin side down, into boiling liquid. Cover pan and remove from heat. Let stand 25 minutes. Do not lift lid. Fish will flake easily when tested with a fork.

Carefully remove the salmon from the liquid. Serve warm or chilled. Serves 6-8.

Calories—201; Saturated fat—3 g.; Total fat—12 g.; Carbohydrates—1 g.; Cholesterol—75 mg.; Sodium—55 mg.; Fiber—0 g.; Protein—23 g.

FISH AND VEGETABLE PLATTER

PAREVE
PASSOVER
SHAVUOT

I first had a platter similar to this in Jerusalem. This version is for the busy cook who wants the meal to look impressive for company. Prepare the poached fish in advance. The rest requires very little cooking.

4 large leaves romaine or
  green lettuce
1 recipe Poached Herb Salmon,
  or poached halibut, sea bass,
  or tuna
1 large green apple,
  cut in thin wedges
1 can hearts of palm, sliced,
  or 1½ cups fresh or frozen
  artichoke hearts, halved

2 carrots, shredded
1 cup frozen corn kernels,
  thawed
8 oz. fresh asparagus, steamed,
  or frozen asparagus, thawed
4 tsp. chopped walnuts or pecans
2-oz. jar capers, drained and
  rinsed

DRESSING (OPTIONAL)

½ cup low-fat mayonnaise
1 garlic clove, chopped
2 tbsp. crumbled feta or
  Roquefort cheese

1 cup buttermilk
1 tbsp. grated onion
¼ tsp. white pepper

Line individual plates with the lettuce leaves. Place cold salmon on each plate. Surround the salmon with apple wedges, hearts of palm or artichokes, carrots, corn, and asparagus.

Top each salad with 1 tsp. nuts and a sprinkling of capers.

Serve with low-fat creamy salad dressing or try the one above if you have time. To make it, combine the mayonnaise, garlic, and cheese. Stir in the remaining ingredients. Serve cold. Serves 4.

Variations:
- The poached fish can also be replaced by Pickled Tuna Salad or Confetti Smoked Whitefish Spread with crackers.
- For Passover, substitute any desired vegetable eaten during Passover, such as steamed and chilled broccoli, for the corn.

Calories—294; Saturated fat—1 g.; Total fat—9 g.; Carbohydrates—38 g.; Cholesterol—23 mg.; Sodium—341 mg.; Fiber—3 g.; Protein—14 g.

PASTICCIO DI TONNO

PAREVE

YOM KIPPUR BREAK-THE-FAST

This is one of Alisa Vardi Benabu's favorite family recipes. Alisa is a very gracious woman who was willing to share some her recipes with me despite her tight schedule in Jerusalem. Alisa is able to switch easily among three different languages—Italian, Hebrew, and English—on the phone, according to the caller. She is active in Jerusalem's Italian-Jewish community as an archivist and cooking teacher. Alisa's mother-in-law, the late Sete Benabu, originally from Gibraltar, used cumin in this tuna dish; her own mother, who was born in Florence before immigrating to Israel, uses nutmeg. Alisa likes to make it for a Brit. It does not freeze, so plan to make it when you want to serve it for an occasion, Shabbat lunch, or weekday dinner.

Olive-oil spray
2 onions, sliced into half-moons
1 carrot, grated
2 cloves garlic, chopped
5 fresh basil or oregano leaves, minced, to taste
¼ tsp. nutmeg or ground cumin, or to taste

1 slice dark bread, such as pumpernickel or dark wheat
2 6½-oz. cans water-packed tuna, drained and crumbled
8 eggs, or 4 whole eggs + 8 egg whites, or egg substitute to equal 8 eggs
Salt and pepper to taste

Spray a skillet with olive-oil spray. Over medium-high heat, sauté the onions, carrot, garlic, basil, and nutmeg or cumin 5-6 minutes or until the onions are translucent.

Soak the bread under running cold water; squeeze and crumble into vegetable mixture.

Remove the pan from the stove and add the tuna.

Beat the eggs and add to the tuna mixture. Add salt and pepper to taste.

Spray a glass baking dish with olive-oil spray. Spoon the mixture into dish. Bake at 350 degrees for 30 minutes until knife inserted comes out clean. Serves 8.

Serving suggestion: There are several ways to serve this dish. It can be served hot with a cold tomato sauce (this is the Italian Sephardic way). It could be served cold with a hot tomato sauce (this is how Alisa often serves it). Another presentation would be served cold with a low-fat mayonnaise dressing on the side. Garnish for a special occasion by sprinkling grated carrot and black olives on top.

Calories—120; Saturated fat—0 g.; Total fat—2 g.; Carbohydrates—7 g.; Cholesterol—61 mg.; Sodium—257 mg.; Fiber—0 g.; Protein—19 g.

PICKLED TUNA SALAD

PAREVE
SHABBAT
YOM KIPPUR BREAK-THE-FAST
TU BISHEVAT

*This is good for breaking the Yom Kippur fast or for a Kiddush-style buffet.
It can be easily doubled for a crowd.*

SALAD

2 6½-oz. cans tuna	6 green olives, diced
1 carrot, minced	3 tbsp. kosher dill pickles, diced
1 stalk celery, minced	⅓ cup reduced-fat mayonnaise
1 cauliflower floret, grated	2 tsp. lemon juice
2 gherkin pickles, diced	1½ tsp. yellow mustard

GARNISH

Parsley sprigs	**Ground sumac or paprika**

Mix all the salad ingredients in a bowl and chill.

Garnish with parsley sprigs and sprinkle either ground sumac or paprika over the top. Serves 8.

Serving suggestion: Serve with pumpernickel bread, pita, or bagels.

*Calories—111; Saturated fat—0 g.; Total fat—1 g.; Carbohydrates—11 g.;
Cholesterol—8 mg.; Sodium—570 g.; Fiber—1 g.; Protein—14 g.*

SEA BASS IN TOMATO SAUCE

PAREVE
SHABBAT
ROSH HASHANAH
PASSOVER

This Sephardic-style dish is of Spanish origin but has traveled through the Mediterranean. This is a beautifully colored display for a holiday table.

2½ lb. sea bass, tuna, or
    salmon fillets
2 onions, sliced in rings
2 carrots, thinly sliced and
    steamed tender crisp
1 small green pepper, chopped
2 tomatoes, chopped
2 medium garlic cloves, chopped

Juice of 2 lemons or 5 tbsp.
    lemon juice
1 cup dry white wine
1 cup tomato sauce
¼ cup chopped parsley
12 small green olives,
    sliced in half

Place the fish in a baking dish and arrange the onions, carrots, green pepper, tomatoes, and garlic around the fish.

Combine the lemon juice, wine, and tomato sauce and pour over the top of the fish.

Bake uncovered at 350 degrees for 20 minutes.

Add the parsley and olives. Continue to bake uncovered for another 15-20 minutes or until the fish is opaque and flakes easily. Serves 6.

Serving suggestion: This is good served hot or cold.

Calories—280; Saturated fat—1 g.; Total fat—5 g.; Carbohydrates—15 g.; Cholesterol—77 mg.; Sodium—320 mg.; Fiber—1 g.; Protein—37 g.

Note: This freezes well.

FISH IN TOMATO-CUMIN SAUCE
WITH EGGPLANT

PAREVE
SHABBAT
ROSH HASHANAH

This is a Tunisian-inspired dish. The eggplant slices fan out around the fish, giving the dish an elegant look for the holidays.

TOMATO-CUMIN SAUCE

1 tsp. cumin seeds
14½-oz. can tomatoes, diced, or
    4 medium tomatoes, diced
4 tbsp. tomato paste
2 tbsp. dry white wine
    (or nonalcoholic)

2 garlic cloves, chopped
¼ tsp. red pepper flakes
4 sprigs cilantro

FISH WITH EGGPLANT

1 large (1½ lb.) eggplant
¾ tsp. curry powder
¾ tsp. ground cumin
1½ lb. cod, bass, or snapper fillet

¼-1/3 cup flour
Mrs. Dash or salt and pepper
Cooking spray
1 tsp. olive oil

In a saucepan, toast the cumin seeds over medium heat about 3 minutes or until lightly browned. Add remaining sauce ingredients except cilantro. Cover and simmer on low heat for approximately 15-20 minutes until flavors meld.

Meanwhile, peel the eggplant. Slice in half lengthwise; continue slicing lengthwise in ¼-inch slices. Sprinkle curry and cumin over both sides. Spread out on a nonstick cookie sheet, and broil 3-5 minutes on each side or until lightly browned. Remove and set aside.

Rinse the fish and pat dry. Lightly coat the fish with flour. Sprinkle the Mrs. Dash or salt and pepper on both sides. Coat a nonstick skillet with the cooking spray, and add olive oil. Over medium-high heat, sauté the fish a few minutes on each side, according to thickness, until the fish flakes easily.

Transfer the fish to the center of a platter. Fan out the eggplant slices, surrounding the fish. Pour the sauce evenly over the eggplant and fish. Garnish with cilantro sprigs.

Serve with couscous or rice. Serves 4.

Calories—224; Saturated fat—0 g.; Total fat—3 g.; Carbohydrates—16 g.; Cholesterol—73 mg.; Sodium—117 mg.; Fiber—1 g.; Protein—33 g.

NORTH AFRICAN POACHED FISH

PAREVE
SHABBAT
ROSH HASHANAH
PASSOVER

This is a very well known North African recipe. The original recipe calls for the fish to be formed into patties and fried. My sister-in-law Joelle Hankin eliminated the grinding, frying, time, and calories. Poaching has faded in popularity but it's a fail-proof way to cook fish, especially for beginners. The water keeps the moisture in the fish so you really can't overcook it. This can be a first course to any holiday meal or a main dish. It can be easily doubled for company.

1 lb. fish fillets (pollack, cod, or orange roughy)

MARINADE

1 tsp. turmeric
1 tsp. paprika

Salt and pepper to taste
1 lemon, peeled and halved

POACHING INGREDIENTS

Water
2 tsp. olive oil
2 carrots, sliced

8 green olives, sliced
½ lemon, peeled and quartered

Rinse and pat dry the fish, and place in a shallow baking dish. Sprinkle the turmeric, paprika, salt, and pepper over the fish. Squeeze half of the lemon evenly over the fish. Cover and marinate in refrigerator about 1 hour.

To poach: Add approximately ½ inch of water to a skillet. Remove fish from marinade and add to skillet. Slice remaining half of lemon and add to skillet with remaining poaching ingredients. Cover and simmer over medium-low heat for approximately 15 minutes or until fish flakes and is opaque.

Carefully transfer the fish to a serving dish. Continue to simmer liquid until reduced by one-half. Pour over the fish. Discard the lemon. Chill fish just to room temperature or slightly cooler to serve.

If chilled overnight, the sauce will congeal. The sauce can be reheated in the microwave for approximately 30 seconds (microwave times may vary), or just to room temperature to loosen the sauce again. Serves 4.

Calories—149; Saturated fat—1 g.; Total fat—4 g.; Carbohydrates—7 g.; Cholesterol—49 mg.; Sodium—243 mg.; Fiber—01 g.; Protein—21 g.

BAHIAN FISH MUQUECA

DAIRY
SHABBAT

Benny Goldstein, our Jewish exchange student from Belo Horizonte, Brazil, missed his comfort foods from home. When I made this, he was delighted. It tasted very similar to his mother's dish.

2 tsp. oil
4 large tomatoes, seeded and chopped
1 green bell pepper, seeded and chopped
1 medium onion, minced
2 lb. firm white fish such as halibut or cod, cut into 1-inch pieces

¾ cup light coconut milk
1 cup nonfat plain yogurt
4 tbsp. lime juice
1 tbsp. cilantro
¼ tsp. cayenne pepper
2 tsp. ground coriander (optional)
2 tsp. minced garlic

In a nonstick skillet, heat the oil over medium heat. Add the onion, tomatoes, green peppers, and fish. Lightly sauté for approximately 5 minutes.

Add the coconut milk, yogurt, lime juice, cilantro, cayenne pepper, coriander, and garlic. Simmer until the fish is cooked through, 8-10 minutes. Serves 6.

Serving suggestion: Spoon Arroz Brasileiro (see index) into the center of individual bowls. Spoon the fish and sauce over the rice.

Calories—233; Saturated fat—4 g.; Total fat—9 g.; Carbohydrates—10 g.; Cholesterol—65 mg.; Sodium—295 g.; Fiber—1 g.; Protein—29 g.

GRILLED HALIBUT IN A CITRUS VINAIGRETTE

PAREVE
LAG B'OMER

*This contemporary recipe is so simple and delicious and summery . . .
and easy to double for company!*

MARINADE

¼ cup orange juice
2 tbsp. grated orange peel
1 tbsp. sodium-reduced soy sauce

1 small bay leaf
⅛ tsp. black pepper
1 lb. halibut or tuna steaks

CITRUS VINAIGRETTE

½ cup orange juice
1 tbsp. lemon juice
1 tbsp. lime juice

1 tbsp. mustard
1 tsp. honey

Combine the marinade ingredients in a shallow bowl.
Rinse and pat dry the fish with a paper towel. Place in the marinade for 30 minutes-1 hour. Grill the fish 4-5 minutes on each side.
Whisk the vinaigrette ingredients and serve with grilled halibut. Serves 4.

*Calories—162; Saturated fat—0 g.; Total fat—1 g.; Carbohydrates—10 g.;
Cholesterol—36 mg.; Sodium—233 mg.; Fiber—0 g.; Protein—25 g.*

CONFETTI SMOKED WHITEFISH SPREAD

DAIRY
SHABBAT
YOM KIPPUR BREAK-THE-FAST
PASSOVER

This is delicious to set out for mishpocha *visiting for brunch or Shabbat.
Serve with bagels, pita chips, or rye bread.*

1 small carrot, coarsely chopped
1 small stalk celery, thickly sliced
2 tbsp. chopped parsley
2 tbsp. minced red onion
8 oz. smoked whitefish
4 oz. nonfat cream cheese or
nonfat yogurt cheese

1 tbsp. nonfat yogurt or
mayonnaise
1 tsp. white horseradish
1 tsp. hot pepper sauce

In a food processor, mince the carrot, celery, parsley, and onion. Set aside.

Use the food processor to pulse the whitefish, cream cheese or yogurt cheese, yogurt, horseradish, and hot sauce until well blended. When mixture is smooth, mix in the chopped vegetables. Spoon into a covered container and refrigerate until serving time. Serves 24.

Per 2 tbsp. serving: Calories—38; Saturated fat—0 g.; Total fat—0 g.; Carbohydrates—4 g.; Cholesterol—7 mg.; Sodium—243 mg.; Fiber—1 g.; Protein—5 g.

Meat Entrees

SWEET AND SAVORY CHICKEN

MEAT
SHABBAT
ROSH HASHANAH
PASSOVER

*This recipe takes advantage of a relatively new convenience food
on the kosher food market. The result is a slightly sweet dish to fulfill
the tradition of sweet foods for the new year, but not too sweet for those
who really do not care for sweet meat dishes.*

2 tbsp. oil
2 onions, sliced
4 apples, cored and sliced
1 pkg. Mrs. Manischewitz Sweet
   Potato Pancake Mix
½ cup egg substitute

2 chickens, cut-up parts, skin
   removed from larger pieces
1 cup chicken broth
1 cup orange juice
½ cup honey

Preheat the oven to 425 degrees. Spread the oil on the bottom of a baking pan. Place the sliced onions and apples in the pan, and mix to coat with the oil. Place the pan in the oven while you prepare the chicken.

Place the sweet potato pancake mix on a plate, and the egg substitute in a shallow bowl. Dip the chicken pieces in the egg substitute, then roll in the pancake mix.

Remove the baking pan from the oven, and arrange the coated chicken pieces on top of the onions and apples.

In a bowl, combine the broth, orange juice, and honey. Pour approximately ⅓ of the mixture in the baking pan around the chicken.

Reduce oven temperature to 350 degrees. Bake chicken for 30 minutes.

Pour the remaining liquid over the chicken and around the sides. Bake another 45 minutes. Serves 8.

Variation: For Latke Chicken, one of our kids' favorites, omit the apples and add 1 extra sliced onion. Substitute 2 pkg. potato pancake (latke) mix for the sweet potato pancake mix. Do not pour any liquid over the top of the chicken, but pour 1 cup chicken broth around the sides of the chicken in the pan. Bake at 400 degrees for 1 hour 15 minutes or 1½ hours.

Calories—511; Saturated fat—2 g.; Total fat—8 g.; Carbohydrates—59 g.; Cholesterol—127 mg.; Sodium—624 mg.; Fiber—1 g.; Protein—50 g.

SHABBAT CHICKEN IN BARBECUE SAUCE

MEAT
SHABBAT

*Unbeknownst to each other, mother and daughter Etta Chaya and
Tzivia Brummel sent me their favorite chicken sauce for Shabbat.
I combined the two recipes, adding my own touches to this American sauce
used for barbecuing. The result was a Shabbat-dinner family pleaser.*

Cooking spray
1 red onion, chopped
½ cup hickory-flavored
    barbecue sauce
1 tbsp. liquid smoke
⅓ cup honey or maple syrup
1 tbsp. chopped garlic
½ cup ketchup

3 tbsp. cider vinegar
¼ cup water
2 tbsp. mustard
1 tbsp. soy sauce
¼ tsp. ground ginger
8 boneless, skinless chicken
    breast halves

In a skillet sprayed with cooking spray, sauté the onions over medium-high heat
5-6 minutes or until brown. Add the remaining ingredients except the chicken, stir
thoroughly, and heat through.

Arrange chicken in a baking dish. Pour sauce over all and bake uncovered at
350 degrees for approximately 40 minutes. Serves 6.

*Calories—254; Saturated fat—1 g.; Total fat—2 g.; Carbohydrates—26 g.;
Cholesterol—78 mg.; Sodium—563 mg.; Fiber—1 g.; Protein—33 g.*

DAFNA'S CHICKEN

My daughter Jennifer learned this delicious recipe from Dafna Sharon, of Efrat, Israel. There is a hint of a Yemenite combination of seasonings—turmeric and pepper. Paprika has replaced the cumin, which, along with the addition of soy sauce, gives this dish a contemporary flavor.

2 tsp. oil	¼ tsp. black pepper
1 large red onion, chopped	1 medium potato, diced
2 tsp. paprika	1 medium zucchini, diced
1½ tsp. turmeric	2 carrots, chopped
2 tsp. garlic powder	1½ cups water
2 lb. skinless chicken breast halves, bone in	3 tbsp. tomato paste
	3 tbsp. soy sauce

In a large pot, heat the oil over medium-high heat, and brown the onion with 1 tsp. each of the paprika, turmeric, and garlic powder for 5-6 minutes. Add the chicken and brown for approximately 15 minutes.

Add the remaining ingredients. Reduce heat to low, cover, and simmer 40-50 minutes or until the chicken is done and the sauce is somewhat thickened. Serves 6.

Variation: Any vegetable combination is good. I even threw in collard greens.

Calories—324; Saturated fat—1 g.; Total fat—5 g.; Carbohydrates—13 g.; Cholesterol—137 mg.; Sodium—412 mg.; Fiber—1 g.; Protein—57 g.

MOROCCAN CHICKEN WITH ALMONDS AND PRUNES

For many Sephardic Jews, this dish is as traditional for Rosh Hashanah as are apples and honey. My good Moroccan friend Marcelle Morgan wouldn't think of serving anything else for Rosh Hashanah. The original recipe calls for cut-up fryers, which gives each serving a fat count of 38 grams. With skinless pieces, I was able to lower the fat grams to 8.

¼ cup slivered almonds
2 tsp. oil
2 onions, sliced
1 cup pitted prunes
2 tsp. cinnamon
2 tsp. sugar
½ tsp. turmeric

2 cups chicken broth
1 tsp. paprika
½ tsp. salt
5 lb. skinless chicken pieces, bone in
¼ cup chopped parsley

Preheat the oven to 350 degrees.

In a dry skillet over medium heat, toast the almonds 2-3 minutes or until lightly golden brown. Set aside.

In a nonstick skillet, over medium heat, heat the oil and sauté the onions for approximately 5 minutes. Add the prunes, cinnamon, sugar, turmeric, and broth. Stir briefly.

Sprinkle the paprika and salt onto the chicken. Set aside.

Spoon half of the skillet mixture onto the bottom of a glass baking dish. Place the chicken pieces on top, breast side down. Spoon the remaining skillet mixture over the chicken.

Bake covered for 40 minutes.

Uncover, turn chicken breasts side up, sprinkle with parsley, and continue to bake for 30 minutes or until the chicken is no longer pink at the bone. Arrange chicken on serving platter. Top with onion sauce mixture. Sprinkle almonds on top. Serves 6-8.

Calories—418; Saturated fat—1 g.; Total fat—8 g.; Carbohydrates—19 g.; Cholesterol—164 mg.; Sodium—334 mg.; Fiber—1 g.; Protein—68 g.

CHICKEN WITH QUINCES OR APPLES

MEAT
SHABBAT
ROSH HASHANAH

This is a popular recipe in parts of the world where quinces are common. The recipe has traveled with Jews from Romania to the Maghreb to Iran. The quince resembles an apple but is more acidic. Sofiya Sandler, a Russian immigrant now living in Denver, uses tart apples. Quinces were unavailable to her in Russia. In the United States, quinces are available during the fall season. To Sofiya's adapted recipe I have added a few spices to color the chicken. The Russian touch is the slight sweet and sour mixture with raisins.

1 tsp. ginger
1 tsp. paprika
⅛ tsp. cinnamon
6 skinless chicken breast halves,
   bone in
1½ tsp. oil
1 large onion, thinly sliced
3 tbsp. natural apricot preserves
2 medium-large tart apples or
   quinces, cored and sliced

½ cup gold raisins
3 tbsp. lemon juice
½ tsp. salt
½ tsp. black pepper
¼ tsp. cinnamon (optional)
1-1½ cups chicken broth
   or water

Combine the ginger, paprika and cinnamon, and rub into the chicken pieces.

In a deep skillet or Dutch oven, heat the oil, add the chicken, and sauté over medium-high heat for 3-4 minutes on each side. Remove and set aside.

Add the onions (coat the skillet with cooking spray if it is too dry) and sauté for 3-4 minutes. Return the chicken to the skillet along with preserves, apples or quinces, raisins, lemon juice, salt, pepper, and cinnamon. Add broth to cover, reduce heat to low, and simmer for 30-35 minutes.

Serve hot on a platter, and surround with steamed rice. Serves 6.

Calories—306; Saturated fat—1 g.; Total fat—3 g.; Carbohydrates—14 g.; Cholesterol—137 mg.; Sodium—351 mg.; Fiber—1 g.; Protein—55 g.

BRAZILIAN-STYLE ARROZ CON POLLO

MEAT
YOM KIPPUR BEFORE THE FAST

*Our Brazilian Jewish exchange student, Benny Goldstein,
really missed his home cooking. This is so easy and quick to make.
It's a pleasantly mild entree to have before the Yom Kippur fast;
it's even mild enough for breaking the fast.*

¾ cup long-grain white rice
1½ lb. boneless skinless
   chicken breast
4-5 green onions, chopped
1 pkg.frozen artichoke hearts or
   hearts of palm
1 medium tomato, chopped

1 cup peas or corn
¼ cup chopped parsley
3 garlic cloves, chopped
¼ tsp. salt
¼ tsp. black pepper
2 cups water

In a large skillet, combine all ingredients. Bring to a boil over high heat. Reduce heat to low. Cover and simmer for 30 minutes. Let sit for approximately 10 minutes before serving. Serves 4.

Variation: For a little contrast, add a few minced green olives to the ingredients.

Calories—261; Saturated fat—1 g.; Total fat—3 g .; Carbohydrates—15 g.; Cholesterol—99 mg.; Sodium—308 mg.; Fiber—2 g.; Protein—44 g.

CHICKEN WITH ARTICHOKES AND OLIVES

MEAT
SHABBAT
PASSOVER

*This is inspired by the famous Moroccan dish of chicken with olives and
preserved lemons. I substituted artichokes for half the Kalamata olives
to reduce the fat and salt. Mushrooms can also be used. Preserved lemons
are high in sodium, so I have not included them in this recipe
but have added lemon juice to retain the lemon flavor
To reduce sodium, always rinse capers before using.*

Cooking spray
1 large onion, chopped
1 tbsp. chopped garlic
½ tsp. ground ginger
½ tsp. paprika
½ tsp. turmeric
6 small skinless chicken breasts, bone in
2 cups chicken broth

⅓ cup sliced Kalamata or green olives
2 tbsp. capers
1-1½ cups frozen or canned artichoke hearts
¼ cup lemon juice
¼ cup snipped cilantro (optional)
¼ cup snipped parsley (optional)
½ tsp. salt (optional)

In a large pot coated with the cooking spray, fry the onion over medium-high heat for approximately 5 minutes. Add the garlic, ginger, paprika, turmeric, chicken breasts, and broth. Reduce heat, cover, and cook over medium-low heat for 40 minutes.

To reduce the salt in the olives, parboil them in a small pot of boiling water for 1 minute. To reduce salt in the capers, rinse and drain them in cold running water.

Add the olives, capers and artichokes to the chicken and continue to cook, covered, for 10-15 minutes. Add the lemon juice, cilantro, parsley, and salt. Serves 6.

Calories—356; Saturated fat—1 g.; Total fat—7 g.; Carbohydrates—10 g.; Cholesterol—153 mg.; Sodium—483 mg.; Fiber—1 g.; Protein—64 g.

HERB CHICKEN IN TOMATO SAUCE

MEAT
SHABBAT
YOM KIPPUR BEFORE THE FAST
PASSOVER

This dish is inspired by one that Bulgarian and Georgian Jews brought to Israel. It is simple enough to make after work, yet sophisticated enough to serve to Shabbat company. Because the sodium is so low, and the dish so easy to make, it's a good Erev Yom Kippur meal.

8-oz. jar (1 cup) roasted peppers
16 oz. fresh or canned
  no-salt-added tomatoes, diced
¼ cup chopped fresh basil
¼ cup chopped fresh cilantro
Cooking spray

1 large onion, chopped
1½ tbsp. minced garlic
1 lb. boneless skinless chicken
  breast, cut into pieces
Several drops hot sauce, or
  to taste (optional)

In a food processor, or with a knife, mince the roasted peppers, tomatoes, basil, and cilantro Set aside.

Coat a nonstick skillet with the cooking spray. Over medium-high heat, sauté the onion and garlic for 2-3 minutes or until onions start turning a light brown.

Add the chicken and cook until white throughout, for approximately 7 minutes.

Add the sauce to the chicken and heat through for another 5 minutes. Add hot sauce to taste if you like it a little hot. Serves 4.

Serving suggestion: This is great served over Onion and Chive Polenta, yolkless egg noodles, or mashed potatoes.

Calories—187; Saturated fat—1 g.; Total fat—2 g.; Carbohydrates—14 g.; Cholesterol—66 mg.; Sodium—95 mg.; Fiber—2 g.; Protein—29 g.

CHICKEN AND PINE NUT SALAD

MEAT
SHABBAT
PASSOVER

*This is a contemporary, easy, tasty Shabbat lunch entree. The pine nuts, lime, and cilantro make a pleasant combination of Mexican flavors.
Just prepare this Friday afternoon and have it ready to serve
over salad greens for Shabbat lunch.*

Cooking spray
1 green pepper, cut in strips
1 red pepper, cut in strips
1 cup sugar snap peas or
  green beans
½ cup steamed julienne carrots
1 lb. skinless chicken breast,
  cooked and cut into strips or
  cubes

2-4 tbsp. chopped cilantro
2½ tbsp. toasted pine nuts
Juice of 2 limes (approximately
  ¼-⅓ cup)
¼ cup dry red wine or sherry
4 cups salad greens

In a skillet coated with the cooking spray, sauté the green pepper, red pepper, and sugar snap peas over medium heat for 2-3 minutes or until tender crisp. Add the steamed carrots and cooked chicken.

Remove from heat. The mixture can be refrigerated overnight at this step.

Add the cilantro and toasted pine nuts and toss briefly to mix. Add the lime juice and wine and toss to coat. Serve over salad greens. Serves 4.

Calories—221; Saturated fat—1 g.; Total fat—5 g.; Carbohydrates—14 g.; Cholesterol—66 mg.; Sodium—127 mg.; Fiber—2 g.; Protein—30 g.

Note: For Passover, omit the sugar snap peas and either increase carrots by ½ cup or use another fresh vegetable, such as steamed broccoli.

BEST MEDITERRANEAN CHICKEN

MEAT
SHABBAT
SIMCHAT TORAH

This is one of Zahava Koll's favorite Shabbat dishes. Zahava, originally from Israel, has a reputation in the Denver Jewish community as an excellent cook and a gracious hostess. It was in her home in the 1970s that my husband, Larry, and I had our first traditional Shabbat lunch in Denver, a delicious meal we still remember. I have turned this recipe into a lighter version but have only sacrificed the fat and calories, not flavor. I omitted ¼ cup of olive oil and reduced 1 cup of green olives to 12 sliced olives.

**1 red onion, peeled and
  sliced into rings
2 garlic cloves, minced
12 sliced green olives
½ cup raisins
6 turkey cutlets or boneless
  chicken breasts**

**1 cup balsamic vinegar
½ cup dry white wine
2 tbsp. honey
1 tbsp. chopped fresh oregano**

On the bottom of a shallow baking dish, place the onions, garlic, green olives and raisins. Place the turkey or chicken on top.

Mix together the balsamic vinegar, wine, honey, and oregano. Pour this mixture over the turkey or chicken.

Bake uncovered at 400 degrees for 25 minutes or until the meat is no longer pink, turning it over halfway through cooking. Serves 6.

Calories—359; Saturated fat—1 g.; Total fat—4 g.; Carbohydrates—22 g.; Cholesterol—137 mg.; Sodium—326 mg.; Fiber—1 g.; Protein—56 g.

SHASHLIK WITH HARISSA SEASONING

MEAT

PASSOVER
YOM HAATZMA'UT
LAB B'OMER

Shashlik and shish kebab both mean skewered meat cooked over an open flame. Shish kebab in Israel is actually the oval-shaped meatballs, and shashlik always refers to cubes of meat on the skewer. Either way, this is not your typical American barbecue.

2 lb. boneless skinless chicken breast, cut into ½-inch cubes
1 tbsp. oil

1-1½ tbsp. Harissa Seasoning recipe
1 tbsp. lemon juice

Place all the ingredients in a bowl. Marinate 2 hours or overnight in the refrigerator.

Prepare the grill or broiler. Thread the meat onto 6 skewers. Grill the kebabs over high heat until the meat lightly browns and is no longer pink (approximately 15 minutes).

Serve in pita halves or with couscous. Serves 6.

Variations:
- Replace the chicken with lamb.
- Add vegetables, or use vegetables only, brushed with the marinade. Try cubes of zucchini, Japanese eggplant, tomatoes, green peppers, and onion wedges.
- Bone-in chicken portions can also be barbecued with this seasoning mix. Cook chicken breasts for approximately 20 minutes. Turn over and cook for another 7 minutes or until the juices run clear when the chicken is pierced with a knife.

Calories—178; Saturated fat—1 g.; Total fat—4 g.; Carbohydrates—0 g.; Cholesterol—88 mg.; Sodium—98 mg.; Fiber—0 g.; Protein—35 g.

AFGHAN-STYLE CHICKEN HAMIN

MEAT
SHABBAT
PASSOVER (SEPHARDIC)

Sephardic hamin or Ashkenazic cholent is the Jewish soul food for Shabbat. What makes this or any variety of this dish unique is the way it is prepared. It is always started on Friday before sundown, cooking at a very low temperature, and is served on Saturday for Shabbat lunch. These recipes are handed down from generation to generation. Sephardic hamin usually includes a combination of rice, split peas, lentils, or chickpeas. Afghani Jews use quinces in their hamin with rosewater or orange-flower water, as do the Iranian and Kurdish Jews. I usually substitute tart apples just because they are more accessible to me. Use quinces in the fall, when you can find them at the market. They really do give the hamin a special taste.

2 tbsp. olive oil
2 onions, thinly sliced
2½ lb. boneless skinless chicken breasts, cut in bite-size pieces
8 oz. or 2½ cups peeled and sliced sweet potatoes or butternut squash
8 oz. or 2½ cups peeled and sliced potatoes
3 large carrots, thinly sliced
1½ cups rice

2 large tart green apples or quinces, peeled, cored, and sliced in wedges
1 tsp. cinnamon
2 tbsp. tomato paste
½ tsp. turmeric
½ tsp. salt
½ tsp. black pepper
6 cups cold water, or enough to just cover
1 tbsp. rosewater (optional)

In a Dutch oven or large pot, heat the olive oil over medium-high heat. Sauté the onions for 7-10 minutes or until golden brown. Add the chicken and brown for 15-20 minutes.

Add the remaining ingredients in the order listed. Bring to a boil. Reduce to medium and cook for 30 minutes.

Place in a 250-degree oven or on a blech (metal tray) on the stove over low heat and cook overnight until Shabbat lunch the next day. Serves 10.

Calories—322; Saturated fat—1 g.; Total fat—5 g.; Carbohydrates—41 g.; Cholesterol—66 mg.; Sodium—320 mg.; Fiber—1 g.; Protein—29 g.

IRANIAN-INSPIRED CROCKPOT HAMIN

MEAT/ PAREVE
SHABBAT

If you're a fan of lamb, this has a mild taste of it, but enough to give this hamin distinction. If you don't care for lamb, this can easily be made with chicken or as a vegetarian dish. I'm a fan of this hamin. This recipe evolved from a cholent recipe given to me by my oldest friend, Etta Chaya Brummel.

2 large onions, sliced
1 cup rice
1 cup split peas
4 carrots, sliced thick
1 cup bulgur wheat
½ lb. lamb, cut in small cubes (optional)

2 tsp. ground cumin
1 tsp. turmeric
½ tsp. black pepper
2 tsp. salt
1 cup pineapple juice
Water to cover

In a Crockpot, layer the onion slices, rice, split peas, carrots, bulgur, and lamb.

Mix the cumin, turmeric, pepper, and salt in the pineapple juice. Pour over the hamin. Add water to cover. Set Crockpot on low starting late Friday afternoon to finish the hamin for Shabbat lunch. Serves 10.

With lamb: Calories—293; Saturated fat—2 g.; Total fat—6 g.; Carbohydrates—48 g.; Cholesterol—16 mg.; Sodium—501 mg.; Fiber—2 g.; Protein—13 g.

Without lamb: Calories—235; Saturated fat—0 g.; Total fat—1 g.; Carbohydrates—48 g.; Cholesterol—0 mg.; Sodium—488 mg.; Fiber—2 g.; Protein—9 g.

THE TAX CHAZZAN'S GREAT CHOLENT

MEAT/PAREVE
SHABBAT

*The Tax Chazzan is just what it sounds like. He is Cantor Isaac Koll, CPA.
With years of experience on the bimah and with the IRS,
Cantor Koll is also adept in the kitchen. I just needed to reduce
the amount of meat in his Lithuanian/Polish recipe from his mother
The prunes are a sweetening agent, but you can substitute ¼ cup honey
if you like. This cholent also works well without any meat. Follow the same
instructions, just omitting the meat and doubling the beans.*

2 onions, halved
1 cup mixed dry beans
5 potatoes
18 (1 cup) pitted prunes
2 lb. brisket, fat removed and
meat cut into bite-size pieces

1 pkg. low-sodium onion soup
mix
2 garlic cloves
½ cup barley
6 cups chicken broth or
water to cover

In a Crockpot or Dutch oven on top of the stove, place the onions, beans, 3 of the potatoes, cut into chunks, and prunes. The prunes will brown the potatoes.

Add the meat, half of the onion soup mix, and garlic. Layer with the remaining potatoes, cut into chunks. Layer the barley. Top with the remaining onion soup mix. Cover with the broth or water.

Set the Crockpot on high for 1 hour, then turn down to low and simmer overnight until Shabbat lunch. If using a Dutch oven, bring the cholent to a boil over high heat, then turn to low and simmer until lunch. Serves 6.

Calories—420; Saturated fat—1 g.; Total fat—4 g.; Carbohydrates—56 g.; Cholesterol—76 mg.; Sodium—81 mg.; Fiber—2 g.; Protein—40 g.

ADOBE CHOLENT

MEAT/PAREVE
SHABBAT

*Ashkenazic cholents usually contain beans, such as kidney and great white Northern beans, and barley. We want to keep the traditional cholents, but it's fun to experiment with new tastes as well.
There are even cholent cookoffs, which introduce new recipes all the time.
This cholent has a hint of American Southwest flavor.*

1 cup red, black, or pinto beans
2 large onions, chopped
1 tbsp. olive oil
1½ lb. boneless skinless chicken
breast, cut into large chunks

½ lb. lean stew meat (optional)
½ cup barley or rice
4 medium potatoes, quartered
20 sun-dried tomatoes
2 mild chili peppers, chopped

SEASONINGS

¾ tsp. oregano
2 tsp. chili powder
½ head garlic, unpeeled
¼ cup chopped cilantro
¼ cup chopped parsley

½ tsp. salt
½ tsp. black pepper
1 tbsp. paprika
3 cups water

Soak the beans in enough water to cover overnight.

In a Dutch oven or skillet, sauté the onions in the olive oil over high heat 3-4 minutes. Add the chicken pieces and stew meat and cook for approximately 8-10 minutes.

Add the beans, barley, potatoes, tomatoes, and peppers.

Combine the seasonings, mix with 3 cups water, and pour over the cholent. Bring to a boil over high heat. Cook on a blech on the stove over low heat or place in a 250-degree oven or a Crockpot set on low overnight. Serves 8.

Variation: For Meatless Chili Cholent, omit the chicken and stew meat. Increase the beans to 2 cups. Omit 2 cups of the water at the end and substitute 2 cups no-salt-added canned chopped tomatoes.

With meat: Calories—284; Saturated fat—1 g.; Total fat—3 g.; Carbohydrates—35 g.; Cholesterol—65 mg.; Sodium—332 mg.; Fiber—2 g.; Protein—31 g.

Without meat: Calories—162; Saturated fat—0 g.; Total fat—1 g.; Carbohydrates—35 g.; Cholesterol—0 mg.; Sodium—262 mg.; Fiber—2 g.; Protein—5 g.

ROASTED TURKEY TZIMMES

MEAT
SHABBAT
ROSH HASHANAH
SUKKOT
CHANUKAH
PASSOVER

4 lb. boneless turkey breast
1 lemon, sliced
2 sprigs each sage, thyme,
  and rosemary
Olive-oil spray
1 onion, coarsely chopped
2 sweet potatoes, peeled and
  cut into chunks
3 carrots, cut into 1-inch pieces

1 large tart apple, cut into
  8 wedges
2 tbsp. brown sugar or honey
1½ cups defatted chicken broth
1/2 cup dry red wine
2 garlic cloves, chopped
2 tsp. cornstarch (or potato
  starch for Passover)

Carefully separate the skin from the turkey breast fillets, and place the lemon slices between the skin and meat. Place 1 sprig of each herb under the skin. Place in a glass baking dish or roasting pan.

Coat a nonstick skillet with the olive-oil spray. Over medium heat, add the onion, sweet potatoes, carrots, and apple, and cook for 5-6 minutes. Sprinkle with the brown sugar.

Arrange the vegetables in the baking dish around the turkey. Bake uncovered at 400 degrees for 40 minutes or until the turkey reaches 185 degrees and the meat is no longer pink.

Remove the vegetables and keep warm.

In a saucepan, combine all but 3 tbsp. of the chicken broth, wine, and garlic. Mix the cornstarch with the remaining broth, and stir into the broth mixture. Bring to a boil to thicken slightly, stirring constantly.

Slice the turkey and transfer it to a platter. Spoon the vegetables around the turkey and drizzle the desired amount of gravy onto the turkey and vegetables.

Garnish with extra herb sprigs and lemon wedges. Serves 8.

Variation: For Passover, replace the cornstarch with potato starch. Stir the potato starch directly into the sauce to blend and thicken just before serving.

Calories—345; Saturated fat—1 g.; Total fat—4 g. Carbohydrates—22 g.; Cholesterol—136 mg.; Sodium—213 mg.; Fiber—1 g.; Protein—55 g.

THE LIGHTER HOLIPSHKES
(Rolled Stuffed Cabbage)

Stuffed cabbage is called by various names, depending on the community's origin. This was my dad's name for it, due to his mother's Ukrainian background. This is a versatile recipe. You don't want meat? Substitute soy protein crumbles, or crumbled frozen veggie burgers. The meat or soy protein and rice filling can be flavored in the style of Jews from the Middle East with cinnamon and allspice, if desired.

1 large head cabbage
Cooking spray
1 large carrot, grated
1 onion, minced
1 garlic clove, chopped
Salt and pepper to taste
1 tsp. paprika

1½ lb. ground white turkey meat, soy crumbles, or crumbled veggie burgers
3 tbsp. uncooked rice
¼ cup water
1 medium onion, sliced

SAUCE

8-oz. can tomato puree
8-oz. can crushed tomatoes with juice, chopped
1 cup water

⅓ cup natural apricot preserves
Juice of 1 lemon
½ tsp. paprika

Microwave the whole cabbage on high for approximately 5 minutes. Rinse with cool water.

Cut approximately 12 leaves from the core end of the cabbage. Set aside.

In a Dutch oven or deep skillet coated with the cooking spray, sauté the carrot, onion, garlic, salt, pepper, and paprika for 6-7 minutes over medium heat, or until golden brown.

In a large bowl, combine the ground turkey or soy crumbles or crumbled veggie burgers with the onion mixture, rice, and water.

To stuff the leaves, place approximately 3 tbsp. of the turkey or soy mixture at the core end. Fold the end over the filling, then fold the sides in, and roll over to complete the roll. Repeat with the remaining leaves until all the filling is used.

Thinly slice any leftover cabbage and place them in the bottom of the Dutch oven. Layer the sliced onions over the leaves. Top with the cabbage rolls, seam side down.

Combine the sauce ingredients and pour over all. Cover and bake at 325 degrees for 2½-3 hours. Baste occasionally. If more liquid is needed, add broth or water in small amounts. Serves 6.

With ground turkey: Calories—324; Saturated fat—0 g.; Total fat—2 g. Carbohydrates—45 g.; Cholesterol—46 mg.; Sodium—212 mg.; Fiber—3 g.; Protein—30 g.

With soy protein: Calories—341; Saturated fat—0 g.; Total fat—1 g.; Carbohydrates—55 g.; Cholesterol—0 mg.; Sodium—81 mg.; Fiber—9 g.; Protein—28 g.

INSIDE-OUT STUFFED CABBAGE

MEAT
SUKKOT

Rolled stuffed cabbage is a classic Ashkenazic dish. It's also very Russian. Jewish stuffed cabbage is more sweet and sour, while the Russian version is more savory. This is an updated version. The meatballs are not encased in the cabbage leaves, but sit on a bed of cabbage. It's haimish and easy to make.

1½ lb. cabbage

MEATBALLS

**1½ lb. extralean ground chicken
   or white turkey meat**
¼ cup breadcrumbs
⅓ cup uncooked rice

1 cup minced onion
2 egg whites
¼ tsp. each salt and pepper
¼ cup ketchup

TAX CHAZZAN'S SAUCE

15-oz. can tomato sauce
16-oz. can natural cranberry
  sauce

2 tbsp. raisins
2 tbsp. lemon juice

Slice the cabbage into a large skillet or pot.

In a bowl, combine the meatball ingredients. With wet hands, form meatballs 1½ inches in diameter. Layer on top of the cabbage.

Whisk together the tomato and cranberry sauce, making sure to break up the cranberry sauce. Pour over the meatballs. Add the raisins. Bring to a boil. Reduce the heat to medium low, cover, and cook for 1 hour.

Add the lemon juice. Cover and continue to simmer for another 30 minutes. Serve with steamed rice or flavored mashed potatoes. Serves 6.

Variation: Of course, you can reverse this, and make stuffed cabbage rolls, using the Tax Chazzan's Sauce as a topping.

With ground turkey breast: Calories—342; Saturated fat—0 g.; Total fat—2 g.; Carbohydrates—59 g.; Cholesterol—46 mg.; Sodium—777 mg.; Fiber—2 g.; Protein—23 g.

STUFFED TOMATOES SYRIAN STYLE

MEAT/PAREVE
SHABBAT
SUKKOT

This is a simple yet pretty dish featuring a Syrian stuffing with a Yemenite accent. Stuffed vegetables of all kinds are common to Sephardic cuisine. The topping is optional. It adds a little texture but the tomatoes are still delicious without it. Stuffed vegetables are made for Shabbat, holidays, and other festive occasions. Many different vegetables are used for stuffing. This filling can be used to stuff onions, eggplant, and zucchini.

⅓ cup rice, any variety
⅔ cup water
Olive-oil cooking spray
1 onion, chopped
½ lb. extra lean ground beef or
  soy protein substitute

2½ tbsp. chopped almonds,
  toasted
1 tsp. cinnamon
4 large or 6 medium tomatoes

TOPPING (OPTIONAL)

Olive-oil spray
2 tbsp. minced onions
2 tbsp. minced parsley

2 tbsp. minced mushrooms
1 tbsp. minced mild chili pepper
2 tbsp. harissa

Cook the rice in water according to package directions.

Meanwhile, over medium-high heat, in a skillet coated with the olive-oil cooking spray, sauté the onion and ground beef for approximately 3 minutes. Add the almonds and cinnamon and continue to cook 5 minutes or until the meat is no longer pink. Remove from stove and mix in cooked rice.

Slice the tops off the tomatoes. Hollow out the tomatoes, leaving ½-inch shells. (Save the tomato pulp for another use.) Spoon the mixture into the tomato shells. Transfer to a baking dish.

In a small skillet, coated with olive-oil spray, sauté the topping vegetables over medium-high heat for approximately 1 minute. Remove from the stove. Add the harissa. Spoon about 1-2 tbsp. on top of the stuffing mixture.

Bake at 350 degrees for 20 minutes or until heated through. Serves 4-6.

Calories—201; Saturated fat—3 g.; Total fat—9 g.; Carbohydrates—20 g.; Cholesterol—20 mg.; Sodium—50 mg.; Fiber—1 g.; Protein—10 g.

Note: Harissa can be found in most Middle Eastern food markets. Otherwise, add 2 tbsp. salsa or Harissa Salsa or ¼-/½ tsp. Harissa Seasoning.

KIBBEH

*Kurdish and Iraqi Jews have brought varieties of kibbeh to Israel.
I have had large ones that were boiled in soup like matzah balls,
but not similar in taste to matzah balls. Many Kurdish and Iraqi dishes are
made with lamb or are vegetarian. This recipe features ground beef and soy
protein to reduce fat. Ground lamb could be used in place of the beef.
The seasoning mixture is Kurdish style. Like falafel, which is more well known
in the United States, kibbeh can be an appetizer or a main dish.*

½ cup bulgur wheat
1 cup boiling water
8 oz. extralean ground beef
  or turkey
½ cup soy meat substitute
  crumbles
2 tbsp. farina or Cream of Wheat
1 cup minced onions
2 garlic cloves, chopped

¼ cup fresh parsley or cilantro,
  or 1 tbsp. dry
1 tsp. dry mint
2 tsp. cumin
1 tsp. allspice
½ tsp. cinnamon
½ tsp. black pepper
Cooking spray

In a small bowl, soak the bulgur in the boiling water for 10 minutes. Drain for 10 minutes.

Meanwhile, in a large bowl, combine the remaining ingredients except the cooking spray. Mix in the bulgur. (It is best to knead it with your hands). Form into 10 small oval patties. Grill or pan fry with cooking spray over medium heat for a total of 10 minutes. Serves 5.

Serving suggestion: These are good stuffed into a pita with Caramelized Onions, Harissa Salsa, and lots of relish fixings.

Calories—141; Saturated fat—0 g.; Total fat—2 g.; Carbohydrates—19 g.; Cholesterol—19 mg.; Sodium—45 mg.; Fiber—1 g.; Protein—12 g.

NORTH AFRICAN STYLE MEATBALLS
OVER COUSCOUS

MEAT/PAREVE

*Meatballs are found in Ashkenazic, Sephardic and Oriental Jewish cuisines.
This is actually how my Ukrainian grandmother made her meatballs—
by cooking them in water and onions. Of course, the similarities end here.
The rest is classic Sephardic. This particular recipe is a specialty from the Jews
of Tunisia and Algeria. Couscous is very common in North Africa. In fact,
it's a staple in Tunisia, where there are many variations of it.*

1 lb. extralean ground beef or
ground white turkey meat or
chicken

1 small potato, grated, or
½ cup breadcrumbs

1 egg white or egg substitute
equaling 1 egg

⅓ cup minced parsley

2 garlic cloves, minced

¼ tsp. nutmeg

Salt to taste

Black pepper to taste

Cooking spray

1 onion, minced

1¾ cups water

2 large fresh tomatoes, diced, or
15½-oz. can diced tomatoes

¾ tsp. turmeric

12-oz. pkg. frozen artichoke
hearts

1½ cups frozen peas

6 cups cooked couscous

In a bowl, combine the ground beef, potato, egg white, parsley, garlic, nutmeg, salt, and pepper and shape into approximately 12 meatballs.

In a nonstick skillet coated with cooking spray, sauté the onion over medium heat for 4-5 minutes. Add 1½ cups of the water and heat until hot but not boiling.

Carefully drop the meatballs into the pan and cook on all sides for approximately 12 minutes. If the water evaporates too quickly, add about ¼ cup more.

Add the undrained can of tomatoes or fresh tomatoes, turmeric, and vegetables. Simmer uncovered over low to medium-low heat for approximately 20 minutes until most of the liquid has evaporated and leaves a thickened red sauce.

Serve over cooked couscous. Serves 6.

Variation: Substitute 1½ cups sliced zucchini or cauliflower florets for the peas.

Pareve/vegetarian variation: Omit the meatballs. Peel small red potatoes and slice them in half. Add zucchini, cauliflower, artichoke hearts, and frozen peas, if desired. Use the same sauce, and serve over couscous.

Calories—277; Saturated fat—1 g.; Total fat—3 g.; Carbohydrates—60 g.; Cholesterol—49 mg.; Sodium—157 mg.; Fiber—2 g.; Protein—28 g.

THE TAX CHAZZAN'S GREAT MEATBALLS

MEAT
SHABBAT
CHANUKAH
PASSOVER

*This is an easy dish that Cantor Isaac Koll enjoys making.
I've lightened it a little, so you get a calorie and fat refund! I call this easy,
versatile sauce the "great American Ashkenazic invention."*

SAUCE

**1 can jellied cranberry sauce
(natural, if available at a
natural-foods store)**

12-oz. can tomato sauce

AMERICAN LOW-FAT MEATBALLS

**¾ lb. ground low-fat white turkey
   or chicken**
½ cup breadcrumbs
½ cup shredded zucchini
¼ cup chopped green onions

1 tsp. Dijon mustard
**1 tsp. chili powder or
   ground cumin**
1 egg white

Combine the cranberry sauce and tomato sauce in a skillet. Turn on medium low while making the tiny meatballs.

Mix the meatball ingredients. Form into 60 tiny meatballs about the size of your thumbnail. (Make larger meatballs if you want to save some time.)

Place the meatballs in the sauce, starting around the edge of the skillet, working in a circular fashion. Cover and cook on low for 1½ hours. Serves 6.

Serving suggestion: Serve over spaghetti, rice, Pareve Mashed Potatoes, couscous, or cooked bulgur wheat.

For Passover: Substitute ½ cup matzah meal for the breadcrumbs and Passover mustard for the Dijon mustard. Substitute 1 tsp. of any seasoning you like for the chili powder.

Calories—223; Saturated fat—0 g.; Total fat—2 g.; Carbohydrates—37 g.; Cholesterol—24 mg.; Sodium—934 mg.; Fiber—1 g.; Protein—15 g.

AMERICAN SPAGHETTI IN A BREAD BOWL

PAREVE/MEAT
SUKKOT

I know . . . it's American-Italian, but it's a good idea for a family Sukkot dinner. The spaghetti can be served from a large bread bowl, or— what's fun for kids—in individual bread rolls. The bread bowls help keep the spaghetti warmer longer in the sukkah, where the evening can be quite cool. These vegetables are only suggestions. Use whatever you have on hand. It's a harvest dish in recognition of Sukkot as the harvest festival.

Cooking spray
1 cup minced onion
1 lb. sliced mushrooms
1 carrot, chopped
½ cup fresh corn
1 small green pepper, chopped
4 garlic cloves, chopped
1 lb. soy protein meat substitute
  or ground white turkey meat
  or chicken
28-oz. can chopped tomatoes

8-oz. can tomato sauce
6-oz. can tomato paste
3 tbsp. chopped fresh basil
  leaves
1 tsp. dry oregano
¼ tsp. crushed red pepper
8 oz. spaghetti
Large round loaf sourdough
  bread or 7 individual hoagie
  or poor-boy rolls

In a skillet sprayed with cooking spray, sauté the onion, mushrooms, carrot, corn, green pepper, and garlic on medium high for 4-5 minutes. Add the soy protein or ground meat to the skillet and brown it until no longer pink.

Add the remaining ingredients except the spaghetti and bread. Bring to a boil over high heat. Reduce heat, cover, and simmer over very low heat for approximately 90 minutes.

Prepare the spaghetti or freeze the sauce until ready to use.

Mix the sauce with the cooked spaghetti.

To make a bread bowl, heat the oven to 325 degrees and warm the bread, just to crisp the outer crust (about 10 minutes). Slice the top off the bread. Hollow out, leaving a ½-inch shell. (Store and use the bread for stuffing, breadcrumbs, or another use.)

Spoon the hot spaghetti into the large bread bowl or individual bread bowls. Serves 7.

Serving suggestion: A green salad completes this meal.

With soy protein: Calories—340; Saturated fat—0 g.; Total fat—3 g.; Carbohydrates—60 g.; Cholesterol—0 mg.; Sodium—207 mg.; Fiber—6 g.; Protein—27 g.

With ground turkey or chicken: Calories—347; Saturated fat—1 g.; Total fat—3 g.; Carbohydrates—54 g.; Cholesterol—39 mg.; Sodium—231 mg.; Fiber—2 g.; Protein—54 g.

Vegetarian
Entrees

FIVE-VEGETABLE STEW WITH COUSCOUS

This dish is a beautiful Rosh Hashanah entree. Moroccan Jews enjoy many symbolic foods for the new year. The symbolism is linked to the names of the food. For example, the Hebrew word for leek is karti, which also means "to cut off." This illustrates the wish that our enemies should be "cut off." In this recipe, three symbolic foods are used: leek (karti, "cut off"), gourd (kraa, "fear"), and carrot (gezeri "tear"). To save time, prepare the artichokes a few days in advance. Include all seven vegetables in the meal by starting with Carrot-Beet Salad "Bi Tahini" or Russian Beet Salad.

6 artichokes, trimmed, boiled or steamed, and choke removed

FILLING

Garlic-flavored cooking spray
1 tsp. olive oil
2 butternut squash, peeled and cubed
1 cup cleaned, sliced leeks
1 cup sliced carrots
1½ cups cooked or canned chickpeas, drained

1 lb. tomatoes
5 tbsp. red lentils
1 cup tomato sauce
1 cup water
¼ cup chopped parsley
½ tsp. paprika
⅛ tsp. cinnamon
⅛ tsp. crushed red pepper flakes

COUSCOUS

1¼ cups water
1 tsp. pareve chicken-flavored bouillon or 1 tsp. seasoning from packet in boxed couscous

¼ tsp. turmeric
Pinch cinnamon and ginger
1 cup uncooked couscous

   In a large skillet coated with garlic spray, add the oil. Cook the squash and leeks over medium-high heat for 5 minutes or until both begin to brown. Add the remaining filling ingredients. Cover and cook on medium low for 25-30 minutes or until vegetables and lentils are tender.

Meanwhile, in a saucepan, bring the water and seasonings for the couscous to a boil. Add the couscous, and remove from heat. Stir briefly. Cover and let stand for 5 minutes.

To serve, place ⅓ cup couscous into each hollowed-out cooked artichoke (the artichoke may be hot or room temperature). Spoon the vegetable stew over the couscous. Serves 6.

Calories—361; Saturated fat—0 g.; Total fat—3 g.; Carbohydrates—69 g.; Cholesterol—0 mg.; Sodium—291 mg.; Fiber—5 g.; Protein—15 g.

LENTIL AND RICE STUFFED PEPPERS

PAREVE
SUKKOT
PURIM
NINE DAYS BEFORE TISHAH B'AV

This is a vegetarian version of the popular Ashkenazic pepper stuffed with meat and rice. Many versions will call for a sweet and sour sauce. Some are more savory. This adaptation is naturally sweetened with fruit-juice concentrate.

½ cup rice
¼ cup red lentils
2 cups water
Cooking spray
1 cup chopped onions
1 tbsp. minced garlic
10-oz. pkg. frozen spinach,
  thawed and drained

4 frozen veggie burgers,
  any flavor
½ cup low-sodium tomato sauce
1 tsp. paprika
3 large green peppers

SAUCE

1 cup low-sodium tomato sauce
2 tbsp. pineapple, apple, or
  orange juice concentrate

3 tbsp. lemon juice
¼ tsp. paprika

In a saucepan, combine the rice, lentils, and water. Bring to a boil over high heat. Reduce heat to low, cover, and simmer for 20 minutes or until the rice is tender and the water is absorbed.

In a nonstick skillet coated with cooking spray, fry the onions and garlic over medium heat for 5-7 minutes.

Remove skillet from heat and add spinach and rice mixture. Crumble the burgers and mix with other ingredients in the skillet. Mix in tomato sauce and paprika.

Slice the green peppers in half lengthwise, and remove the seeds. Spoon the filling mixture into each pepper half. Place the peppers in a baking dish. Cover the bottom of the baking dish with approximately ¼ inch water.

Combine the sauce ingredients and pour over the stuffed peppers. Bake at 350 degrees for 50 minutes. Serves 6.

Calories—217; Saturated fat—0 g.; Total fat—1 g.; Carbohydrates—35 g.; Cholesterol—0 mg.; Sodium—64 mg.; Fiber—5 g.; Protein—18 g.

POLENTA-STUFFED PEPPERS

PAREVE
SHABBAT
SUKKOT
NINE DAYS BEFORE TISHAH B'AV

This contemporary Italian-style vegetarian dish is strikingly colorful for a holiday. It is made easier by using commercial roasted peppers and spaghetti sauce. Polenta comes in a box, as well, but this is easy enough to make yourself. The polenta and layers can be made a day or two in advance, stuffed into the peppers, and stored covered in the fridge. The sauce can also be made in advance. Actually, I have baked the dish, stored it in the refrigerator, and rewarmed it the next day, and it was still very good.

2 roasted red peppers
2 tbsp. tomato paste
2 garlic cloves
1 cup fresh or frozen chopped spinach
½ cup chopped basil

4 cups Vegetable Broth
1½ cups cornmeal
2 each of red, yellow, and green bell peppers
¾ cup water

SAUCE

Cooking spray	**15-oz. jar roasted peppers**
1 onion, chopped	**½ cup spaghetti sauce,**
1 garlic clove, chopped	**jar or homemade**
1 tsp. oregano	**Salt and pepper to taste**
½ tsp. red pepper flakes	

Set 3 bowls out. In a food processor, puree the roasted peppers, tomato paste, and 1 garlic clove. Place into the first bowl.

Place the chopped spinach, basil, and remaining garlic clove in the clean food processor. Coarsely puree. Place into the second bowl.

In a saucepan, combine the Vegetable Broth and cornmeal. Bring to a boil over high heat. Reduce heat to low, stir, and cook for 10 minutes. Divide and mix the polenta evenly into the 3 bowls. (One bowl will have only the polenta.)

To stuff the peppers, slice off the tops, seed, and rinse. Distribute the red pepper mixture into the bottoms of all 6 peppers. Layer the plain mixture into the peppers. Top with the basil mixture.

Place the peppers in a casserole dish and bake at 350 degrees for 25-30 minutes. Remove and slice the peppers in halves lengthwise. Lay the halves in a baking dish. Add the water to the bottom of the dish and bake for 20-25 minutes longer.

Meanwhile, make the sauce. In a saucepan coated with the cooking spray, sauté the onion for 3-4 minutes over medium-high heat. Add the garlic and sauté for another minute.

Add the remaining sauce ingredients and simmer for 10 minutes on medium-low to low heat.

To serve, spoon the sauce in plates or on a platter and place the pepper halves on top. Serves 6.

Variation: For protein, add ½ cup mashed low-fat tofu to the cooked polenta before adding the stir-in ingredients.

Calories—281; Saturated fat—0 g.; Total fat—1 g.; Carbohydrates—57 g.; Cholesterol—0 mg.; Sodium—198 mg.; Fiber—4 g.; Protein—10 g.

ONION AND CHIVE POLENTA

PAREVE/DAIRY

NINE DAYS BEFORE TISHAH B'AV

*Polenta is so versatile. It can be made dairy or pareve, so it can fit
into any meal. This is just a base, as is pasta, so be creative!
Serve it as a side or main dish, depending upon your choice of toppings
and stir-ins. For dairy, stir in your choice of low-fat cheese.*

Cooking spray
½ cup minced onion
3 cups vegetable broth

1 cup cornmeal
Salt and pepper (optional)
¼ cup minced fresh chives

Coat a small pan with cooking spray. Over medium heat, cook the onions for a few minutes until they just begin to turn brown. Remove from heat.

In a saucepan, add the vegetable broth and cornmeal. Bring to a boil over high heat. Reduce heat to low, stir, and cook for 10 minutes. (Bringing the ingredients to a boil together eliminates lumps.) Season with a light sprinkling of salt and pepper if desired. Stir in the chives and onions.

Serve immediately or mold it by spreading it into a greased 8-inch square baking pan. Chill for 1 hour. Slice into 6 squares. Can reheat in oven before serving. Sometimes polenta is reheated by sautéing it in a pan with cooking spray, or broiling it, coating the tops with cooking spray, to a light golden brown. Serves 6.

Serving suggestions: Just a couple of the popular stir-ins include roasted garlic and plumped sun-dried tomatoes. For a vegetarian main dish, stir in 8 oz. pureed light tofu with the chives and onions.

Variation: To microwave, use 1 cup cornmeal and 3½ cups water or broth. Microwave on high for 12 minutes. Stir for 1 minute. Let it rest 3 minutes. Serve hot, or coat an 8-inch square baking pan with cooking spray, spread the mixture in, and chill.

Calories—136; Saturated fat—0 g.; Total fat—1 g.; Carbohydrates—29 g.; Cholesterol—0 mg.; Sodium—138 mg.; Fiber—2 g.; Protein—4 g.

RICE-STUFFED ZUCCHINI

PAREVE
SUKKOT

*This Greek-style stuffing is usually wrapped in grape leaves for dolmas.
Variations of this stuffing are found from Greece to Turkey and Syria to
Yemen. Sometimes ground beef or lamb is added. This dish has bulgur wheat
to add more texture. This stuffing could also be a side dish or
stuffed into other vegetables. The sun-dried tomatoes are
a contemporary touch for taste and color.*

8 medium zucchini

STUFFING

1 cup boiling water	**¼ cup chopped parsley or mint**
½ cup sun-dried tomatoes	**2 tbsp. currants or raisins**
2 tsp. olive oil	**2 tbsp. chopped toasted almonds**
1 onion, chopped	**¼ tsp. allspice**
½ cup long-grain white rice	**½ tsp. salt**
1/2 cup bulgur wheat	
2½ cups pareve chicken-flavored	
bouillon or vegetable broth	

TOPPING

¼ cup tomato puree	**1 tbsp. lemon juice**
2 cups pareve chicken-flavored	**1 tsp. minced garlic**
bouillon or vegetable broth	**⅛ tsp. cayenne pepper**

In a bowl of boiling water, rehydrate the tomatoes, and set aside.

In a nonstick skillet, heat the oil, add the onion, and brown for 3 minutes on medium high. Add the rice and bulgur and sauté for another 3 minutes to lightly brown.

Add the remaining stuffing ingredients, including the sun-dried tomatoes. Bring to a boil over high heat. Reduce heat to low, cover, and simmer for 20 minutes or until the rice is tender and the liquid is absorbed.

Cut each zucchini in half lengthwise. Using a melon-ball scoop (it's easiest), scrape the pulp from the center of each zucchini half.

Place the hollowed-out zucchini in a baking pan and fill each with rice mixture, about a heaping tablespoon each.

In a saucepan, bring the topping ingredients to a boil over high heat. Remove from heat, and pour a little over each zucchini half.

Cover and bake at 350 degrees for 30 minutes. Uncover and bake for 20 more minutes. Serves 6.

Calories—163; Saturated fat—0 g.; Total fat—2 g.; Carbohydrates—31 g.; Cholesterol—0 mg.; Sodium—231 mg.; Fiber—1 g.; Protein—6 g.

Note: Tomato puree comes in cans.

STUFFED EGGPLANT

PAREVE
ROSH HASHANAH
YOM KIPPUR BEFORE THE FAST
SUKKOT
NINE DAYS BEFORE TISHAH B'AV

Stuffed vegetables are a Sephardic tradition, especially for holidays.

¼ cup pine nuts
3 small eggplants or
   6 Japanese eggplants
Olive-oil spray
8 oz. reduced-fat firm silken tofu, crumbled
10-oz. pkg. frozen chopped spinach, thawed and drained

1 cup instant roasted-garlic-flavored couscous
1 tsp. mild curry
⅛ tsp. turmeric
⅛ tsp. cinnamon

In a small nonstick skillet over medium heat, toast the pine nuts 3-5 minutes or until lightly toasted. Set aside.

Trim the tops off the eggplants. Cut eggplants in half lengthwise. Discard as much of the seeds as possible to remove the bitter taste.

Cut and scoop out pulp, leaving ¼ inch of the shells. Cut pulp into small cubes.

In a large nonstick skillet coated with olive-oil spray, cook eggplant cubes, tofu, spinach, and nuts over medium heat for approximately 15 minutes or until the eggplant is tender.

Meanwhile prepare the couscous according to package directions. Add seasonings to water when preparing couscous. Set aside while it absorbs the water (approximately 5 minutes). Add this to the eggplant mixture and stuff back into the eggplant skins. Bake at 350 degrees for 20-30 minutes until heated through. Let sit for 5-10 minutes before serving. Serves 6.

Calories—194; Saturated fat—1 g.; Total fat—5 g.; Carbohydrates—29 g.; Cholesterol—0 mg.; Sodium—43 mg.; Fiber—1 g.; Protein—8 g.

DOLMAS (STUFFED GRAPE LEAVES)

PAREVE
SUKKOT
YOM HATZMA'UT

Rice is the usual stuffing for this Greek classic. This version is a little simpler.

¼ cup pine nuts
Cooking spray
½ small onion, chopped
2 garlic cloves, chopped
½ tsp. oregano
¼ tsp. cinnamon
¼ tsp. cumin

3 cups water
1½ cups cracked bulgur wheat
¼ cup raisins
2 tbsp. minced mint or parsley
24 grape leaves (approximately
    ½ jar), rinsed and drained
3 tbsp. lemon juice

In a dry skillet, toast the pine nuts over medium heat 4-5 minutes or until golden. Set aside.

Coat the skillet with cooking spray. Add the onion, garlic, oregano, cinnamon, and cumin, and sauté over medium heat for 5 minutes or until the onions are soft.

Bring the water to a boil over high heat. Add the pine nuts, cracked bulgur wheat, and raisins. Reduce heat to low and simmer for 10 minutes or until the liquid is absorbed.

Cover the pot and set aside for approximately 20 minutes.

Stir in the mint or parsley and onion mixture.

Preheat the oven to 325 degrees. To stuff the grape leaves, spread out each leaf, vein side down. Spoon 1 tbsp. of filling into the center of each leaf. Fold in the sides and, starting from the stem end, roll leaf up.

Place the stuffed leaves in a lightly oiled casserole dish. Drizzle the lemon juice over the top. Bake covered for 15 minutes. Serves 8.

Calories—147; Saturated fat—0 g.; Total fat—3 g.; Carbohydrates—26 g.; Cholesterol—0 mg.; Sodium—72 mg.; Fiber—1 g.; Protein—4 g.

SYRIAN MEJADARRA (Lentils and Rice)

PAREVE
YOM KIPPUR BEFORE THE FAST
PURIM
NINE DAYS BEFORE TISHAH B'AV

A common weekday vegetarian dish eaten by Sephardic Jews,
influenced by Arab host countries. This is a mild, unadorned dish.
In this version, the spices and flavors have been enhanced.

Olive-oil cooking spray
1 onion, chopped
1 stalk celery, chopped
1 carrot, chopped
3 garlic cloves, chopped
1 cup long-grain and wild rice
  mix, including contents
  of seasoning packet

½ cup brown lentils
3½ cups water
½ tsp. cumin seed
½ tsp. curry powder
¼ tsp. ground cardamom
¼ tsp. salt
⅛ tsp. black pepper
3 tbsp. toasted pine nuts

In a saucepan coated with the olive-oil cooking spray, sauté the onion, celery, carrot, and garlic over medium heat for 7 minutes or until the vegetables are soft.

Add the remaining ingredients. Bring to a boil over high heat. Reduce the heat to medium low. Cover and simmer for 40 minutes or until the lentils and rice are tender. Serves 6.

Serving suggestion: This is delicious served as a main dish with dollops of yogurt and Caramelized Onions. Serve hot.

Variation: For a lower-sodium version, omit the seasoning packet from the rice mix and increase the spices to 1 tsp. cumin seed, ¾ tsp. curry powder, ½ tsp. ground cardamom, ½ tsp. salt, and ¼ tsp. black pepper.

Calories—176; Saturated fat—1 g.; Total fat—4g.; Carbohydrates—27 g.; Cholesterol—3 mg.; Sodium—499 mg.; Fiber—3 g.; Protein—8 g.

FAVA BEANS WITH RICE

*The Sephardic Algerian version of this dish does not include lemon like the
Moroccan and Tunisian versions, although two seasonings common
to North African cuisine, cumin and paprika, are included. I took the liberty
of including my own additions, which I leave optional for you.
This is also found in Iranian Jewish cuisine and was brought to Israel.*

2 cups cooked or
   canned fava beans
1½ tsp. cumin
½ tsp. paprika
2 tsp. olive oil

2 tbsp. lemon juice (optional)
2 tbsp. minced parsley
¼ tsp. red pepper flakes
   (optional)
2 cups cooked rice

In a saucepan, combine all ingredients except the rice and heat through. Serve
with rice or mash in your plate and serve with pita bread. Serves 4.

Variation: Baby lima beans or kidney beans can be substituted for the fava beans.

*Calories—254; Saturated fat—0 g.; Total fat—3 g.; Carbohydrates—47 g.;
Cholesterol—0 mg.; Sodium—428 mg.; Fiber—3 g.; Protein—10 g.*

VEGETARIAN SENEYEH
WITH APRICOT-TOMATO CHUTNEY

PAREVE
*SHABBAT
ROSH HASHANAH
SUKKOT
NINE DAYS BEFORE TISHAH B'AV*

*This is a vegetarian version of a well-known Yemenite dish of ground meat
baked with a tahini sauce topping. The tahini is a kosher substitute
for a creamy dairy sauce. Since tahini is high in fat, you can substitute this
Indian chutney. This recipe, and the accompanying chutney recipe,
comes from Dr. Gratia Meyer Solomon, a generous dear friend and hostess
who is known for her creativity with vegetarian cuisine.*

1 tsp. olive oil
2 cups chopped onion
2 garlic cloves, chopped
4 cups beef-flavored seitan
8 oz. soft tofu
½ cup whole-wheat flour
5 tbsp. matzah meal or
    breadcrumbs
2 tbsp. wheat gluten (helps
    texture; available at natural-
    foods stores)

¼ cup chopped fresh parsley or
    cilantro
¾ tsp. cinnamon
½ tsp. cayenne pepper
¼ cup toasted pine nuts
Cooking spray
Apricot-Tomato Chutney
    (recipe follows)

In a nonstick skillet, heat the oil over medium-high heat and sauté the onions and garlic until golden brown, approximately 5 minutes.

In a food processor or blender, puree the tofu. Add all the ingredients but only half the pine nuts and not the cooking spray or chutney. Blend. Stir in remaining pine nuts.

Coat a 9-inch round baking pan with the cooking spray and pour in the mixture. Spoon the chutney over the top. Bake at 350 degrees for 35 minutes or until the chutney bubbles. Serves 8.

Calories—201; Saturated fat—0 g.; Total fat—4 g.; Carbohydrates—22 g.; Cholesterol—0 mg.; Sodium—151 mg.; Fiber—1 g.; Protein—20 g.

APRICOT-TOMATO CHUTNEY

PAREVE

*This condiment is inspired by the chutneys that the Bene Israel
community from India brought to Israel.*

½ lb. dried apricots, halved
½ lb. fresh tomatoes, chopped
¼ cup golden raisins
¼ cup sugar
½ cup white-wine vinegar
½ cup orange juice
1 tsp. minced fresh ginger

2 garlic cloves, chopped
1 small hot green chili pepper,
  chopped, or ½ tsp. cayenne
  pepper
½ tsp. ground coriander
½ tsp. ground cardamom
⅛ tsp. salt

In a skillet, combine all the ingredients and simmer over low heat, covered, for
20 minutes.

Cool to room temperature for 1-2 hours before using. Store in a covered container in the refrigerator. Serve as a topping for Vegetarian Seneyeh. Makes 1 cup.

Variation: If using for Rosh Hashanah, omit the vinegar and increase the orange
juice to 1 cup.

*Per 2 tbsp.: Calories—164; Saturated fat—0 g.; Total fat—g.; Carbohydrates—
38 g.; Cholesterol—0 mg.; Sodium—45 mg.; Fiber—2 g.; Protein—2 g.*

SOUTH AFRICAN MALAYSIAN
VEGETABLE CURRY

PAREVE
SIMCHAT TORAH
NINE DAYS BEFORE TISHAH B'AV

*Indonesian and Malaysian curries are popular in Holland, and South African
cooking has been influenced by the Dutch. South African Jews, in turn, have
brought these tastes to Israel. There is a lot of cross-culture fusion going on in
this dish from neighboring countries: curry from Indonesia and Malaysia,
and coconut milk from Thailand and India. All of this in one dish!*

CURRY SAUCE

3 shallots, peeled
1-2 small red chili peppers, seeded and coarsely chopped, or ½ tsp. cayenne pepper

3 tbsp. curry powder
½ cup light coconut milk (if unavailable, use ½ cup pureed apricot baby food)

VEGETABLES

Cooking spray
2 onions, chopped
3 cups unpeeled, sliced Japanese eggplants
3 carrots, sliced
8 oz. fresh green beans

½ head napa cabbage, sliced
1 large tomato, sliced in half-moons
1 cup cooked chickpeas
4 cups steamed rice

GARNISHES

2 bananas, sliced
⅓ cup raisins

Mango chutney

In a food processor, pulse the shallots and red chili peppers. Add the curry powder and coconut milk and coarsely puree. Set aside.

In a skillet coated with cooking spray, sauté the onions over medium-high heat for approximately 5 minutes. Add the eggplants and sauté for approximately 7 minutes.

Add the carrots, green beans, cabbage, tomatoes, chickpeas, and curry sauce. Cover and simmer on low for another 5 minutes or until all the vegetables are tender.

Serve curry over rice on a platter and serve the garnishes in attractive bowls. Serves 6.

Variation: If fresh curry leaves are available, add a few leaves to the vegetables.

Calories—382; Saturated fat—0 g.; Total fat—2 g.; Carbohydrates—81 g.; Cholesterol—0 mg.; Sodium—105 mg.; Fiber—4 g.; Protein—10 g.

GARDEN VEGETABLES WITH COUSCOUS

PAREVE
SHABBAT
YOM KIPPUR BEFORE THE FAST
NINE DAYS BEFORE TISHAH B'AV

*I found a similar recipe, which is common to the North African Jews,
in a fundraising cookbook for the Herzl Jewish School in Belo Horizonte,
Brazil. It inspired my own version and actually became one of my favorite
combinations of vegetables. It is a quick and easy meal that tastes
as though you've worked on it a long time.*

2 cups cauliflower florets
4 small red potatoes, halved
1 cup baby carrots
1 onion, cut into wedges
1 cup vegetable broth or water
2 tbsp. minced parsley
1 tsp. turmeric
½ tsp. cumin
¼ tsp. black pepper

Pinch cinnamon
½ cup water
1 tbsp. Harissa Salsa (optional)
1 large stalk celery, sliced thick
1½ cups cooked or canned chickpeas
2 tomato wedges
1 medium zucchini, cubed
1 box flavored instant couscous

In a soup pot, combine the cauliflower, red potatoes, carrots, onion wedges,
broth, parsley, turmeric, cumin, pepper, and cinnamon. Add the water and Harissa
Salsa, cover, and, over medium heat, steam the vegetables for 3-4 minutes.

Add the remaining vegetables and continue to steam until they reach desired tenderness.

Meanwhile prepare the instant couscous. Spoon the vegetables over the couscous. Serve with additional Harissa Salsa if desired. Serves 4.

*Calories—389; Saturated fat—0 g.; Total fat—3 g; Carbohydrates—77 g.;
Cholesterol—0 mg.; Sodium—240 mg.; Fiber—5 g.; Protein—13 g.*

SARA'S SPINACH PIE

DAIRY/PAREVE
SHABBAT
YOM KIPPUR BREAK-THE-FAST
PURIM
PASSOVER
SHAVUOT
NINE DAYS BEFORE TISHAH B'AV

Sara Kishoni and her family are well versed in vegetarianism. She and her husband, Israelis now living in Colorado, have followed this way of eating since the 1970s. Sara's attitude about food is, it's not what you eat, it's the portion size that's important. This is one of her favorite recipes because of its ease of preparation and, most importantly, its flavor. She suggests creating a rice shell, which I have done below. Use a kosher readymade pie shell as a delicious alternative (although it's higher in fat). Sara recommends this as a festive dairy dish for Shabbat, Shavuot, or even Rosh Hashanah.

RICE SHELL

1 cup white rice
2 cups water
¼ tsp. salt

¼ cup egg substitute or
   1 egg or 2 egg whites
Butter-flavored cooking spray

SPINACH FILLING

Butter-flavored cooking spray
2 large onions, chopped
4-6 garlic cloves, chopped
1 carrot, grated (optional for
   extra color and sweetness)
2 10-oz. pkg. frozen spinach,
   thawed, chopped, but not
   drained

½ cup nonfat sour cream or
   yogurt, or soft tofu
⅔ cup combination of your
   choice of low-fat grated cheese:
   cheddar, Muenster, Gruyere or
   feta, or soft tofu

In a saucepan, combine the rice, water, and salt. Bring to a boil over high heat. Reduce heat to low and simmer, covered, 18 minutes or until the water is absorbed and rice is tender.

Set the oven rack to the bottom position. Preheat the oven to 400 degrees.

Add the egg to the rice and mix thoroughly.

Coat a 9-inch pie pan with butter-flavored cooking spray. Press the rice mixture on the bottom and up the sides of the pie pan to form a crust. Spray the top of the rice with the butter spray. Place on the bottom oven rack and bake for 20 minutes.

Prepare the spinach filling. Coat a skillet with the cooking spray. Sauté the onions, garlic, and carrot on medium until soft, for 7-8 minutes.

Add spinach and cook until much of the moisture evaporates. Remove from the skillet.

Set the oven to 375 degrees.

Mix the sour cream and cheese into the spinach mixture. Pour into the rice shell. Bake for 30 minutes. This is best served hot. Serves 6.

Calories—201; Saturated fat—1 g.; Total fat—2 g.; Carbohydrates—34 g.; Cholesterol—5 mg.; Sodium—246 mg.; Fiber—1 g.; Protein—11 g.

Note: For Passover, omit Rice Shell. Use Potato Shell (see index). Use nonfat yogurt.

FALAFEL TWO WAYS

PAREVE
YOM HAATZMA'UT

These quintessentially Israeli chickpea croquettes can be served with a variety of relishes and toppings. For a more authentic flavor, use a little oil. These are usually deep fried, but I enjoy them baked.

1¼ cups chickpeas, soaked
   overnight (will become
   approximately 3 cups)
2 tsp. chopped garlic
½ cup bulgur, soaked
   10 minutes and drained
1 small onion, chopped
1½ tsp. ground cumin

1 tsp. ground coriander
2 tbsp. snipped parsley
¼ tsp. cayenne pepper
¾ tsp. salt
2 tbsp. canola oil (optional)
1 tbsp. olive oil (optional)
Cooking spray (optional)

In a food processor, blend all the ingredients except the oils until smooth. Refrigerate the mixture 1 hour until it is firm.

Form into about 30 croquettes. Over medium-high heat, fry 10 at a time, using 2 tsp. canola oil and 1 tsp. olive oil. Fry on both sides until golden. Repeat with the remaining croquettes using remaining oil.

To avoid the oil, bake at 425 degrees on the bottom oven rack. Spray the falafel balls with cooking spray and bake 20 minutes or until lightly browned on both sides. It becomes only 3 grams of fat.

Serve in a pita half with your choice of fixings. Serves 8.

Serving suggestion: Make a relish with diced cucumbers, diced tomatoes, diced chili or banana peppers, and hot sauce. Or try some American taco-style fixings with the falafel, such as low-fat shredded cheddar cheese, chopped lettuce, chopped tomato, low-fat ranch dressing, and salsa.

Variation: You can omit the cumin, and add 1 extra tsp. garlic and one finely grated carrot.

Calories—201; Saturated fat—1 g.; Total fat—7 g.; Carbohydrates—27 g.; Cholesterol—0 mg.; Sodium—232 mg.; Fiber—2 g.; Protein—7 g.

AUSTRIAN-HUNGARIAN EGGPLANT GOULASH

PAREVE
PASSOVER
NINE DAYS BEFORE TISHAH B'AV

This makes a good vegetarian main meal, although originally the chief ingredient was beef. Everything else is authentic—there are no changes. This is a savory version. The sweet and sour variation below is another choice. The onions become the thickening agent, rather than flour as in other sauces.

2 tsp. oil
1 lb. onions (2 medium), minced
½ lb. eggplant, cubed, or seitan, drained and cubed (not for Passover)
½ lb. mushrooms, quartered
1 large green pepper, cut in 1-inch squares
2 tbsp. tomato puree

1 tbsp. Hungarian paprika
½ tsp. caraway seeds (optional)
½ tsp. minced garlic
1 bay leaf
⅛ tsp. black pepper
1 cup vegetable broth or water
1 lb. cooked yolk-free egg noodles or Passover noodles

In a large nonstick skillet, heat the oil over medium heat and cook the onions for approximately 2 minutes.

Add the eggplant, mushrooms, and green pepper. Continue cooking for approximately 5 minutes.

Add the remaining ingredients except the noodles and bring to a boil over high heat. Reduce heat to low, cover, and simmer for 30 minutes.

Serve over yolk-free egg noodles or, for Passover, mashed potatoes. Serves 6.

Variation: For Sweet and Sour Israeli Style, after cooking the eggplant, mushrooms, and green pepper for 5 minutes, omit all other ingredients and add ½ cup ketchup, 2 tbsp. vinegar, 2 tbsp. brown sugar, 2 tbsp. Worcestershire sauce, and 1 tsp. paprika. (This is not for Passover.)

Calories—54; Saturated fat—0 g.; Total fat—2 g.; Carbohydrates—7 g.; Cholesterol—0 mg.; Sodium—311 mg.; Fiber—1 g.; Protein—2 g.

Sweet and Sour Israeli Style: Calories—103; Saturated fat—0 g.; Total fat—2 g.; Carbohydrates—19 g.; Cholesterol—0 mg.; Sodium—254 mg.; Fiber—1 g.; Protein—2 g.

GRILLED VEGGIE SANDWICH

PAREVE/DAIRY
YOM HAATZMA'UT
LAG B'OMER

This is my favorite summer quick dinner. It can be made for a picnic as well.

1 large red pepper
1 large green pepper

4 portobello mushroom slices
4 steak rolls or kaiser rolls

SANDWICH FIXINGS

Baba Ghanouj recipe or
  Roasted Pepper Dip recipe
Caramelized Onions recipe
4 lettuce leaves
4 tomato slices
2 banana peppers, halved
Fresh basil leaves

Nonfat Italian dressing
4 slices white low-fat cheese,
  such as Muenster or
  mozzarella, or 2 tbsp.
  crumbled low-fat feta cheese on
  each sandwich (optional)

Grill or broil the red and green peppers and portobello mushroom slices 6-7 minutes each side or until brown on both sides. Let peppers steam in a plastic bag a few minutes to loosen skins. Peel skins from peppers. Slice peppers and mushrooms for sandwiches.

Spread both halves of the steak rolls with Baba Ghanouj or Roasted Pepper Dip. Layer on Caramelized Onions, lettuce, tomato, banana peppers, and basil leaves. Layer on the roasted vegetables. Drizzle the dressing over the veggies. Add the cheese, if desired. Serves 4.

Variation: For a complete nutritional meal with protein, grill a veggie burger and add to sandwich.

Without cheese: Calories—182; Saturated fat—1 g.; Total fat—3 g.; Carbohydrates—33 g.; Cholesterol—2 mg.; Sodium—428 mg.; Fiber—2 g.; Protein—6 g.

With cheese: Calories—239; Saturated fat—3 g.; Total fat—7 g.; Carbohydrates—33 g.; Cholesterol—2 mg.; Sodium—492 mg.; Fiber—2 g.; Protein—11g.

CREAMY EGG SALAD

PAREVE
YOM KIPPUR BREAK-THE-FAST

Egg salad has always been essential in Jewish cuisine. It's pareve and fits well into Shabbat Kiddushes, lunches, or shalosh seudot because it can be made a day in advance. This cholesterol-free egg salad can be easily doubled, or more.

6 hardboiled eggs
8 oz. low-fat tofu
1 carrot, peeled and shredded
¼ cup low-fat mayonnaise
2 tsp. yellow mustard
½ tsp. onion powder

¼-½ tsp. turmeric
¼ tsp. salt
⅛ tsp. black pepper
**1 scallion, chopped,
    or more to taste**
Paprika for garnish

Remove and discard the yolks from the hardboiled eggs.

In a bowl, mash the egg whites with a fork. Crumble the tofu with a fork, and add it to the whites.

Fold in the remaining ingredients and garnish with paprika. Serves 6.

Variation: Try some optional add-ins, such as ½ cup sautéed chopped onion, 1 chopped celery stalk, 1 tbsp. pickle relish or a small chopped dill pickle, or ½-¾ tsp. curry powder.

Calories—48; Saturated fat—0 g.; Total fat—1 g.; Carbohydrates—4 g.; Cholesterol—0 mg.; Sodium—281 mg.; Fiber—0 g.; Protein—6 g.

TORTILLA DE PATATA FRITA

PAREVE
PASSOVER

One of the most common Spanish dishes, this egg dish is a combination of whole eggs, egg whites, and egg substitute. It reduces the cholesterol but keeps the texture and flavor intact. My son, who doesn't go for fake, never questions this mixture.

Cooking spray
3 medium baking potatoes, thinly sliced into rounds, then cut into half-moons
1 medium onion, thinly sliced into wedges
1 large red pepper, thinly sliced into strips
4 large eggs or 1 whole egg + 5 egg whites + ¼ cup egg substitute

Coat a baking sheet with the cooking spray. Spread out the potatoes, onion, and red pepper strips in a single layer. Bake at 450 degrees on bottom shelf for approximately 25 minutes or until the vegetables begin to soften and brown.

Heat a large iron skillet over medium heat.

In a bowl, beat the egg mixture together. Add the vegetables to the eggs.

Spray the skillet with the cooking spray, and pour the vegetable-egg mixture into the skillet. Spread around to even out the egg mixture and let cook for 8-10 minutes until the eggs begin to set.

Set the oven to broil. Transfer the skillet to the middle rack in the oven and broil until the vegetable-egg mixture begins to brown. After 5-8 minutes, with an oven mitt, remove the skillet from the oven and turn mixture out onto a serving dish. Serves 4.

Serving suggestion: This is really good topped with salsa.

With 4 whole eggs: Calories—267; Saturated fat—2 g.; Total fat—5 g.; Carbohydrates—44 g.; Cholesterol—213 mg.; Sodium—77 mg.; Fiber—1 g.; Protein—10 g.

With egg mixture: Calories—238; Saturated fat—0 g.; Total fat—2 g.; Carbohydrates—45 g.; Cholesterol—53 mg.; Sodium—121 mg.; Fiber—1 mg.; Protein—12 g.

Note: If you do not have a large skillet, you can make this in two batches.

ARTICHOKES FOR STUFFING

*This is a contemporary flavoring of artichokes. Different herbs can be used—
Jews all over the Mediterranean have various combinations.*

6 artichokes
2 lemons, halved
½ head garlic, unpeeled
⅓ cup chopped parsley

3 tbsp. fresh rosemary
1 tbsp. olive oil (optional)
2 cups water

Cut stems and outer leaves off the artichokes, but do not discard. (Trim tips if desired.)

Place the artichokes in a large pot.

Squeeze the juice of 2 lemons onto the artichokes. Add the garlic, herbs, and olive oil to the pot. Add the water. The olive oil gives the artichokes added flavor and helps them retain their flavor when stored in the refrigerator.

Bring to a boil. Reduce heat to medium low, cover, and cook until the artichokes are tender, 35-40 minutes. Remove from pot but reserve the liquid. Cool enough to gently spread the center leaves and remove the fuzzy choke underneath the center leaves. A melon baller works well for this.

The artichokes are ready for filling the centers now. If storing for later, remove the garlic and herbs from the cooking liquid. Keep the artichokes in their cooking liquid in the refrigerator for up to 4 days before stuffing.

When preparing for stuffing, peel the tough outer skin of the reserved artichoke stems. Cut stems into slices and use in the stuffing mixture of your choice. It's a delicious surprise addition. Serves 6.

Each unstuffed artichoke: Calories—91; Saturated fat—0 g.; Total fat—0 g.; Carbohydrates—17 g.; Cholesterol—0 mg.; Sodium—132 mg.; Fiber—2 g.; Protein—5 g.

BRAISED FENNEL AND ARTICHOKES

PAREVE
SHABBAT
PASSOVER

*Fennel is also called anise and has a licorice flavor. The simple combination
of fennel and artichoke gives this dish a mellow yet complicated flavor
that will get your guests' attention. This French Algerian dish
is a Shabbat favorite of my sister-in-law Joelle.*

1½ lb. fennel (about 2 bulbs)
2 garlic cloves
1 lemon, sliced

**1 box frozen artichoke hearts or
3 fresh artichoke hearts**
½ cup water

Slice off the bottom of the fennel bulbs and any other tough skin. Quarter the
bulbs.

Add to a pan with remaining ingredients. Cover. Simmer over low heat for 25
minutes or until tender. Serves 4-6.

*Calories—58; Saturated fat—0 g.; Total fat—0 g.; Carbohydrates—10 g.;
Cholesterol—0 mg.; Sodium—155 mg.; Fiber—1 g.; Protein—3 g.*

SWEET PUMPKIN AND CHICKPEAS

PAREVE
ROSH HASHANAH
SUKKOT

*Usually, this Sephardic dish contains pumpkin and chickpeas with a little
honey and cardamom to your taste. Here is an Ashkenazic tzimmes-inspired
version although the Moroccans flavor their sweet potatoes in this fashion.*

Cooking spray
1 onion, chopped
**1 lb. pumpkin, skinned and cut
into chunks**
**1 lb. sweet potatoes, peeled and
cut into chunks**
1 cup cooked chickpeas

1 cup water
**2-3 tbsp. honey (or pomegranate
syrup, found in Middle Eastern
food markets)**
½ tsp. cinnamon
¼ tsp. ground cloves (optional)
¼ cup raisins or dried cherries

Coat a nonstick skillet with cooking spray. Sauté the onion over medium-high heat for 5-7 minutes until translucent. Add the remaining ingredients. Cover and simmer over low heat for 30 minutes or until the vegetables are tender. Serves 6.

Calories—210; Saturated fat—0 g.; Total fat—1 g.; Carbohydrates—45 g.; Cholesterol—0 mg.; Sodium—79 mg.; Fiber—3 g.; Protein—5 g.

BRAISED CARROTS AND LEEKS

PAREVE
SHABBAT
PASSOVER
SHAVUOT

This is a variation on Apio, a Turkish dish of celery root and carrots.

2 tsp. olive oil
¾ cup vegetable broth
3 cups sliced carrots
2 cups sliced leeks, white part

¼ cup lemon juice
Salt and pepper, to taste
2 tbsp. chopped fresh parsley

Heat a nonstick skillet over medium-high heat. Add the olive oil and ¼ cup of the vegetable broth. When hot add the carrots and leeks. Sauté for 7 minutes or until the liquid evaporates and the vegetables start turning a light golden brown.

Add the remaining broth and lemon juice, scraping the pan to mix the flavors. Cover, reduce heat to low, and simmer for 20 minutes or until the vegetables reach the desired tenderness.

Season with salt and pepper and sprinkle with parsley before serving. Serves 6.

Calories—78; Saturated fat—0 g.; Total fat—2 g.; Carbohydrates—14 g.; Cholesterol—0 mg.; Sodium—67 mg.; Fiber—2 g.; Protein—2 g.

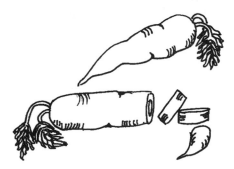

INDIAN CARROT CURRY

PAREVE
ROSH HASHANAH
CHANUKAH

This is a typical technique of preparing Indian vegetables.
The seasonings are heated to release maximum flavor, then the vegetables
are added and coated with those spices. It's an easy and effective technique.
This traditional recipe is easy to double or triple for company.
It is popular with Indian Jews for Rosh Hashanah.

1 tbsp. cumin seeds
2 tsp. coriander powder
2 tsp. cardamom pods or
   ¼ tsp. ground cardamom
1 tsp. turmeric
½ tsp. curry powder or cinnamon
2 whole cloves or
   ¼ tsp. ground cloves
Pinch cayenne

1 tbsp. canola oil
2 large onions, coarsely chopped
1½ lb. carrots, cut into 1-inch
   slices
¼ cup raisins
1½ cups water
½ tsp. grated ginger
Banana slices

Combine the cumin seeds, coriander, cardamom, turmeric, curry powder, cloves, and cayenne pepper in a small dish.

In a skillet, heat the oil over medium heat. When the oil is hot, add seasoning mixture and sauté about 30 seconds. Add the onions and sauté for 3-4 minutes.

Add the carrots, raisins, water, and ginger. Reduce to medium low. Cover and simmer for approximately 25 minutes until the carrots are tender and the water is absorbed. If the carrot mixture is too dry before it is done, add 1-2 tbsp. water to keep it from sticking.

Garnish with banana slices. Serves. 6

Calories—155; Saturated fat—0 g.; Total fat—4 g.; Carbohydrates—28 g.; Cholesterol—0 mg.; Sodium—53 mg.; Fiber—2 g.; Protein—3 g.

CARAMELIZED ONIONS

PAREVE
YOM KIPPUR BEFORE THE FAST
SUKKOT
PASSOVER
NINE DAYS BEFORE TISHAH B'AV

This goes well with Syrian Mejadarra (Lentils and Rice). The onions are so aromatic that they can stand on their own as a side dish or topping. Try mixing them with mashed potatoes, steamed rice, or vegetables. They are also good on sandwiches.

2 tsp. olive oil
4 medium yellow onions, halved
   then thinly sliced
4 garlic cloves, minced

3 tbsp. water or balsamic vinegar
¼ tsp. black pepper
1 tsp. sugar

In a large, heavy skillet, heat the oil over medium heat. Sauté the onions for approximately 7-8 minutes, stirring occasionally.

Add the garlic and continue to stir another few minutes.

Add the water or vinegar. Reduce heat to low. Add the pepper and sugar. Cover and slowly steam the onions for 25-30 minutes. Makes 2 cups.

Calories—131; Saturated fat—0 g.; Total fat—3 g.; Carbohydrates—24 g.; Cholesterol—0 mg.; Sodium—8 mg.; Fiber—2 g.; Protein—3 g.

BROCCOLI IN LEMON-SOY SAUCE

MEAT
SHABBAT
ROSH HASHANAH
YOM KIPPUR BEFORE THE FAST

This is a contemporary side dish with an Asian flavor that will blend with many different meals.

½ cup chicken broth
2 tbsp. dry sherry
1½ tbsp. lemon juice
1 tbsp. soy sauce
½ tsp. sesame oil

6 cups broccoli florets
Olive-oil cooking spray
1 tbsp. minced fresh ginger
1 large garlic clove, minced
¾ cup canned water chestnuts

In a small bowl, combine the chicken broth, dry sherry, lemon juice, soy sauce, and sesame oil. Set aside.

In a pot, cook the broccoli in boiling water to cover over medium-high heat for 4-5 minutes. Drain.

Coat a nonstick skillet with the olive-oil cooking spray. Heat over medium-high heat. When hot, add the ginger and garlic and cook for approximately 30 seconds. Add the broccoli and cook for another 2 minutes. Add the water chestnuts. Stir in the broth mixture. Stir to coat the broccoli with the sauce. Serve immediately. Serves 6.

Calories—51; Saturated fat—0 g.; Total fat—1 g.; Carbohydrates—8 g.; Cholesterol—0 mg.; Sodium—114 mg.; Fiber—1 g.; Protein—3 g.

BROCCOLI LATKES

PAREVE
CHANUKAH

The combination of curry, coriander, and cumin gives these latkes a touch of Indian flavor.

4 cups chopped broccoli or 20-oz. bag frozen chopped broccoli
1 tsp. curry powder
1 tsp. each coriander and cumin or 2 tsp. chili powder
⅓ cup matzah meal
3-4 egg whites
1 tbsp. lemon juice
Cooking spray
4 tsp. oil

In a pot with a few tablespoons of water, steam the broccoli over medium-high heat until heated through. Drain.

In a food processor, mince the broccoli. Add the seasonings, matzah meal, egg whites, and lemon juice. Pulse just until well mixed.

Coat a skillet with cooking spray, and add 1 tsp. oil. Heat the skillet over medium high. When the oil is hot, drop four ¼ cupfuls of the latke mixture into the skillet. Slightly flatten each of the patties with a spatula. Fry the latkes for 3-4 minutes on each side.

Repeat with three more batches, adding 1 tsp. oil for each batch. Makes 16 latkes; serves 8.

Calories—73; Saturated fat—0 g.; Total fat—3 g.; Carbohydrates—8 g.; Cholesterol—0 mg.; Sodium—38 mg.; Fiber—1 g.; Protein—4 g.

ITALIAN BUTTERNUT-SQUASH LATKES

PAREVE
SUKKOT
CHANUKAH
PASSOVER

This has such a naturally sweet flavor that you can serve it on the side as mashed squash instead of fried into latkes, if desired.

2 tbsp. sliced almonds
1 butternut squash (2 lb.) or
  2 pkg. frozen squash
Olive-oil spray

2-3 shallots, chopped
¼ tsp. black pepper
Salt to taste
¼ cup golden raisins

In a dry nonstick skillet, toast the almonds over medium heat for 2-3 minutes until lightly browned.

Pierce the squash several times with a fork, and microwave it on high for 10-12 minutes or until tender, or steam until tender. Cool and peel skin, or spoon out of shell. Mash in a mixing bowl.

Add the toasted almonds to the squash. Set aside.

Coat a nonstick skillet with the olive-oil spray and sauté the shallots over medium heat for 3-4 minutes. Remove and transfer to the mashed squash and add the remaining ingredients.

Form squash mixture into 8 patties. Coat same skillet again with olive-oil spray and sauté the patties over medium heat for a few minutes on each side or until golden. Serves 8.

Variation: For Syrian Pumpkin Latkes, use 2 lb. pumpkin. Omit the almonds, pepper, and raisins and add ½ tsp. allspice and ½ tsp. baking powder.

Calories—120; Saturated fat—0 g.; Total fat—2 g.; Carbohydrates—24 g.; Cholesterol—0 mg.; Sodium—7 mg.; Fiber—2 g.; Protein—2 g.

RED CABBAGE WITH ORANGE

PAREVE
ANY HOLIDAY

*Cooked cabbage is notably Ashkenazic. The cumin seeds here replace
the caraway seeds that are often combined with cabbage,
and orange is a nice complement to the cumin.
This flavorful winter side dish is easy to double for a crowd.*

**4 cups red cabbage or 2 cups
  each of red and green cabbage,
  thinly sliced
2 tbsp. cider vinegar
¼ cup orange juice**

**1 tsp. whole cumin seeds
2 tsp. orange zest or peel
2 small oranges, peeled and
  sectioned**

In a large skillet, combine the cabbage, cider vinegar, and orange juice over
medium heat. Cover.

Meanwhile, in a small, dry skillet, toast the cumin seeds over medium heat until
they just start to turn a light brown. Add the cumin seeds and orange zest to the
cabbage mixture. Continue to cook, covered, until the cabbage is tender, approximately 20 minutes. During the last few minutes, add the oranges. Serve warm.
Serves 4.

*Calories—68; Saturated fat—0 g.; Total fat—0 g; Carbohydrates—14 g.;
Cholesterol—0 mg.; Sodium—9 mg.; Fiber—1 g.; Protein—2 g.*

NORTH AFRICAN GREEN BEANS
IN TOMATO SAUCE

PAREVE
*SHABBAT
SUKKOT*

*Originally from Spain, this is a common Sephardic dish found all along
the North African coast, as well as in Turkey and Syria. This variation
is from Joelle Hankin with an Algerian touch.*

**Cooking spray
1 onion, sliced in half-moons
16 oz. frozen French-style green
  beans, thawed**

**2 small tomatoes, sliced in
  half-moons
1 large garlic clove, chopped
2 tbsp. minced parsley**

Coat a nonstick skillet with the cooking spray, and sauté the onion slices over medium heat for 3-4 minutes. Add the green beans and tomatoes and cook for 7-8 minutes or until heated through.

Add the garlic and parsley. Turn off heat and let stand for approximately 5 minutes, covered. This will lightly steam the garlic and parsley, which need very little cooking in this dish.

Serve immediately. Serves 6.

Variation: You can use 1 lb. fresh green beans. Simply add a small amount of water to help steam the green beans.

Calories—127; Saturated fat—0 g.; Total fat—1 g.; Carbohydrates—24 g.; Cholesterol—0 mg.; Sodium—189 mg.; Fiber—2 g.; Protein—6 g.

SUGAR SNAP PEAS WITH ROASTED PEPPERS

PAREVE
SHABBAT
PURIM
SHAVUOT

If you use garden-fresh vegetables, this is a summer treat for Shabbat.
The combination of rosemary, basil, and sage can be found in Iraqi cuisine.
I combined these herbs with a vegetable medley, and it works very nicely.

1 lb. fresh or frozen sugar snap peas
2 tsp. chopped garlic
1 tsp. rosemary
1 tsp. dried basil
½ tsp. sage

⅛ tsp. crushed red pepper flakes
1 tsp. canola oil
1 roasted yellow or red pepper, cut into strips
1-2 tbsp. toasted pine nuts
Salt and black pepper, to taste

Drop the snap peas into a pot of boiling water, and cook them for 4 minutes. Drain and rinse in cold water.

In a small dish, combine the garlic, rosemary, basil, and sage. Have the crushed red pepper close at hand. Set aside.

In a skillet, heat the oil over medium-low heat. Add the seasoning mixture and cook for 1 minute. Add the crushed red pepper flakes and cook for another 15 seconds.

Add the roasted pepper strips and snap peas. Cover and simmer over low heat for approximately 20 minutes, stirring often, or until the peas reach desired tenderness.

Top with the pine nuts. Season with a tiny amount of salt and pepper. Serve warm or at room temperature. Serves 6.

Calories—64; Saturated fat—0 g.; Total fat—2 g.; Carbohydrates—9 g.; Cholesterol—0 mg.; Sodium—8 mg.; Fiber—2 g.; Protein—3 g.

COCHIN-STYLE OKRA

PAREVE
SHABBAT
PASSOVER

The combination of okra and tomatoes is very popular with Sephardim and the Cochin Jews, an Indian community who are now in Israel and contributing spicy new flavors to the Israeli culinary palette. Chili peppers, turmeric, and ginger give this vegetable dish its distinctly Indian flavor.

1½ tsp. olive oil
1 large onion, minced
2 large garlic cloves, chopped
2 tsp. finely diced green chili
   peppers, or more to taste
1½ tsp. turmeric

2 10-oz. pkg. frozen okra
1½-2 lb. tomatoes, chopped,
   or 1 28-oz. can peeled,
   chopped tomatoes
½ tsp. chopped fresh ginger
   (optional)

Heat a nonstick skillet over medium-high heat and add the oil. Sauté the onions with the garlic, chili peppers, and turmeric for approximately 4-5 minutes.

Reduce heat to medium low and continue to cook for 5-10 minutes. Add the okra, tomatoes, and ginger and cook just until the vegetables are heated through, approximately 8-10 minutes. The texture might change if cooked too long. Serves 6.

Serving suggestion: Serve with steamed rice.

Calories—95; Saturated fat—0 g.; Total fat—2 g.; Carbohydrates—16 g.; Cholesterol—0 mg.; Sodium—19 mg.; Fiber—2 g.; Protein—3 g.

EGGPLANT AND TOMATOES

PAREVE
PASSOVER

*Inspired by the Cochin Indians, the combination of cumin and coriander
is what makes this an out-of-the-ordinary side dish.
Try using unpeeled Japanese eggplants.*

1½ lb. eggplant, peeled if
    desired, sliced
2 tsp. olive oil
¾ tsp. cumin
1½ tsp. coriander

1 large onion, cut into wedges
8 oz. tomatoes, chopped
1 tsp. chopped fresh ginger
1 small green chili, minced
1 tsp. honey

In a saucepan, steam the eggplant slices in a small amount of water over medium heat for 10 minutes. Remove. Set aside.

In a nonstick skillet, heat the olive oil over medium heat and cook the cumin and coriander for 1 minute. Add the onion and continue cooking for 4-5 minutes or until transparent. Do not brown.

Add the tomatoes, ginger, chili, and honey. Cook for approximately 2 minutes. Add the eggplant. Cover and simmer for 10-15 minutes or until desired tenderness is reached. Serves 4.

*Calories—130; Saturated fat—0 g.; Total fat—3 g.; Carbohydrates—23 g.;
Cholesterol—0 mg.; Sodium—16 mg.; Fiber—3 g.; Protein—3 g.*

Potatoes

GLAZED SWEET POTATOES

PAREVE
ROSH HASHANAH

*This dish has a delicious glaze based on apricots and cranberries,
but the fruit can be cooked with the sweet potatoes as a tzimmes, as well.*

1 cup apricots
1 cup fresh or frozen cranberries
1½ cups orange juice
⅓ cup water
¼ cup brown sugar or natural
  apricot preserves

½ tsp. cinnamon
1 tbsp. lemon juice
2½ lb. sweet potatoes, cooked,
  peeled, and cubed

In a saucepan, combine the apricots, cranberries, orange juice, water, brown sugar and cinnamon. Bring to a boil over high heat. Reduce heat to low, cover, and simmer for 15-20 minutes or until the apricots are tender. Add lemon juice.

Place the apricot mixture in a blender, and puree.

Arrange the cooked sweet potatoes in a large skillet. Pour the glaze over the potatoes. Cover and simmer on medium low, basting frequently, until the potatoes are heated through and glazed, approximately 15 minutes. Serves 8.

Variation: Do not puree the fruit mixture and simmer fruit and potatoes for approximately 30 minutes.

Calories—244; Saturated fat—0 g.; Total fat—2 g.; Carbohydrates—54 g.; Cholesterol—0 mg.; Sodium—58 mg.; Fiber—1 g.; Protein—3 g.

SOUTH AFRICAN VEGETABLE TZIMMES

PAREVE
SHABBAT
ROSH HASHANAH
PASSOVER

*What differentiates this from American tzimmes is its two steps:
boiling to cook the vegetables, then baking with a little honey over the top
to help slightly glaze the vegetables. Increase the honey if you like
your tzimmes sweeter.*

1½-2 cups water
1 lb. sweet potatoes, peeled and
    cut in chunks
1 lb. winter squash, such as
    butternut squash, cut in chunks
1 white potato, cubed
1 lb. carrots, sliced

1 small onion, cut in wedges
2 parsnips, sliced
1 tsp. cinnamon
¼ tsp. ginger
2 tbsp. brown sugar
2 cinnamon sticks
2 tbsp. honey

In a Dutch oven, with the water over medium-high heat, bring the sweet potatoes, squash, potatoes, carrots, onion, parsnips, cinnamon, ginger, and brown sugar to a boil. Reduce heat to medium low. Cover and simmer for approximately 45 minutes or until little liquid is left.

Add cinnamon sticks and honey. Place in oven and bake at 350 degrees, uncovered, for 30 minutes. Serves 8.

Calories—173; Saturated fat—0 g.; Total fat—1 g.; Carbohydrates—39 g.; Cholesterol—0 mg.; Sodium—34 mg.; Fiber—3 g.; Protein—3 g.

ROASTED VEGETABLES
WITH SEPHARDIC TASTE

PAREVE
SHABBAT
SUKKOT
PASSOVER

This is a good fall, winter, and even early spring dish, when root vegetables are sweeter. Be creative! Use your favorite vegetables of the season. Try roasting a cut-up apple with the vegetables. Just add it in halfway through roasting time.

DRESSING

1 tbsp. honey
2 tsp. oil
1½ tsp. cumin
½ tsp. ground fennel

¼ tsp. ground cardamom
⅛ tsp. paprika
Dash hot pepper sauce

VEGETABLES

1 onion, peeled and
    cut into 6 wedges
2 cups peeled and cubed
    sweet potatoes

2 cups peeled and cubed white
    sweet potatoes or garnets
2 cups peeled and sliced carrots
Cooking spray

Preheat the oven to 425 degrees. Set the rack in the bottom position.

Combine the dressing ingredients. Toss the vegetables in the dressing, coating them evenly.

Coat a baking sheet with cooking spray. Spread the vegetables in a single layer on the baking sheet. Spray a thin coating of cooking spray over the vegetables.

Place on the bottom oven rack. Bake for 55-60 minutes. Serves 6.

Variation: You can replace the potato mixture with 1 lb. eggplant, cubed; 1 whole garlic head, sectioned; ½ lb. whole mushrooms; 1-2 zucchinis, sliced; and 1-2 tomatoes, quartered. Bake for 30-35 minutes until vegetables are brown and tender.

Calories—173; Saturated fat—0 g.; Total fat—2 g.; Carbohydrates—33 g.; Cholesterol—0 mg.; Sodium—42 mg.; Fiber—2 g.; Protein—3 g.

CRUSTY BROWNED POTATOES

PAREVE
SHABBAT

Nutritional yeast gives this dish its crusty texture, almost like a Parmesan crust. It tastes like the higher-fat version.

2 lb. new potatoes, peeled and halved
Olive-oil spray
3 tbsp. breadcrumbs
3 tbsp. nutritional yeast

¼ tsp. onion powder
1 tbsp. Mrs. Dash, Spike, or other seasoning blend
½ tsp. paprika

Boil the potatoes in water for 10 minutes until tender-crisp. Drain.

Preheat the oven to 425 degrees. Coat a 9-by-13-inch baking pan with the olive-oil spray. Place the seasonings in a plastic bag. Place 4-5 potato halves in the plastic bag and shake until well coated. Repeat until all the potatoes are coated.

Place the potatoes on the prepared baking pan. Spray 1 layer of the olive-oil spray over the potatoes.

Bake for 35-40 minutes. Serves 6.

Calories—212; Saturated fat—0 g.; Total fat—0 g.; Carbohydrates—47 g.; Cholesterol—0 mg.; Sodium—126 mg.; Fiber—2 g.; Protein—6 g.

POTATOES WITH CAPER-DILL SAUCE

PAREVE
SHABBAT
PASSOVER

2½ lb. red, Yukon, or
  new potatoes
1½ tsp. oil
2 shallots, peeled and chopped
2 garlic cloves, peeled and
  chopped
⅓ cup Vegetable Broth

3 tbsp. lemon juice
1½ tbsp. capers, drained and
  rinsed
1 tbsp. chopped fresh dill or 1
  tsp. dry dill
¼ tsp. each salt and pepper

In a pot, boil the potatoes whole in water until fork tender, about 20 minutes. Drain. Cool. Peel. Cut into cubes. Set aside.

In a nonstick skillet, heat the oil over medium heat and sauté the shallots and garlic for 2-3 minutes. Add the broth, lemon juice, capers, dill, salt, and pepper. Continue to simmer for 15-20 minutes until the sauce slightly thickens.

Add the potatoes, stir to coat the potatoes with the sauce, and heat through. Serves 6.

Calories—187; Saturated fat—0 g.; Total fat—1 g.; Carbohydrates—39 g.; Cholesterol—0 mg.; Sodium—176 mg.; Fiber—2 g.; Protein—4 g.

LOW-FAT CLASSIC POTATO LATKES

PAREVE/DAIRY
CHANUKAH
PASSOVER

*I had always grated my potatoes for latkes with a hand grater,
until I discovered someone making "mincemeat" of the potatoes in a food
processor, achieving a coarsely ground texture. I was such a purist.
I had never considered the food processor as an alternative. I still hand grate
them first even without peeling them, but sometimes I put them in several
batches into the food processor and pulse 2-3 times to chop them more finely.
It also helps to mince the onion. Whatever your tradition is, this way of oven
frying latkes can be added to your choices. Applesauce is a classic partner.*

5 large potatoes	2 tbsp. matzah meal
1 large onion	½ tsp. black pepper
1 egg	½ tsp. salt
2 egg whites	Cooking spray

Preheat the oven to 425 degrees.

Grate the potatoes and onion into a colander, or use a food processor to grate, and transfer to a colander. Let drain for 5-10 minutes. It helps to squeeze the liquid out with your hands.

Transfer to a large mixing bowl and add the remaining ingredients, except cooking spray.

Generously spray a nonstick baking sheet with cooking spray.

Make 20 patties and place on baking sheet. Place the baking sheet on the bottom rack of the oven and bake for 10-15 minutes or until bottoms are brown.

Spray latkes with cooking spray and turn over. Bake for another 10-15 minutes or until bottoms are golden. Remove from oven onto serving tray. Makes 20 latkes.

Serving suggestion: Serve with yogurt cheese, low-fat or nonfat sour cream, or applesauce.

Variations: Flavor here is open to your imagination. Here are two examples. For an Indian flavor, try adding 1 tsp. chopped garlic, ¾ tsp. cumin, ½ tsp. turmeric, ¼ tsp. crushed red pepper, and ¼ tsp. ground ginger. For a Russian-Polish twist, add 1 tsp. dry dill, or to taste, and 1 tsp. dry parsley.

Calories—64; Saturated fat—0 g.; Total fat—0 g.; Carbohydrates—13 g.; Cholesterol—11 mg.; Sodium—72 mg.; Fiber—0 g.; Protein—2 g.

HERBED HOME FRIES

PAREVE
CHANUKAH
PASSOVER

Do you miss the taste of fried potatoes? This contemporary dish will truly satisfy. Home fries are haimish but the presentation and taste here say: serve it for company. These potatoes are at home at a formal Seder or you can serve them in place of latkes one night of Chanukah.

1 tbsp. olive or canola oil
1½ lb. potatoes, peeled and cut into small cubes
2 garlic cloves, crushed
⅔ cup dry white wine

12 cherry tomatoes, quartered
2 tbsp. minced fresh basil or 1 tsp. dried basil
2 tbsp. minced fresh parsley
Salt and pepper to taste

In a skillet, heat the oil over medium heat. Brown the potatoes for approximately 5 minutes on each side. Add the garlic the last 5 minutes of frying the potatoes.

Add the wine, cover, reduce heat to low, and cook for 7 minutes or until the potatoes are tender.

Turn off heat, but leave skillet on the stove, and toss the remaining ingredients with the potatoes. Cover and let sit for another minute for the flavors to meld. Serves 6.

Calories—185; Saturated fat—0 g.; Total fat—2 g.; Carbohydrates—37 g.; Cholesterol—0 mg.; Sodium—13 mg.; Fiber—1 g.; Protein—4 g.

GARLIC MASHED POTATOES

PAREVE
CHANUKAH
PASSOVER

These mashed potatoes are different. The seasoning is added to the cooking liquid.

2 lb. baking potatoes, peeled and cubed
1 tbsp. dry minced onion
3 large garlic cloves

1 tsp. hot sauce or ⅛ tsp. cayenne pepper, or to taste
Salt and pepper to taste

Place all ingredients in a pot and add 4 cups water. Bring to a boil.

Reduce heat to medium low and cover until the potatoes are tender, approximately 20 minutes.

Drain, reserving the water. In a bowl, mash all ingredients and add the reserved liquid as needed for smoothness. Add more hot sauce to taste. Serves 7.

Variations: To make low-fat dairy mashed potatoes, add buttermilk or nonfat cream cheese. Also try flavoring with curry powder, or mix Caramelized Onions into the potatoes.

Calories—143; Saturated fat—0 g.; Total fat—0 g.; Carbohydrates—34 g.; Cholesterol—0 mg.; Sodium—11 mg.; Fiber—1g.; Protein—3 g.

Note: If you never add any salt to your cooking, the hot sauce is a good substitute. Just adjust the amount to taste.

Rice and Grains

IRAQI RICE

This is a mellow-tasting traditional dish for Iraqi Jews.

Olive-oil cooking spray
1 onion, chopped
1 tsp. turmeric
¼ tsp. black pepper
2-3 small zucchinis, sliced
1 cup long-grain rice

3 cups vegetable broth
1 tbsp. tomato paste
¼ tsp. salt
3 tbsp. slivered almonds, toasted
3 tbsp. raisins or currants

Coat a skillet with the olive-oil cooking spray. Sauté the onions on medium high for approximately 3-5 minutes or until transparent.

Add the turmeric, black pepper, and zucchini and continue cooking for approximately 15 minutes.

Add a small amount of water to the zucchini if it is sticking. Add the rice and stir for approximately 5 minutes. Add the broth, tomato paste, and salt. Cover and simmer on low for approximately 45 minutes.

Stir in the toasted almonds and raisins or currants. Serves 6.

Calories—166; Saturated fat—0 g.; Total fat—3 g.; Carbohydrates—33 g.; Cholesterol—0 mg.; Sodium—156 mg.; Fiber—1 g.; Protein—3 g.

EGYPTIAN RICE PILAF

*The typical Sephardic way of cooking rice is to sauté it with onion,
then add water to the skillet. Rice is a staple in Egyptian cuisine,
as couscous is in Tunisian and Moroccan cooking. This is a basic pilaf
that will accompany many favorite holiday dishes elegantly.*

Cooking spray
1 onion, chopped
⅓ cup vermicelli noodles
1½ cups basmati rice
2½ cups fat-free chicken broth
  or water

½ tsp. turmeric
¼ tsp. ground coriander
⅛ tsp. cayenne pepper
Salt and pepper to taste

Coat a nonstick skillet with cooking spray. Over medium-high heat, sauté the onion 1-2 minutes. Coat skillet again with cooking spray. Add the noodles and continue to cook 2 minutes or until golden. Add the rice and sauté another 2 minutes.

Add the broth and seasonings. Cover and cook for 20 minutes on low until rice is tender and water is absorbed. Serves 6.

Variation: Fruits and nuts are added for special occasions. For Festive Rice Pilaf, mix into the cooked pilaf 2 tbsp. each of toasted walnuts and almonds, ⅓ cup raisins, and a splash of lemon juice. This is a good dish to incorporate into Tu Bishevat.

Calories—140; Saturated fat— 0 g.; Total fat—0 g.; Carbohydrates—31 g.; Cholesterol—0 mg.; Sodium—2 mg.; Fiber—0 g.; Protein—3 g.

ARROZ BRASILEIRO (BRAZILIAN RICE PILAF)

PAREVE
SHABBAT
YOM KIPPUR BEFORE THE FAST

This rice pilaf variation is served by Sephardim.

2 tsp. canola or olive oil
1 onion, chopped
2 garlic cloves, chopped
2 cups long-grain white rice

1 lb. fresh tomatoes, chopped, or
   15-oz. can chopped tomatoes
3 cups boiling water
½ tsp. salt

In a medium saucepan, heat the oil over medium heat. Add the onion and sauté for approximately 5 minutes until onion is translucent. Add the garlic and rice and sauté for another 2 minutes.

Add the remaining ingredients. Reduce heat to low, cover, and simmer for 30-35 minutes or until the rice is tender. Serves 8.

Calories—206; Saturated fat—0 g.; Total fat—2 g.; Carbohydrates—44 g.; Cholesterol—0 mg.; Sodium—154 mg.; Fiber—1 g.; Protein—4 g.

MUSHROOM BARLEY PILAF

PAREVE
SHABBAT
SUKKOT
TU BISHEVAT

*This is a haimish comfort food. It is also very attractive,
with the carrots and peas giving it color.*

3 cups vegetable broth
¾ cup uncooked barley (not
   quick barley)
Cooking spray
1 cup sliced leeks
1 cup coarsely chopped variety
   mushrooms, such as shiitake
   or enoki

1½ cups frozen carrots and peas,
   or mixed vegetables
1 tsp. dry thyme

In a saucepan, bring the vegetable broth to a boil. Add the barley. Cover, reduce heat to low, and cook for 30-35 minutes until the barley is tender.

Meanwhile, in a large skillet coated with cooking spray, sauté the leeks and mushrooms over medium heat for 3-4 minutes or until the leeks are softened.

Add the carrots and peas, thyme, and barley mixture. Mix and heat through. Serves 6.

Calories—154; Saturated fat—0 g.; Total fat—1 g.; Carbohydrates—31 g.; Cholesterol—0 mg.; Sodium—936 mg.; Fiber—1 g.; Protein—4 g.

ORZO RICE PILAF

MEAT/PAREVE
SHABBAT
ROSH HASHANAH
YOM KIPPUR
SIMCHAT TORAH

Orzo is a rice-shaped pasta found in the pasta aisle. This is a contemporary side dish that nicely complements Roasted Turkey Tzimmes. Being a combination of two complex carbohydrates, this dish can serve you well before the Yom Kippur fast.

½ cup chopped sun-dried tomatoes without oil
1 cup orzo
2 tsp. olive oil
1 onion, chopped
2 garlic cloves, chopped
1 lb. mushrooms, sliced
½ cup long-grain rice
2 cups chicken or vegetable broth

Set the sun-dried tomatoes in a bowl of hot water. Set aside.

Bring a pot of water to a boil for the orzo. Cook according to package directions. It will later be mixed into the cooked pilaf.

Meanwhile, in a large nonstick skillet, heat the olive oil on medium-high heat and sauté the onion and garlic for approximately 10 minutes. Add the mushrooms and continue to sauté until the mushrooms wither, 5-7 minutes.

Drain the tomatoes and add to the skillet along with the rice and broth. Bring to a boil over high heat. Cover, reduce heat, and simmer over low heat for 20-25 minutes or until the rice is tender. Stir in the drained orzo and heat through. Serves 8.

Calories—135; Saturated fat—0 g.; Total fat—2 g.; Carbohydrates—26 g.; Cholesterol—0 mg.; Sodium—85 mg.; Fiber—2 g.; Protein—4 g.

KASHA VARNISHKES

PAREVE
SHABBAT
CHANUKAH

Kasha, buckwheat groats, is a Russian grain central to Slavic cuisine, but Jews who left the Slavic lands popularized this grain so much that it now associated with Russian-Jewish cooking in particular. When I was growing up, it was simply kasha and bow-tie noodles or seashells. Now, sometimes I add ½ lb. sliced mushrooms to the onions and/or 1 cup frozen peas at the end. My kids Jennifer and Michael have always been purists when it comes to this dish. It is their comfort food when they are home. So I don't mess with a perfect food when they are here. If you are vegan, you can omit the egg. Using egg is the traditional Jewish way of making kasha but it won't affect the texture or taste if you leave it out.

1 cup medium-grain kasha
2 egg whites
2 cups bow ties or medium pasta seashells
2 tsp. canola oil
1 large onion, minced

2 cups boiling water
½ tsp. salt
Black pepper to taste
3 tbsp. parsley for garnish (optional)

In a bowl, thoroughly coat the kasha grains with the egg whites. Set aside.

In a pot of boiling water, cook pasta according package directions. Drain.

Meanwhile, in a nonstick skillet, heat 1 tsp. of the oil over medium heat and brown onions for approximately 8 minutes. Remove from pan.

Add the remaining 1 tsp. oil and brown the kasha for approximately 8 minutes.

Holding a lid over the skillet to prevent splattering, add the 2 cups boiling water, onions, salt and pepper.

Reduce heat to low, cover, and simmer for 20 minutes or until kasha fluffs and water is absorbed. Stir in cooked and drained pasta. Garnish with parsley. Serves 6.

Calories—160; Saturated fat—0 g.; Total fat—2 g.; Carbohydrates—29 g.; Cholesterol—0 mg.; Sodium—218 mg.; Fiber—0 g.; Protein—6 g.

FESTIVE COUSCOUS

PAREVE

ROSH HASHANAH
SUKKOT
CHANUKAH
TU BISHEVAT

Sephardim add fruits and nuts to their couscous for special occasions and holidays. A dish like this is traditional for Sukkot.

2½ cups water
2 cups or 2 5.8-oz. boxes instant couscous (discard any seasoning packets)
⅓ cup low-sugar apricot preserves
⅓ cup toasted slivered almonds

½ cup mixture of raisins, dried cranberries, chopped dried apricots, and chopped dates
1 tsp. cinnamon
½ tsp. salt
½ tsp. cardamom
⅛ tsp. turmeric

Bring the water to a boil. Stir in the couscous and apricot preserves. Remove from the stove and let stand covered for 5 minutes. Stir in the remaining ingredients. Serves 8-10.

Calories—254; Saturated fat—0 g.; Total fat—3 g.; Carbohydrates—49 g.; Cholesterol—0 mg.; Sodium—7 mg.; Fiber—1 g.; Protein—7 g.

MAMAGLIA

DAIRY
PURIM
SHAVUOT
NINE DAYS BEFORE TISHAH B'AV

Mamaglia is a Romanian staple now catching on in the United States. The beauty of this basic dish is that it can be as casual or as dressed up as you like, depending on the stir-ins or toppings that you add.

6 cups skim milk
2 cups cornmeal
1 cup nonfat yogurt cheese (strained 1 hour)

4 tsp. butter-flavored granules, or to taste

In a saucepan, bring the milk and cornmeal to a boil. Reduce the heat to low to medium low and cook while stirring frequently, for approximately 10 minutes or until the mixture thickens and pulls away from the saucepan.

Remove from heat. Stir in the cheese and butter-flavored granules. Either serve it hot out of the pan or spread the mixture on a baking sheet and cool until firm, then cut into squares. Serve as a side dish to a dairy meal. Serves 6-8.

Serving suggestion: If you want a topping, try a tomato sauce or Austrian Mushroom Sauce.

Variation: Other cheese stir-ins could include Greek cheeses such as kaskaval, kasseri, or halumi, which are popular with Israelis, as well as American cheese, or drained and mashed cottage cheese.

Calories—257; Saturated fat—0 g.; Total fat—1 g.; Carbohydrates—49 g.; Cholesterol—4 mg.; Sodium—134 mg.; Fiber—0 g.; Protein—12 g.

CORNMEAL LATKES

DAIRY/PAREVE
CHANUKAH

These Romanian latkes can be made into a delightfully different kind of side dish or a quick and easy vegan main dish—or even breakfast. I am presenting this recipe two ways, and there is virtually no difference in taste. It's merely a

*matter of preference. When they are made on the griddle like this
rather than in ½ inch of oil in a pan, they resemble the American johnnycakes.
These latkes are very good with cinnamon and sugar sprinkled
on them and with Sweet Apples in Date Sauce on the side. Applesauce
is just as tasty when time is short.*

**½ cup egg substitute or
 4 egg whites**
**2 cups nonfat sour cream or
 nonfat plain yogurt**
2 tbsp. honey

1 cup whole-wheat pastry flour
1 cup cornmeal
1 tsp. baking soda
½ tsp. salt
Butter-flavored cooking spray

In a bowl, mix the egg substitute, sour cream, and honey. Stir in the remaining ingredients except the spray.

Heat a griddle over medium-high heat. When hot, coat the griddle with the cooking spray.

Spoon the batter onto the griddle in two batches of 9 pancakes, and lightly brown for about 1-2 minutes. Spray the tops with the cooking spray before turning, then brown another 1-2 minutes. Serves 9.

Variation: For Vegan Cornmeal Latkes, combine 1 cup whole-wheat pastry flour, 1 cup cornmeal, 1 tsp. baking soda, and ½ tsp. salt. Blend ⅓-½ cup apple juice, 2 tsp. vinegar, and 2 cups low-fat soft tofu. Follow directions as above. Serves 9.

Nonvegan: Calories—154; Saturated fat—0 g.; Total fat—1 g.; Carbohydrates—14 g.; Cholesterol—0 mg.; Sodium—283 mg.; Fiber—0 g.; Protein—8 g.

Vegan: Calories—108; Saturated fat—0 g.; Total fat—1 g.; Carbohydrates—23 g.; Cholesterol—0 mg.; Sodium—224 mg.; Fiber—0 g.; Protein—3 g.

Kugels

ONION-VEGETABLE KUGEL

PAREVE
SHABBAT

In the United States, the kugel has really evolved. It started in Central and Eastern Europe as a noodle pudding baked in a slow oven over Friday nights as a side dish to cholent. Today, kugels combine many different ingredients. Friday night or Shabbat afternoon are still the traditional times to serve them. Normally, this kugel depends upon a lot of oil. This version is flavorful without the additional oil. This kugel goes nicely with poultry dishes.

Cooking spray
2 tbsp. oil
2 large onions, chopped
3 garlic cloves, chopped
14 oz. fine noodles
2 packed cups chopped spinach
2 large carrots, shredded

¼ cup chopped parsley
5 egg whites
1 egg
1 tsp. paprika
¾ tsp. salt
¼ tsp. black pepper

Generously coat a 9-by-13-inch baking pan with the cooking spray. Set aside.

In a skillet, heat the oil over medium-high heat. Sauté the onions and garlic for 5-7 minutes or until golden brown.

Boil the noodles for 3-5 minutes or according to package directions. Rinse in a colander with cold running water, and transfer to a mixing bowl with the onion mixture and remaining ingredients.

Add the mixture to the prepared baking pan. Sprinkle the top with more paprika for color.

Bake at 350 degrees for 45-55 minutes until the top is lightly golden and the kugel is firm to the touch. Serves 8.

Calories—135; Saturated fat—0 g.; Total fat—4 g.; Carbohydrates—18 g.; Cholesterol—27 mg.; Sodium—198 mg.; Fiber—1 g.; Protein—5 g.

ROMANIAN ZUCCHINI KUGEL

DAIRY
PASSOVER
SHAVUOT

*Not all kugels are made of noodles. This adaptation was inspired
by a kugel recipe from Felicia Herscovici.*

About 1½ lb. (3-3½ cups)
   zucchini or summer squash,
   cut into chunks
1 small onion, chopped

½ small green pepper, chopped
½ small red pepper, chopped
1 tbsp. fresh dill or 1 tsp. dry dill

BATTER

1 cup flour
1 cup skim milk
½ cup egg substitute + 2 egg
   whites or 1 egg + 4 egg whites
¼ tsp. salt

¼ tsp. black pepper
½ cup crumbled low-fat feta
   cheese
¼ cup grated low-fat
   Parmesan cheese

In a food processor, grate the zucchini and onion. Set aside, and let drain in colander for approximately 30 minutes.

Squeeze out any remaining liquid. Transfer to a bowl and add peppers and dill.

In a bowl, blend all the batter ingredients except the Parmesan cheese. Add the zucchini mixture to batter and mix well.

Transfer to a greased 11-by-9-inch glass dish. Sprinkle top with Parmesan cheese. Bake at 375 degrees for 45 minutes or until top is golden brown. Serves 6.

*Calories—154; Saturated fat—1 g.; Total fat—3 g.; Carbohydrates—23 g.;
Cholesterol—10 mg.; Sodium—292 mg.; Fiber—1 g.; Protein—10 g.*

ROASTED-GARLIC POTATO KUGEL

PAREVE
SHABBAT
ROSH HASHANAH
SUKKOT
PASSOVER

*These potatoes could be hand grated like latkes, but with a food processor,
it is faster and the dish comes out just right.*

2 onions, minced
2 tbsp. oil
6 cups peeled grated potatoes,
well drained
1 egg
4 egg whites

2 small heads roasted garlic,
peeled and mashed
½ cup flour
1 tsp. salt
½ tsp. black pepper
Cooking spray

Preheat the oven to 350 degrees.

In a nonstick skillet, sauté the onions in 1 tbsp. oil over medium-high heat until golden brown, 4-5 minutes.

In a bowl, combine the potatoes, onions, eggs, garlic, flour, salt, and pepper.

Coat the sides and bottom of a 9-by-13-inch baking pan with the cooking spray, then the remaining tbsp. of oil. Heat the pan in the oven for a few minutes until the oil becomes hot.

Pour the potato mixture into the baking dish. Bake uncovered for 1½ hours or until the top is golden brown. Serves 8.

Serving suggestion: For a special accompaniment (after all, it is *yom tov*) make a dish of Caramelized Onions and serve alongside this savory kugel.

Calories—230; Saturated fat—0 g.; Total fat—3 g.; Carbohydrates—44 g.; Cholesterol—27 mg.; Sodium—343 mg.; Fiber—2 g.; Protein—8 g.

Note: The potatoes can be grated the night before. Store them in cold water with 1 tbsp. flour added to the water. This will help keep the potatoes white. It is best, however, not to bake the kugel in advance.

PEACHES 'N' CREAM KUGEL

DAIRY/PAREVE
SHABBAT
YOM KIPPUR BREAK-THE-FAST
TU BISHEVAT
SHAVUOT

This is a contemporary American-style dairy kugel that can be changed to pareve to fit your menu.

KUGEL

Cooking spray, butter flavor
   or regular
12 oz. yolk-free wide noodles
⅔ cup chopped dried peaches
⅓ cup golden raisins
⅔ cup nonfat plain yogurt
⅔ cup skim ricotta cheese or
nonfat yogurt cheese
1 cup low-sugar orange
   marmalade or apricot
   preserves

⅓ cup brown sugar or honey
1 whole egg
6 egg whites
½ cup egg substitute
1 tsp. cinnamon
⅛ tsp. cardamom or nutmeg
2 tsp. vanilla extract
1 tsp. almond extract

TOPPING

1 tsp. cinnamon

Coat a 9-by-13-inch baking pan with cooking spray.

Boil the noodles according to package directions until tender. Drain and cool by placing in colander under cool running water. Transfer to a bowl.

Stir in the remaining kugel ingredients and spoon into the prepared baking pan. Sprinkle the top with 1 tsp. cinnamon.

Cover and bake at 350 degrees for ½ hour. Uncover, reduce heat to 325 degrees, and bake 30 minutes more. Serves 12.

Variation: For pareve Peach Kugel, omit the yogurt, ricotta cheese, and almond extract. Increase the vanilla to 1 tbsp. Add to the noodles 8 oz. crushed pineapple, undrained, and 3 tbsp. oil.

Calories—197; Saturated fat—0 g.; Total fat—1 g.; Carbohydrates—40 g.; Cholesterol—20 mg.; Sodium—74 mg.; Fiber—0 g.; Protein—8 g.

CHERRY DAIRY KUGEL

DAIRY
SHABBAT
YOM KIPPUR BREAK-THE-FAST
SHAVUOT

This sweet kugel is sweetened only with pineapple-juice concentrate.

8 oz. yolk-free noodles
8 oz. (1 cup) low-fat cottage
  cheese, drained
½ cup nonfat sour cream or
  plain yogurt
½ cup pineapple-juice
  concentrate

1 whole egg
5 egg whites
1 cup canned cherries, drained
1½ tsp. vanilla
½ tsp. almond extract
Cooking spray

TOPPING

½ cup crushed corn flakes

3 tbsp. chopped toasted almonds

Boil the noodles according to package directions and drain.

In a bowl, combine the noodles with the remaining kugel ingredients except the spray.

Coat a 9-inch square, glass baking dish with the cooking spray. Pour in the noodle mixture.

Combine the topping ingredients and sprinkle over the noodle mixture.

Bake at 350 degrees for 1 hour to 1 hour and 15 minutes. Serves 12.

Calories—102; Saturated fat—0 g.; Total fat—3 g; Carbohydrates—12 g.; Cholesterol—19 mg.; Sodium—126 mg.; Fiber—0 g.; Protein—12 g.

CRANBERRY-APPLE KUGEL

PAREVE
ROSH HASHANAH
SUKKOT
CHANUKAH

The freshly baked apples in this kugel create a delightful fragrance. This is a good holiday pareve kugel that will fit in anywhere from Rosh Hashanah to Chanukah to winter Shabbats, when apples are in their season. Cranberries have a very short season—middle to late fall. I buy and store them raw in their bag in my freezer, ready to use any time of the year. If cranberries are unavailable, use frozen rhubarb and chop it into smaller pieces. Vicki-Bluma Olesky was glad to give me this recipe to see what I could do to lighten yet still retain the character of this kugel.

Cooking spray
6 apples, peeled and sliced
16-oz. bag cranberries or
   frozen rhubarb
⅓ cup sugar

½ cup apple-juice concentrate
¾ cup egg substitute
1 tbsp. lemon juice
1 tsp. vanilla
1¼ cups flour

TOPPING

⅔ cup crushed sweetened cereal,
   such as Frosted Flakes or
   Rice Krispies

Preheat the oven to 350 degrees. Coat a 9-by-13-inch baking pan well with cooking spray.

In a bowl, combine the apples, cranberries, sugar, apple-juice concentrate, egg substitute, lemon juice, and vanilla. Mix in the flour and stir well to coat. Pour into the prepared baking pan.

Sprinkle topping over all and baking for 1 hour. Serves 16.

Calories—115; Saturated fat—0 g.; Total fat—0 g.; Carbohydrates—26 g.; Cholesterol—0 mg.; Sodium—2 mg.; Fiber—1 g.; Protein—2 g.

Condiments and Sauces

CURRY APRICOT SALSA FOR GEFILTE FISH

PAREVE
SHABBAT
ROSH HASHANAH

*This is a popular chunky condiment from South Africa. Although
the traditional recipe calls for half of the onions to be cooked
only 1 minute, I prefer my onions well done, so I cook them together.
This salsa will give a punch to any broiled or poached mild fish.*

1 cup white vinegar
Syrup from 15-oz.-can light-syrup
    apricots, apricots reserved
2 tsp. curry powder
2 whole cloves

2 large onions, sliced
6 low-fat gingersnaps
1 cup golden raisins
2 tbsp. tomato sauce
Pinch salt

In a saucepan, bring the vinegar, apricot syrup, curry powder, cloves, and onions
to a boil over high heat.

Reduce heat to medium low, cover, and simmer for 20 minutes. Add the remaining ingredients except the apricots and continue to simmer another 10 minutes or until the gingersnaps dissolve. This thickens the salsa and adds flavor. Serve the apricots on the side. Makes approximately 2½ cups.

*Per 2 tbsp. serving: Calories—87; Saturated fat—0 g.; Total fat—0 g.;
Carbohydrates—20 g.; Cholesterol—0 mg.; Sodium—37 mg.; Fiber—1 g.;
Protein—1 g.*

HARISSA SALSA

PAREVE
YOM HAATZMA'UT

*Normally, hot red peppers are processed with olive oil to make this sauce.
I omitted this step by using a jar of Mexican salsa with some of the flavors
already in it. By doing this, I eliminated the oil and therefore the fat. This
simple harissa salsa has the same consistency as canned harissa from Israel.*

½ tsp. minced garlic
½ tsp. ground cumin
⅛ tsp. caraway seeds, crushed
2 tsp. ground coriander

⅛ tsp. cayenne pepper, or
   to taste
Pinch cinnamon
½ cup medium-hot salsa

Stir the seasonings into the salsa. Store in refrigerator and use as a condiment as you would salsa or ketchup. It's good on falafel. Makes ½ cup.

Per tbsp.: Calories—5; Saturated fat—0 g.; Total fat—0 g.; Carbohydrates—1 g.; Cholesterol—0 mg.; Sodium—32 mg.; Fiber—0 g.; Protein—0 g.

HARISSA SEASONING

PAREVE
YOM HAATZMA'UT
LAG B'OMER

If harissa is not available to you and you will not be using it often enough to make the salsa at home, try this seasoning mix for adding flavor to your meals. This can also be used as a rub for grilled meats, poultry, and vegetables.

2 tbsp. coriander seeds
2 tbsp. cumin seeds
½ tsp. crushed hot red pepper
   flakes, or to taste

¼ tsp. dry minced garlic
1½ tsp. paprika

In a coffee grinder, grind the seeds, pepper flakes, and garlic to a finer texture. Transfer to a small container and add paprika. Store in a covered container or zipper storage bag. Makes 6 tbsp.

Variation: For Tunisian Tabil Mix, grind together 2 tbsp. coriander seeds, ½ tsp. (or to taste) crushed hot red pepper flakes, 2 tsp. dry minced garlic, and 2 tbsp. caraway seeds.

Per teaspoon: Calories-15 g; Saturated fat—0 g.; Total fat—1 g.; Carbohydrates—2 g.; Cholesterol—0 mg.; Sodium—4 mg.; Fiber—1 g.; Protein—1 g.

HORSERADISH (CHRAINE)

PAREVE
SHABBAT
ROSH HASHANAH
PASSOVER

This is a classic Ashkenazic condiment to go with fish.

½ to ¾ lb. horseradish root, peeled and cut into chunks

1 large beet, peeled
½ cup cider vinegar

In a food processor, grate the horseradish and beets. Mix in vinegar. Chop it further in food processor for a finer consistency. Makes 1½ cups

Calories-1 g; Saturated fat—0 g.; Total fat—0 g.; Carbohydrates—2 g.; Cholesterol—0 mg.; Sodium—3 mg.; Fiber—0 g.; Protein—1 g.

DAIRY HORSERADISH SAUCE

DAIRY

This is good on salmon or gefilte fish. It's an excellent addition to any yom tov dairy meal.

1 cucumber, peeled and cut into chunks
¾ cup nonfat plain yogurt
¼ cup low-fat mayonnaise
4 tsp. prepared white horseradish

1½ tbsp. minced onion
2 tbsp. white vinegar
2 tbsp. chopped parsley or cilantro
1 tsp. fresh dill or ¼ tsp. dry dill

Combine all the ingredients in a food processor and pulse several times until the cucumber is minced. Serves 8.

Calories—31; Saturated fat—0 g.; Total fat—1 g.; Carbohydrates—5 g.; Cholesterol—0 mg.; Sodium—80 mg.; Fiber—0 g.; Protein—1 g.

AUSTRIAN MUSHROOM SAUCE

DAIRY
PASSOVER

This is typical of the rich cream sauces of Austria. This is so good it makes everything taste extraspecial. Try it on baked potatoes, noodles, or Onion and Chive Polenta.

Cooking spray
1 small onion, chopped
2 cups sliced mushrooms
1 cup dry white wine
    (non-alcoholic is good)

¼ cup minced parsley
1 tsp. capers
2 tsp. Dijon mustard
½ cup low-fat sour cream or
    yogurt cheese

In a nonstick skillet coated with the cooking spray, sauté the onion over medium-high heat 3-4 minutes. Add the mushrooms and cook over medium heat 10 minutes or until moisture evaporates from the mushrooms. Add the wine, parsley, capers, and Dijon mustard, scraping the bits from the bottom of the pan. Remove from the stove and whisk in the sour cream. Makes 1¼ cups.

Per 2 tbsp.: Calories—21; Saturated fat—0 g.; Total fat—1 g.; Carbohydrates—2 g.; Cholesterol—1 mg.; Sodium—24 mg.; Fiber—0 g.; Protein—1 g.

CITRUS CINNAMON SAUCE

PAREVE
PASSOVER

Very low in sugar, this is a versatile sauce that goes nicely over Rosewater Angel Food Cake, or omit the cornstarch and bake apples with it. It's based on nature's sweeteners.

¾ cup orange juice
1 tbsp. honey
1 cinnamon stick
2 tbsp. water

1 tbsp. lemon juice
1 tbsp. lime juice
2 tsp. cornstarch or potato starch

In a saucepan, combine orange juice, honey, and cinnamon stick. Bring to a boil. Reduce heat to medium low and simmer for 5 minutes.

In a small bowl, blend together the water, lemon juice, lime juice, and cornstarch. Stir into the sauce and stir for 1 minute just until it begins to thicken. Chill with the cinnamon stick. Discard the cinnamon stick before serving. Makes about 1 cup.

Per 2 tbsp.: Calories—24; Saturated fat—0 g.; Total fat—0 g.; Carbohydrates— 6 g.; Cholesterol—0 mg.; Sodium—0 mg.; Fiber—0 g.; Protein—0 g.

HONEY-ALMOND SAUCE

DAIRY
SHABBAT
ROSH HASHANAH
CHANUKAH
TU BISHEVAT
PASSOVER
SHAVUOT

Not everybody wants cake for dessert. This no-fuss, simple, yet sophisticated topping for fresh fruits is good for any time of the year. You can use this for Passover even if almond flavoring is not available.

¾ cup nonfat plain yogurt
2 tbsp. honey
½ tsp. almond extract or vanilla
  flavoring

2 tbsp. chopped almonds, toasted

Mix the yogurt, honey, and almond extract. Spoon over fruit and sprinkle on the almonds. Makes 1 cup of sauce.

Per 2 tbsp.: Calories—43; Saturated fat—0 g.; Total fat—1 g.; Carbohydrates— 6 g.; Cholesterol—0 mg.; Sodium—17 mg.; Fiber—0 g.; Protein—2 g.

RICH 'N' DARK CHOCOLATE SYRUP

DAIRY/PAREVE

½ cup unsweetened cocoa
  powder
1 cup corn syrup
3 tbsp. brown sugar

1 tbsp. pareve creamer or
  nonfat sour cream
2 tsp. vanilla extract or
  any liqueur

In a saucepan combine the cocoa, corn syrup and brown sugar. Cook 1-2 minutes over medium heat. Remove from heat and stir in the pareve creamer and vanilla. Makes 1½ cups.

Serving suggestion: Serve over low-fat frozen yogurt or angel-food cake. Drizzle over a dessert dish of fresh strawberries.

Per 2 tbsp.: Calories—86; Saturated fat—0 g.; Total fat—0 g.; Carbohydrates— 20 g.; Cholesterol—0 mg.; Sodium—41 mg.; Fiber—0 g.; Protein—1 g.

ORANGE-BLOSSOM SYRUP

PAREVE

This is a typical Sephardic syrup, usually combined with ice and club soda for a cool drink. There are many flavors of syrups—almond, fruit, mint, and flower essence. A cinnamon syrup is more an Ashkenazic sweetener that I have included as a variation. Originally, I paired this syrup with the Ashkenazic-Sephardic combination of Pita Blintzes (see index), but this is also an aromatic topping over plain cake, waffles, pancakes, or frozen yogurt.

1½ cups sugar
¾ cup water
½ tbsp. fresh lemon juice

½ tsp. orange-blossom water, or more to taste

Combine the sugar, water, and lemon juice in a saucepan. Bring to a boil over high heat, stirring frequently. Reduce heat to low and cook uncovered for approximately 20 minutes or until a candy thermometer registers 212 degrees.

Immediately remove from heat and let cool. Stir in the orange-blossom water. Serve the syrup at room temperature. Makes 1 cup.

Variation: For Cinnamon Syrup, add about ½ tsp. ground cinnamon with the sugar and omit the orange-blossom water. Add 1 cinnamon stick to the syrup after reducing the heat to low.

Fruit Dishes

CAROL JOY'S MICROWAVED FRUIT COMPOTE

PAREVE
SUKKOT
CHANUKAH
PASSOVER
ANY HOLIDAY

Like most compotes, this is so versatile, but the secret sweetening ingredient here is bananas. Use fruits in season, so that this compote travels with you throughout the year. Carol Joy Shaffer says that this is her favorite way to use fruit that would otherwise go to waste. Another tip is that she buys bananas whenever they go on sale and then freezes them. This way she can use them for cooking at any time. To freeze, just skin the bananas and store them in zipper storage bags.

Cooking spray
3 large apples, peeled, cored, and cut in small cubes
2 large bananas, peeled and thickly sliced
1 large orange with peel, quartered
2 pears or peaches (when in season), sliced
¼ cup chopped dried apricots (optional)
1 2-inch cinnamon stick or ¼ tsp. ground cinnamon
2 tbsp. brandy or orange liqueur, or to taste (optional)
¼ cup dried cranberries or raisins (optional)

Coat a baking dish with cooking spray. Place the apples, bananas, orange wedges, pears, apricots, cinnamon stick, and brandy in the dish. Cover with plastic wrap. Microwave on high for approximately 15 minutes.

Add the cranberries. Continue microwaving, covered, 5 minutes longer. The mixture will bubble, and the bananas will almost dissolve.

Serve warm or cold as a dessert or side dish. Serves 6.

Serving suggestion: For an extraspecial dessert treat, serve with nonfat frozen vanilla yogurt.

Variation: This can also be baked all together including cranberries at 300 degrees for 1-2 hours. If the sauce seems dry, add ½ cup apple or orange juice.

Calories—202; Saturated fat—0 g.; Total fat—1 g.; Carbohydrates—45 g.; Cholesterol—0 mg.; Sodium—2 mg.; Fiber—2 g.; Protein—1 g.

FLOWER-SCENTED FRUIT COMPOTE

PAREVE

SHABBAT
ROSH HASHANAH
TU BISHEVAT
SHAVUOT

Here is a well-known compote with an exotic touch.

1 cup or 4 oz. dried apple rings
½ cup or 4 oz. pitted prunes
½ cup or 5 oz. dried apricots or peaches
⅓ cup or 3 oz. dried cherries, cranberries, blueberries, or raisins

1 cup orange juice
½ tbsp. orange-blossom water
2 tbsp. toasted pine nuts (optional)
1 tbsp. toasted chopped almonds or chopped pistachios (optional)

In a saucepan, combine the fruit and orange juice. Cook over low heat for 15-20 minutes, just until fruit plumps. Remove from stove.

Add the orange-blossom water. Chill. Garnish with nuts, if desired. Serves 6.

With nuts: Calories—293; Saturated fat—0 g.; Total fat—3 g.; Carbohydrates—64 g.; Cholesterol—0 mg.; Sodium—32 mg.; Fiber—3 g.; Protein—3 g.

Without nuts: Calories—265; Saturated fat—0 g.; Total fat—0 g.; Carbohydrates—63 g.; Cholesterol—0 mg.; Sodium—30 mg.; Fiber—3 g.; Protein—3 g.

MELON FRUIT SALAD

PAREVE

PURIM
PASSOVER
YOM HAATZMA'UT
ANY HOLIDAY

*There is nothing easier or more refreshing than fresh fruit for a buffet or holiday table. This fruit salad is delicious by itself but if you want just a little something extra, try the light fruit dressing.
It enhances the salad as a frame does a painting.*

FRUIT SALAD

2 cups watermelon
in 1-inch chunks
1 small cantaloupe,
cut 1-inch chunks

4 kiwis, peeled and cubed
1 pt. strawberries, quartered

WATERMELON DRESSING

1 cup watermelon in chunks
1½ tsp. balsamic vinegar

2 tbsp. lime juice
1 tbsp. fresh or 1 tsp. dry mint

Place the fruit-salad ingredients in a serving bowl and chill until ready to serve.

In a food processor, blend the watermelon, vinegar, and lime juice until smooth. Stir in the mint. Chill. Pour desired amount over salad and serve. Serves 6.

Variation: As for any fruit salad, combine fruits that are in season. In the fall you can sprinkle pomegranate seeds over the salad.

Calories—102; Saturated fat—0 g.; Total fat—1 g.; Carbohydrates—22 g.; Cholesterol—0 mg.; Sodium—10 mg.; Fiber—1 g.; Protein—2 g.

MOROCCAN ORANGES RIMONIM

PAREVE
ROSH HASHANAH
SUKKOT

*A Moroccan custom is to combine sesame seeds and pomegranate seeds
for Rosh Hashanah to symbolize the fertility of the Jewish people.
Moroccan Jews eat the mixture as is, but it makes a nice,
refreshing topping for this simple dessert.*

**5 oranges, peeled, sectioned,
then cut in half**

Orange-blossom water

TOPPING

½ large pomegranate
1 tbsp. sesame seeds

1 tsp. sugar

Arrange oranges in a bowl. Sprinkle on orange-blossom water lightly to taste.

Spoon the seeds from the pomegranate, separating as much of the white rind from it as you can. Add sesame seeds and sugar to the pomegranate seeds. Pass around to spoon about 1 tbsp. on top of oranges. Serves 6.

Calories—70; Saturated fat—0 g.; Total fat—0 g.; Carbohydrates—15 g.; Cholesterol—0 mg.; Sodium—0 mg.; Fiber—1 g.; Protein—1 g.

SUMMER'S FRUIT IN A CLOUD

DAIRY

*Any summer fruit will do. The sour-cream mixture can be made a day
in advance. Just add the fruit 2-3 hours before serving.*

1 cup nonfat yogurt cheese or
  sour cream
2 tbsp. brown sugar or 1½ tbsp.
  maple syrup
2 tbsp. sherry

½ tsp. vanilla extract
3 cups sliced nectarines or
  peaches
2 cups blueberries

In a blender or food processor, blend the nonfat yogurt cheese or sour cream,
brown sugar, sherry, and vanilla until smooth.

In a fruit bowl, mix the fruits and fold in the yogurt-cheese or sour-cream mixture. Chill for 3 hours before serving. Serves 6.

*Calories—114; Saturated fat—0 g.; Total fat—1 g.; Carbohydrates—22 g.;
Cholesterol—0 mg.; Sodium—33 mg.; Fiber—1 g.; Protein—4 g.*

MOROCCAN DATES DIPPED IN CHOCOLATE

PAREVE
*ROSH HASHANAH
SUKKOT
TU BISHEVAT
YOM HAATZMA'UT
ANY HOLIDAY*

*This treat is especially appropriate for Tu Bishevat. What could be a quicker
bite-size dessert than these no-bake goodies? They can be an addition
to a holiday dessert tray as well. Stuffed dates are an ancient treat.
The chocolate gives a contemporary twist.*

10 whole blanched almonds
10 whole pitted dates or prunes

½ cup semisweet or bittersweet
  chocolate chips

Create a slit in each date or prune. Insert a nut in each.

Melt the chocolate, dip half of each fruit and nut into the chocolate, and set it out on a foil- or wax-paper-covered cookie sheet. Chill before serving. Makes 10.

Calories—49; Saturated fat—2 g.; Total fat—3 g.; Carbohydrates—5 g.; Cholesterol—0 mg.; Sodium—0 mg.; Fiber—0 g.; Protein—0 g.

SWEET APPLES IN DATE SAUCE

PAREVE
ROSH HASHANAH
CHANUKAH
TU BISHEVAT
PASSOVER

*This recipe is inspired by cooks in the Oriental Jewish community
who make a date syrup in large quantities before Passover
It is used in* charoset *and throughout the week. Here, the syrup
has been changed to a sauce to eliminate the sugar.*

2 cups water
3 tbsp. chopped dates
1 cinnamon stick

**4 apples, peeled, cored,
and sliced**

In a large pot or skillet, combine the water, dates, and cinnamon stick. Bring to a boil. Reduce heat to low, cover, and simmer for 25 minutes. It should reduce the sauce by ½ cup.

Add the apples. Bring to a boil again. Reduce heat, cover, and simmer over low heat for approximately 45 minutes or until the apples are tender. Serve warm as a side dish or chilled as a dessert. Serves 6.

Variation: Add 2 tsp. lemon juice or rosewater.

Calories—103; Saturated fat—0 g.; Total fat—1 g.; Carbohydrates—24 g.; Cholesterol—0 mg.; Sodium—0 mg.; Fiber—1 g.; Protein—0 g.

ISRAELI BAKED APPLES

PAREVE

YOM KIPPUR BEFORE THE FAST
SIMCHAT TORAH
CHANUKAH
ANY HOLIDAY

Baked apples are a mainstay in Ashkenazic cooking. My mom offered
them as a dessert for most holidays dinners. For added spice
in this sweet dessert, sprinkle a dash of cinnamon and cardamom
or ginger into each apple. And . . . enjoy!

6 apples
⅓ cup raisins, plumped
in white wine
2 tbsp. apricot or cherry
preserves
1 tbsp. grated lemon peel

½ cup white wine such as white
or pink zinfandel (I use non-
alcoholic wine)
½ cup water
2 tbsp. honey

Preheat oven to 350 degrees. Core and seed apples.

Mix the raisins, preserves, and lemon peel. Spoon about 1 tsp. of the mixture into each apple.

In a measuring cup, combine the wine, water, and honey. Microwave on high for approximately 10 seconds or less, just to warm the mixture. Spoon it over the apples.

Bake and baste every 10-15 minutes until apples are tender, approximately 50 minutes. Serve warm or at room temperature. Serves 6.

Calories—200; Saturated fat—0 g.; Total fat—1 g.; Carbohydrates—48 g.;
Cholesterol—0 mg.; Sodium—2 mg.; Fiber— 2 g.; Protein—1 g.

WATERMELON-ADE

PAREVE
YOM KIPPUR BREAK-THE-FAST
PASSOVER

This is a popular contemporary drink. I've served it at my break-the-fast buffet table and it was very refreshing and appreciated.

4 cups watermelon, seeded
2 cups juice of choice, such as raspberry, apple, or pineapple orange

Juice of 3 lemons or ⅓ cup lemon juice
Mint leaves

Combine watermelon and juices in a food processor and blend until smooth. Garnish with mint leaves. Serves 6.

Calories—53; Saturated fat—0 g.; Total fat—0 g.; Carbohydrates—11 g.; Cholesterol—0 mg.; Sodium—8 mg.; Fiber—0 g.; Protein—1 g.

Desserts

APPLE-PLUM CRISP

DAIRY/PAREVE
SHABBAT
CHANUKAH
TU BISHEVAT

*German crisps are popular all over the U.S. They make a delicious
haimish dessert any time of the year. Use fruits of the season.
If you want to serve this with a meat meal, there is a reduced-fat
kosher pareve margarine on the market at this writing.*

3 cups pitted and sliced plums
4 cups peeled, cored, seeded,
  and sliced apples

1½ tsp. cinnamon
1 cup apple-juice concentrate

TOPPING

½ cup flour or whole-wheat
  pastry flour
⅔ cup oatmeal
½ cup brown sugar

3 tbsp. low-fat margarine (dairy
  or pareve)
1½ tsp. cinnamon
½ tsp. nutmeg

Combine the plums, apples, and cinnamon. Stir in the apple-juice concentrate.
Set aside.

Combine the topping ingredients, and stir well to mix in margarine to resemble a
coarse meal. Place the fruit mixture in a 10-inch square baking pan. Sprinkle the
topping over the fruit.

Bake at 375 degrees for 40-45 minutes or until the fruit is tender and topping is
lightly browned. Serve warm. Serves 8.

Variation: For a summer crisp, use a combination of seasonal fruits such as plums,
peaches, raspberries, blueberries, and strawberries.

*Calories—153; Saturated fat—1 g.; Total fat—3 g.; Carbohydrates—28 g.;
Cholesterol—0 mg.; Sodium—53 mg.; Fiber—1 g.; Protein—3 g.*

PINEAPPLE-APRICOT STRUDEL

DAIRY/PAREVE
SUKKOT
CHANUKAH

*Strudels can be laden with sugar, but not this one.
It's naturally sweetened by the fruit.*

½ cup crushed pineapple,
  drained
¾ cup diced dried apricots or
  diced dried mixed tropical fruit
¼ cup grated unsweetened
  coconut
1 tsp. grated lemon rind
¾ cup diced dates or whole
  golden raisins

2 tbsp. any variety nuts,
  toasted and crushed
½ cup naturally sweetened
  cereal flakes, crushed
5 sheets phyllo dough
Butter-flavored cooking spray
¾ cup natural or reduced-sugar
  apricot jam, melted
1 tsp. cinnamon

TOPPING

1½ tbsp. low-fat margarine
1 tbsp. honey (optional)

Cinnamon

In a bowl, combine the pineapple, dried fruit, coconut, and lemon rind.

Process the dates until coarsely ground. (If using raisins, do not grind them.) Add the dates to the pineapple mixture and set aside.

Combine the crushed nuts and cereal. Set aside.

Place 1 phyllo sheet on a work surface. Lightly coat with the butter spray. Repeat with a second phyllo sheet, and sprinkle ½ of the nut mixture on top. Repeat with 2 more sheets and butter spray. Sprinkle on the remaining nut mixture. Layer the last phyllo, brush on the melted jam, and sprinkle on the cinnamon.

Spoon the pineapple mixture evenly over the phyllo, leaving a 1½-inch border all around. Roll over once from the long side. Fold in the shorter edges, and continue to roll from the long side until the roll is completed.

Place the strudel, seam side down, on a nonstick baking sheet. Combine the margarine and honey. Melt for 5-10 seconds in the microwave. Brush over strudel and sprinkle the top of the strudel with a little extra cinnamon.

Slice at 1-inch intervals through the top layers of the strudel. Do not slice all the way through to the bottom.

Bake at 375 degrees for approximately 30 minutes or until the top is golden brown. Makes 12 slices.

Calories—177; Saturated fat—1 g.; Total fat—3 g.; Carbohydrates—37 g.; Cholesterol—0 mg.; Sodium—54 mg.; Fiber—1 g.; Protein—1 g.

Note: To freeze, wrap in foil after baking, then place in plastic bags

PITA BLINTZES WITH SYRUP

DAIRY

YOM KIPPUR BREAK-THE-FAST
CHANUKAH
SHAVUOT

This is a perfect example of "fusion cuisine." Blintzes are classically Ashkenazic, but pita bread comes from the Middle East and is found in Sephardic cuisine. And the Orange-Blossom Syrup is "Oriental" (Iran, Iraq, Syria). Serve these for breakfast or brunch or with Turkish coffee as a special dessert. They can be served as blintzes with fresh fruit, fruit coulis (pureed fruit), or Citrus Cinnamon Sauce. Assemble these in advance. The pitas will come out nice and soft if kept in the refrigerator overnight. To cook, just spray with butter-flavored cooking spray and microwave 1 minute.

**1½ cups low-fat or nonfat ricotta
cheese, or yogurt cheese,
drained for 48 hours**
1 tbsp. sugar
**1 tbsp. grated orange or
lemon peel**

5 pitas
Butter-flavored cooking spray
Orange-Blossom Syrup

Blend the ricotta or yogurt cheese with the sugar and peel.

Square off the pitas by trimming off the four rounded sides. You will have two square halves per pita.

Spoon about 2 tbsp. of the cheese mixture on each of the pita squares. Roll each pita square over once. Line up the rolls seam side down in a baking dish. Spray with butter-flavored cooking spray.

Bake uncovered at 350 degrees for 10-15 minutes until warmed through, or microwave until warmed through, approximately 1 minute.

Serve warm, topped with Orange-Blossom Syrup. If desired, sprinkle with berries and orange peel. Makes 10 blintzes. Serves 5.

Variations: Other toppings include Rich 'n' Dark Chocolate Syrup or melted low-sugar apricot jam.

Calories—188; Saturated fat—0 g.; Total fat—1 g.; Carbohydrates—9 g.; Cholesterol—9 mg.; Sodium—255 mg.; Fiber—0 g.; Protein—15 g.

TRUFFLES (KARTOSHKA)

DAIRY
SHABBAT
CHANUKAH
PURIM

These confections are based on the popular chocolate truffle but have added vitamins and calcium. In the original recipe, these are held together with butter and lots of sugar. Sofiya Sandler, a Russian-Jewish newcomer to Denver suggests the dry milk. If you want a festive look for a party, try rolling them in chocolate sprinkles or colored granulated sugar.

½ cup raisins
½ cup orange or apple juice
½ cup reduced-calorie maple
   syrup or honey
1 cup chocolate chips
⅓ cup cocoa powder
1 cup nonfat dry milk

1½ cups crushed low-fat vanilla
   wafer cookies (about 24
   cookies)
2 tbsp. rum extract or almond
   extract
⅔ cup crushed crisped rice cereal

Plump the raisins in the juice by warming them in the microwave on high for 1 minute. Set aside for 10 minutes.

In a saucepan, combine the raisins and juice, syrup, chocolate chips, and cocoa. Over medium-low heat, stir the contents until the chocolate chips just begin to melt.

Remove from heat and stir in the dry milk, cookie crumbs, and extract. Refrigerate the dough for 1 hour. (You can leave it in the same saucepan.) Prepare a plate with the crushed cereal (or other coating).

Shape dough into 1-inch balls and roll in the coating. Store in a covered container. Do not freeze. Makes approximately 4 dozen.

Serving suggestion: Sofiya makes her balls larger and places them in decorative minimuffin cups for special events.

Variation: Replace the extract with ¼ cup bourbon, rum, or other liquor.

Calories—53; Saturated fat—1g.; Total fat—2 g.; Carbohydrates—9 g.; Cholesterol—0 mg.; Sodium—30 mg.; Fiber—0 g.; Protein—1 g.

HAMANTASCHEN

PAREVE
PURIM

*There is a delicious filling used by Sephardic Jews to fill phyllo dough.
It's reminiscent of pumpkin-pie filling. I didn't have phyllo dough one time,
so I made a hamantasch dough. This is Jewish fusion cuisine—
a Sephardic-style filling in an Ashkenazic cookie. Try these unique, tasty
hamantaschen for Purim. They're high in flavor but much lower in fat
than traditional hamantaschen.*

PUMPKIN FILLING

1 lb. canned pumpkin or
   mashed sweet potatoes
6 tbsp. Solo pecan filling

1 tsp. cinnamon
¼ tsp. ground cloves

DOUGH

½ cup orange or apple juice
⅓ cup oil
2 egg whites
1 egg

2¾ cups flour (or 2 cups flour
   and ¾ cups whole-wheat flour)
½ cup sugar
1 tsp. baking powder

Mix all filling ingredients.

Preheat the oven to 350 degrees.

In a bowl, mix the juice, oil, and eggs. Add the remaining dough ingredients and mix until the dough forms a ball.

Knead for 1-2 minutes until very smooth. Place the ball in a covered bowl and refrigerate for 1-2 hours.

Roll dough out to ⅛ inch thick. Cut out circles with a 4-inch round mold. (A glass works well.) Place approximately 2 tsp. of filling onto each center. Form a triangle by folding in the edges at three points, leaving a space in the center to view the filling.

Bake at 375 degrees for 15-20 minutes. Makes 18.

*Calories—172; Saturated fat—0 g.; Total fat—5 g.; Carbohydrates—28 g.;
Cholesterol—12 mg.; Sodium—56 mg.; Fiber—1 g.; Protein—3 g.*

CHOCOLATE MANDELBROIT (BISCOTTI)

These cookies are called mandelbroit or mandel bread by Ashkenazim. Biscotti are very similar although Italian biscotti rarely contain any fat, and Jewish mandel bread always has fat. This delicious version has just a little fat. Enjoy!

⅓ cup slivered almonds
Cooking spray
½ cup sugar
2 tbsp. low-fat pareve margarine, softened
2 tbsp. oil
3 tbsp. orange-juice concentrate
½ cup egg substitute

1 tsp. vanilla
1¾ cups flour
4 tbsp. cocoa
1 tsp. baking powder
⅛ tsp. cinnamon
⅓ cup reduced-fat chocolate chips

Toast the almonds in a dry skillet over medium heat, turning to make sure they are lightly browned. Transfer to a grinder or small food processor and coarsely grind. Set aside.

Preheat oven to 350 degrees. Coat a baking sheet with cooking spray.

Using a food processor or electric mixer, mix the sugar, margarine, oil, orange-juice concentrate, egg substitute, and vanilla. Pulse until well combined. Add the flour, cocoa, baking powder, and cinnamon. Stir in the reserved almonds and chocolate chips.

Divide the dough in half. Shape into 2 loaves approximately 12 inches long by 2 inches wide and ¾ inch high. Place on baking sheet and bake for 25 minutes.

Remove from oven, but leave oven on. Cool loaves for 10 minutes.

Slice the loaves diagonally into 1-inch slices. Turn over on baking sheet so cut side is down, with all the slices facing the same direction. Bake for 10 minutes on both sides.

After baking, these can be easily frozen in zipper storage bags. Makes 24 slices.

Variation: Substitute pineapple-juice concentrate or chocolate syrup for the orange-juice concentrate.

Calories—70; Saturated fat—0 g.; Total fat—2 g.; Carbohydrates—12 g.; Cholesterol—0 mg.; Sodium—44 mg.; Fiber—0 g.; Protein—2 g.

CINNAMON MANDELBROIT

PAREVE

YOM KIPPUR BREAK-THE-FAST
SUKKOT
SIMCHAT TORAH
TU BISHEVAT

The classic Ashkenazic cookie usually has a lot of either eggs or oil.
This has little fat—lotsa flavor.

⅓ cup chopped pecans or almonds
Cooking spray
½ cup sugar
⅓ cup egg substitute
¼ cup low-fat pareve margarine
1½ tsp. vanilla

1 tsp. almond extract or
  ½ tsp. anise extract
1¾ cups flour
1½ tsp. baking powder
1 tbsp. cinnamon
⅓ cup reduced-fat chocolate
  chips (optional)

Toast the nuts in a toaster oven at 325 degrees for 7 minutes or in a dry skillet over medium heat until lightly toasted. Transfer to a food processor and mince. Set aside.

Preheat the oven to 350 degrees. Coat a baking sheet with cooking spray.

In a bowl, mix the sugar, egg substitute, margarine, vanilla, and almond extract.

Combine flour, baking powder, and cinnamon and mix into the egg mixture. Fold in the nuts and chocolate chips if you are using them.

Divide the dough in half. Shape into 2 loaves approximately 12 inches long by 2 inches wide and ¾ inch high. Place on a baking sheet and bake for 25 minutes.

Remove from oven; keep oven on. Cool loaves for 10 minutes. Slice the loaves diagonally into 1-inch slices. Turn over onto the baking sheet so the cut side is down. Bake for 10 minutes on each side or 15 minutes if crisper cookies are desired.

After baking, these can be easily frozen in zipper storage bags. Makes 24 slices.

Calories—72; Saturated fat—0 g.; Total fat—2 g.; Carbohydrates—12 g.; Cholesterol—0 mg.; Sodium—51 mg.; Fiber—0 g.; Protein—1 g.

ANISETTE COOKIES

PAREVE
SHABBAT
SUKKOT
SIMCHAT TORAH
PURIM

These are North African Sephardic cookies. Aniseeds are also used to sweeten challah on special occasions. I have reduced the oil and liqueur amounts. These cookies are good with tea as a refreshing dessert.

5 tbsp. sugar	**1½ tsp. anise extract**
5 tbsp. oil	**½ tbsp. aniseeds**
3 egg whites	**2 cups flour**
¼ cup anisette liqueur	**½ tsp. baking powder**

Combine the sugar, oil, egg whites, liqueur, extract, and aniseeds in a bowl and mix well.

Combine the flour and baking powder and stir into the mixture, blending well. Drop by tablespoonfuls onto a nonstick cookie sheet. Bake at 350 degrees for 15-20 minutes. Remove to wire rack to cool. After baking, these will freeze well stored in an airtight container or zipper storage bag. Makes 24 cookies.

Calories—83; Saturated fat—0 g.; Total fat—3 g.; Carbohydrates—12 g.; Cholesterol—0 mg.; Sodium—14 mg.; Fiber—0 g.; Protein—2 g.

RICE PUDDING

DAIRY
SHAVUOT

Rice pudding is found in the Middle East and as far north as Sweden. Of course, there are differences in this widely popular dessert. In the Middle East, short-grain rice is generally used, rather than long grain. Eggs usually are not included but flower water or a hint of lemon and cinnamon commonly are. Another difference is a sprinkling of pistachios or almonds as a topping.

2½ cups skim milk
½ cup water
2 tbsp. honey
Pinch salt
1 cinnamon stick
1 cup arborio (short-grain) rice

¼ cup raisins
2 tsp. cornstarch
2 tbsp. water
1 tbsp. rosewater, or
   more to taste

GARNISH

Cinnamon to taste
2 tsp. minced pistachios or
   almonds, or 4 tbsp. minced
   fresh seasonal fruit

In a saucepan, combine the milk, water, honey, salt, cinnamon stick, rice and raisins. Bring to a boil. Reduce heat to low and simmer uncovered for 30-40 minutes until the liquid is absorbed.

Combine the cornstarch and water. Stir into the rice and continue to cook for another minute or so until it slightly thickens. Remove from heat and stir in the rosewater.

Spoon into 4 custard cups or a larger serving bowl. Garnish with a sprinkling of cinnamon and a ½ tsp. nuts on each serving. Serve warm or chilled. Serves 4.

Calories—188; Saturated fat—0 g.; Total fat—1 g.; Carbohydrates—38 g.; Cholesterol—3 mg.; Sodium—80 mg.; Fiber—0 g.; Protein—7 g.

LEMON CREAM PUDDING

PAREVE
SHABBAT
SIMCHAT TORAH
PASSOVER
YOM HAATZMA'UT

Most popular with Syrian, Iraqi, and Iranian Jews, this pudding is served throughout the Middle East. It is usually eaten warm with a sprinkling of nuts on top but, when chilled, it is the perfect consistency for lemon pie, which is a favorite of mine. Try topping this with a spoonful of Honey-Almond Sauce for a dairy treat.

2½ cups orange juice
⅓ cup cornstarch or potato starch
⅓ cup lemon juice

⅓ cup sugar
4 tbsp. any flavor baby-food fruit puree (optional)

In a bowl, combine ½ cup of the orange juice and all of the cornstarch. Mix well. Transfer to saucepan. Over medium heat, add the remaining orange juice and the lemon juice and sugar, stirring while cooking until it begins to boil. Reduce heat to medium low and simmer for 2 more minutes.

Remove from heat and either serve warm or let it thicken as it cools to room temperature. If you like it sweeter, add the baby-food fruit puree now. (This just sweetens the pudding a little more without adding refined sugar.) If serving the pudding chilled, cover the dishes with plastic wrap before refrigerating.

Garnish with chopped pistachios or almonds, or a spoonful of fresh fruit. Serves 4.

Calories—185; Saturated fat—0 g.; Total fat—0 g.; Carbohydrates—45 g.; Cholesterol—0 mg.; Sodium—3 mg.; Fiber—0 g.; Protein—15 g.

LEMON POPPY-SEED CREAM-CHEESE BARS

DAIRY
YOM KIPPUR BREAK-THE-FAST
CHANUKAH
TU BISHEVAT
PURIM
SHAVUOT

Poppy seeds are extremely popular in the Ashkenazic culture and are an ancient sweetener. Lemon and poppy seeds have become a favorite combination among Americans. These delicate bars might remind you of lemon poppy-seed muffins. They are a sweet satisfier for dessert after any dairy meal, buffet, break-the-fast, or on Purim.

3 egg whites
1 cup sugar
6 oz. (½ cup) nonfat lemon yogurt (or ½ cup nonfat plain yogurt + 1 tbsp. lemon extract)
2½ tbsp. lemon juice

1 tsp. lemon extract
2 tbsp. grated lemon peel
1¼ cups cake flour
2 tbsp. poppy seeds
½ tsp. baking powder
Cooking spray

TOPPING

6 oz. (½ cup) low-fat cream cheese	**1 egg white**
¼ cup sugar	**1 tsp. lemon juice**
	1 tsp. vanilla extract

Whisk together the egg whites, sugar, yogurt, lemon juice, extract, and peel.

Combine the flour, poppy seeds, and baking powder and stir in egg-white mixture.

Coat a 9-inch square baking dish with the cooking spray and pour the batter in, spreading evenly.

In a blender or food processor, combine the topping ingredients. Spoon over batter. Swirl a knife through the batter to marbleize. Bake at 350 for 30 minutes. Cool on wire rack. Cut into bars. These will freeze well. Makes approximately 16.

Calories—71; Saturated fat—1 g.; Total fat—2 g,; Carbohydrates—11 g.; Cholesterol—5 mg.; Sodium—48 mg.; Fiber—0 g.; Protein—2 g.

SUGARLESS PINEAPPLE CHEESECAKE

DAIRY
SHAVUOT

Cheesecakes are an ancient dessert going back to the second century B.C.E. Even back then, this dessert was associated with Shavuot because of its whiteness, symbolizing purity. This ancient Greek dessert has traveled far and evolved much since then. Every country has its unique way to thicken the cheese base. Americans use cornstarch.

CRUST

24 low-fat gingersnaps, vanilla wafers, or natural fruit-juice-sweetened cookies, equaling 1½ cups crushed	**1 egg white**

FILLING

2 8-oz. pkg. nonfat cream cheese
1 cup nonfat sour cream or
   nonfat plain yogurt
⅔ cup pineapple-juice
   concentrate

2 tbsp. cornstarch
3 egg whites
2 tsp. vanilla
3 tbsp. lemon juice

TOPPING

1 pkg. instant vanilla pudding

1 cup pineapple juice

Process or crush the cookies into crumbs. Mix in the egg white. Pat the crumb mixture into an 8-inch springform pan. Bake at 350 degrees for 8 minutes. Set aside to cool.

In a food processor, puree all the filling ingredients until very smooth. Pour over the crust.

Bake at 375 degrees for 1 hour. Turn the oven off and let the cheesecake sit in the oven for 30 minutes.

Remove and cool completely.

Beat the pudding and juice according to the package directions, substituting the juice for the milk called for in the directions. Spread over the cake. Serves 12.

Calories—55; Saturated fat—0 g.; Total fat—0 g.; Carbohydrates—7 g.; Cholesterol—0 mg.; Sodium—193 mg.; Fiber—0 g.; Protein—7 g.

MOCHA CHOCOLATE CHEESECAKE

DAIRY
SHAVUOT

*The cookie-crumb crust is an American creation. Jews in Europe
have traditionally used a baked pie crust.*

CRUST

24 low-fat vanilla or chocolate
   wafers, equaling 1½ cups
   crushed

1 egg white
½ tsp. instant coffee granules
⅛ tsp. cinnamon

CHEESE FILLING

2 8-oz. pkg. nonfat or
   low-fat cream cheese
8 oz. low-fat cottage cheese
1 cup nonfat plain yogurt
¾ cup sugar

2 tbsp. cornstarch
2 tsp. vanilla extract
1½ tsp. instant coffee granules
3 egg whites
¼ cup egg substitute

CHOCOLATE FILLING

3 tbsp. cocoa
3 tbsp. sugar

½ tsp. vanilla extract

TOPPING

1 box sugar-free instant
   chocolate pudding mix
1 cup skim milk

½ tsp. instant coffee granules
   (optional)

Process or crush the vanilla wafers into crumbs. Mix in the remaining crust ingredients. Pat into an 8-inch springform pan, and bake at 350 degrees for 10 minutes. Cool.

In a food processor, puree all the cheese filling ingredients until very smooth.

Remove ½ cup of the cheese filling to a small bowl, add the chocolate filling ingredients, and mix thoroughly.

Spread half of the white cheesecake mixture onto the crust. Spread the chocolate mixture over it. Pour remaining cheese mixture evenly over the chocolate. Run a knife through the batter in a swirling fashion.

Bake at 325 degrees for 1 hour. Turn off the oven and allow the cheesecake to sit in oven for 30 minutes. Cool the cake completely before spreading on the topping.

Beat the pudding mix, milk, and coffee granules (if using) together according to package directions. Spread over the cheesecake. Refrigerate for 3-4 hours before serving. Serves 12.

Calories—192; Saturated fat—1 g.; Total fat—1 g.; Carbohydrates—36 g.; Cholesterol—3 mg.; Sodium—263 mg.; Fiber—0 g.; Protein—9 g.

CHEESECAKE IN PHYLLO POUCHES

This is so easy to make and so nice for company. Key lime is from Florida but bottled key lime juice is available in many places in the United States.

Butter-flavored cooking spray
14-oz. can fat-free sweetened
  condensed milk
4 oz. nonfat cream cheese

5 tbsp. key lime juice
4 sheets phyllo dough
Powdered sugar

RASPBERRY COULIS (OPTIONAL)

18 oz. or 3 containers (½ pt.
  each) fresh or frozen
  raspberries
2 tbsp. orange-juice concentrate

2 tbsp. fruit liqueur
Approximately 5 tsp. powdered
  sugar

Coat the cups in a muffin tin with the butter-flavored cooking spray.

Preheat the oven to 350 degrees. In a food processor or blender, blend the condensed milk, cream cheese, and key lime juice until smooth.

On a work surface, spray one phyllo sheet with the butter spray. Stack on 3 more sheets, spraying between each sheet. Cut the stack in half lengthwise, then in 3 equal squares per strip. Tuck each stack of squares into a prepared cup of the muffin tin. Spoon 2 tbsp. of the cheese filling into each cup. Twist the corners of the phyllo dough to form little pouches.

Bake at 400 degrees for 10 minutes or until golden. Turn out onto wire rack to cool. To serve, sprinkle each pouch with powdered sugar.

For a holiday presentation, puree 2 cups of the raspberries. Stir in the orange-juice concentrate, liqueur, and sugar. Spoon the raspberry mixture around each pouch on a plate. Place some whole raspberries on the sauce. Serves 6.

Calories—203; Saturated fat—2 g.; Total fat—3 g; Carbohydrates—39 g.; Cholesterol—11 mg.; Sodium—109 mg.; Fiber—0 g.; Protein—4 g.

APPLE CAKE

Apple cake for Rosh Hashanah is almost as traditional as honey cake. It is customary to use apples in cooking to symbolize hopes for a sweet new year. This recipe came from Israel. Apple cake is a great haimish pareve cake that is nice to serve for any of the fall holidays. And it's easy to make!

Cooking spray
1 tsp. cinnamon
2 tbsp. lemon juice
3 cups peeled, thickly sliced, then coarsely chopped apples
⅓ cup honey
1 cup brown sugar
¾ cup orange juice
¾ cup egg substitute

½ cup applesauce
¼ cup oil
2 tsp. vanilla extract
1½ cups flour
1 cup whole-wheat pastry flour
2 tsp. baking powder
½ tsp. nutmeg
¼ tsp. salt

GLAZE

½-¾ cup powdered sugar   **1 tbsp. orange juice**

Preheat the oven to 350 degrees. Coat a 10-inch tube pan with the cooking spray.

In a bowl, mix the cinnamon and lemon juice with the apples. Set aside.

In a mixing bowl, whisk together the honey, sugar, orange juice, egg substitute, applesauce, oil, and vanilla until well blended.

Combine the flours, baking powder, nutmeg, and salt, and mix into the egg mixture to make a smooth batter.

Fold in the apples and pour the batter into the prepared baking pan. Bake for 1 hour or until a toothpick comes out clean when inserted into the cake.

Cool the cake for 10 minutes, then invert onto a wire rack to cool completely.

To garnish, mix the powdered sugar and orange juice to form a thin glaze, and drizzle over the cake. The cake can be made a couple of days in advance and frozen. Serves 14.

Variation: For a natural sweetener, replace the brown sugar and honey with 1 cup maple syrup.

Calories—192; Saturated fat—0 g.; Total fat—4 g.; Carbohydrates—36 g.; Cholesterol—0 mg.; Sodium—113 mg.; Fiber—1 g.; Protein—4 g.

ROSEWATER ANGEL FOOD CAKE

PAREVE/DAIRY
PASSOVER
SHAVUOT

This is an example of the Arab influence on the Oriental (Mizrachi) Jews (those from Iran, Iraq, and Syria). This cake has a delicate roselike flavor Rosewater is a popular sweetener in those regions. Increase or decrease the amount of rosewater, depending on what you are accustomed to.

¾ cup cake flour
4 tbsp. cornstarch or potato
  starch
¼ tsp. baking soda
1 tsp. cinnamon

1 cup sugar
11 egg whites
3 tbsp. rosewater, room
  temperature
1 tsp. cream of tartar

In a bowl, mix the flour, cornstarch, baking soda, cinnamon, and ½ cup of the sugar. Set aside.

In a large bowl, beat the egg whites until foamy. Add the rosewater and cream of tartar; continue beating until soft peaks form. Gradually add the remaining sugar while beating until stiff peaks form.

Sprinkle ⅓ of the flour mixture over the top and carefully fold in. Repeat until all of the flour mixture is used.

Spoon batter into an ungreased 10-inch tube pan or angel cake pan, spreading evenly. Bake at 325 degrees for 40-45 minutes or until the cake springs back when touched.

Invert the cake pan to cool on a wire rack for 40 minutes. Loosen the sides of the cake and remove from pan. Serves 12.

Serving suggestion: Serve with Citrus Cinnamon Sauce or Dairy Chocolate Sauce for those who just have to have something chocolate for dessert.

Calories—116; Saturated fat—0 g.; Total fat—0 g.; Carbohydrates—25 g.; Cholesterol—0 mg.; Sodium—87 mg.; Fiber—0 g.; Protein—4 g.

ORANGE SPONGE CAKE

PAREVE
SHABBAT
ROSH HASHANAH

This is an age-old Jewish soaked sponge cake, originally from the Jews of Spain, with a tender texture and a delicate orange flavor. I've lowered the sugar content, since soaked cakes are drenched in a sugar syrup. Don't forget to add the orange extract—it intensifies the flavor. This is good for any holiday!

10 eggs, room temperature	**1 cup sugar or ¾ cup maple**
2 tsp. grated orange peel	**syrup**
¼ cup orange juice	**1 cup cake flour or**
1 tsp. orange extract	**whole-wheat pastry flour**

SAUCE

1 cup orange juice	**1 tsp. rum extract (optional)**

GARNISH

Vanilla sugar or powdered sugar	2 tsp. grated orange peel

Have ready an ungreased 10-inch tube pan with a removable bottom. If you do not own one, a greased Bundt pan will work as well.

Separate the eggs, placing 10 whites in one bowl, and 2 egg yolks in another bowl. Discard the 8 remaining yolks. To the egg yolks, add the orange peel, orange juice, and orange extract. Set aside.

Beat the egg whites until soft peaks begin to form. Gradually add the sugar, ¼ cup at a time, while beating the egg whites to stiff peaks, but not dry.

Using a spatula, fold in alternately the egg-yolk mixture and cake flour, ¼ cup at a time.

Gently pour the batter into the tube pan. Bake at 324 degrees for 45-55 minutes or until the top springs back when lightly touched.

Remove sides of pan, and invert cake over a wire rack. If using a Bundt pan, carefully work the cake out by running a sharp knife along the sides and center, and carefully turn the cake onto a flat platter.

Cool for approximately 15 minutes. With a metal skewer, poke holes randomly in the cake. Pour the orange-juice mixture over the cake. The cake should still be warm to absorb the liquid.

Garnish with a sprinkling of vanilla sugar and top with a sprinkling of orange peel. Serves 8-10.

Variation: For a contemporary modification, fold in ½ package sugar-free orange-flavored gelatin to beaten egg whites.

Calories—119; Saturated fat—0 g.; Total fat—1 g.; Carbohydrates—26 g.; Cholesterol—23 mg.; Sodium—38 mg.; Fiber—0 g.; Protein—3 g.

HONEY DATE ORANGE CAKE

DAIRY/PAREVE
SHABBAT
ROSH HASHANAH
TU BISHEVAT
YOM HAATZMA'UT

This is like a honey cake using ginger rather than cinnamon, something like an English ginger cake. All the other ingredients—dates, figs, orange juice, and honey—are reminiscent of Israel.

Cooking spray
2¼ cups flour
1 tsp. baking powder
1 tsp. baking soda
2 tsp. ground ginger
½ tsp. allspice
6 oz. (1 cup) dates, chopped
½ cup diced dried figs (optional)

2 egg whites or ¼ cup egg substitute
2 tbsp. reduced-fat pareve or dairy margarine
2 tbsp. oil
1 cup orange juice
¾ cup honey

Coat a 9-by-9-inch square, glass baking dish with cooking spray.
Preheat the oven to 350 degrees.
In a mixing bowl, mix the flour, baking powder, baking soda, ginger, and allspice. Add the dates and figs and toss to coat.
In another bowl, beat egg whites, margarine, oil, orange juice, and honey. Stir into the flour mixture to blend.
Pour into the prepared baking dish. Bake for 40-45 minutes or until the cake springs back to a light touch. Serves 16.

Variation: If baked in a 9-by-13-inch dish, this cake can be cut into 24 slices for dessert or as part of a buffet for a bigger party. The calories will be lower because the pieces are smaller.

Calories—179; Saturated fat—0 g.; Total fat—3 g.; Carbohydrates—36 g.; Cholesterol—0 mg.; Sodium—99 mg.; Fiber—0 g.; Protein—3 g.

PINEAPPLE HONEY CAKE

PAREVE
SHABBAT
ROSH HASHANAH
YOM KIPPUR BREAK-THE-FAST
SUKKOT
CHANUKAH

Honey cakes are probably the oldest cakes around, as honey, dates, poppy seeds, and pistachios were among the earliest natural sweeteners. Jews always needed pareve desserts to go with meat meals, so they devised a combination of strong-tasting spices, such as cinnamon, allspice, and ginger, to flavor cakes, which became spice cakes. This is also probably how coffee developed as a flavoring for Jewish honey cakes. I have taken it a step farther by adding fruit-juice concentrate.

Cooking spray
1 cup honey
1 cup sugar
6 egg whites
1 cup brewed coffee,
    double strength
½ cup pineapple-juice
    concentrate
¼ cup oil

3½ cups flour
2 tsp. baking powder
2 tsp. baking soda
4 tsp. cinnamon
½ tsp. salt
½ tsp. allspice
8-oz. can crushed pineapple,
    drained

Preheat the oven to 350 degrees. Spray and flour a 10-inch tube pan.

In a large mixing bowl, beat the honey, sugar, egg whites, coffee, pineapple-juice concentrate, and oil until blended.

In another bowl, combine the flour, baking powder, baking soda, cinnamon, salt, and allspice and mix into the honey mixture to make a smooth batter. Fold in the pineapple. Pour the batter into the prepared pan.

Bake for 1 hour until the cake springs back to a light touch. Let stand for 10 minutes. Invert onto a wire rack to cool. May be baked a couple of days in advance and frozen. Serves 16.

Calories—246; Saturated fat—0 g.; Total fat—4 g.; Carbohydrates—49 g.; Cholesterol—0 mg.; Sodium—170 mg.; Fiber—0 g.; Protein—4 g.

ROOT-BEER SPICE CAKE

PAREVE/DAIRY
SHABBAT
SUKKOT
CHANUKAH

This inspired cake has an intriguing origin. I found it in an heirloom cookbook that belonged to my grandmother entitled Tempting Kosher Dishes, *published by the Manischewitz Company in 1933. Half the book is in English, half in Yiddish for the then-new Americans. Originally, this recipe called for matzah cake meal and milk. I replaced the milk with root beer and reduced the sugar, but root-beer concentrate and spices are part of the original recipe.*

2 cups flour
1 tsp. baking soda
1 tsp. baking powder
1 tsp. cinnamon
1 tsp. cardamom
1 tsp. allspice
1 cup sugar

4 egg whites or ½ cup egg
   substitute
⅔ cup unsweetened applesauce
1 cup flat root beer
4 tsp. root-beer concentrate
½ cup raisins
Cooking spray

GLAZE

1¾ cups powdered sugar
¼ cup cocoa powder
1 tbsp. root beer or skim milk
2 tbsp. low-fat margarine or
   2 tbsp. low-fat cream cheese,
   softened

1 tsp. root-beer concentrate

In a bowl, mix flour, baking soda, baking powder, cinnamon, cardamom, and all-spice.

In another bowl, blend sugar and egg whites or egg substitute. Mix in apple-sauce, root beer, and root-beer concentrate. Add to dry mixture and mix well. Fold in raisins.

Lightly spray an 8-by-8-inch square or Bundt pan with cooking spray. Add batter to pan. Bake at 350 degrees for 40-45 minutes or until a toothpick comes out clean.

Cool in pan for 10 minutes. Turn out on cake rack and cool completely. This cake can be frosted with the glaze or served plain.

To make the glaze, combine the powdered sugar and cocoa. Mix in the root beer, margarine, and root-beer concentrate until a spreadable mixture is achieved. Drizzle the glaze over the cake. Serves 8.

Calories—380; Saturated fat—0 g.; Total fat—2 g.; Carbohydrates—85 g.; Cholesterol—0 mg.; Sodium—277 mg.; Fiber—0 g.; Protein—5 g.

CHOCOLATE MARBLE POUND CAKE

DAIRY
SHABBAT
SHAVUOT

This is a popular "plain" cake to go with coffee or tea at any dairy table. The butter extract helps to give this cake that rich taste without so much butter.

2½ cups flour	**2 tbsp. butter or margarine**
1 tsp. baking soda	**2 tsp. vanilla extract**
¼ tsp. salt	**1 tsp. almond extract**
1⅓ cups sour cream	**½ tsp. butter extract**
1 cup applesauce	**⅔ cup sugar or honey**
1 egg	**5 tbsp. cocoa powder**
6 egg whites	**3 tbsp. water**

Preheat the oven to 350 degrees.
Oil and flour an 8-cup loaf pan.
In a bowl, combine the flour, baking soda, and salt. Set aside.
In another bowl, combine the sour cream, applesauce, egg and egg whites, butter or margarine, extracts, and sugar. Beat for 1 minute or until well mixed. Add flour mixture and mix well.
Remove 1½ cups of the batter to a smaller bowl. Add the cocoa powder and water. Mix until well blended.
Pour the white batter into the prepared pan. Pour the chocolate batter over the white batter. Marbleize the batter with a knife by swirling it side to side.
Bake for 1 hour. Cool in the pan for 10 minutes. Turn out onto a cake rack and cool completely. Serves 10.

Calories—245; Saturated fat—2 g.; Total fat—3 g.; Carbohydrates—45 g.; Cholesterol—27 mg.; Sodium—238 mg.; Fiber—0 g.; Protein—9 g.

SOUR-CREAM COFFEECAKE

DAIRY
YOM KIPPUR BREAK-THE-FAST
SHAVUOT

A staple in Ashkenazic cuisine, this simple yet rich-tasting cake is good for brunches, break-the-fast, and after a dairy holiday meal with coffee or tea.

3 egg whites
1 cup nonfat sour cream
⅔ cup sugar
3 tbsp. nonfat cream cheese
2 tsp. vanilla extract
1 tsp. almond extract

2 cups flour
1 tsp. baking powder
1 tsp. baking soda
¼ tsp. salt
Cooking spray

TOPPING

½ cup Grape Nuts cereal
⅓ cup brown sugar

½ tbsp. cinnamon

In a mixing bowl, blend the egg whites, sour cream, sugar, cream cheese, vanilla and almond extracts with an electric mixer until creamy.

Combine the flour, baking powder, baking soda, and salt and stir into the wet mixture until well blended.

Coat a 10-inch round baking pan with cooking spray and spoon the batter into the pan evenly.

To make the topping, combine the Grape Nuts, brown sugar, and cinnamon and sprinkle over the batter. Bake at 350 degrees for 30 minutes or until the cake springs back to a light touch. Serves 12.

Variation: For Cream-Cheese Topping, blend 8 oz. nonfat or light cream cheese, ⅓ cup sugar or 3 tbsp. apple-juice concentrate, and 2 egg whites. Spoon on top of cake batter evenly. Dot with ½ cup natural apricot preserves. Top with 1 cup frozen blueberries. Then bake as directed.

Calories—124; Saturated fat—0 g.; Total fat—0 g.; Carbohydrates—27 g.; Cholesterol—0 mg.; Sodium—16 mg.; Fiber—0 g.; Protein—3 g.

ITALIAN CHEESECAKE

DAIRY
SHAVUOT

This recipe has been circulating in Israel—it comes from Italy originally. It's not like American cheesecake. Its taste is between a cheesecake and an angel-food cake. You can top it with melted apricot or peach preserves.

5 egg whites
½ cup sugar
½ cup flour
¼ cup cornstarch
1 tsp. baking powder
1 lb. light ricotta cheese,
    drained low-fat cottage cheese,
    or yogurt cheese

3 tbsp. cognac
1 tbsp. vanilla
2 egg whites
Cooking spray
⅓ cup breadcrumbs
1 tbsp. sugar

TOPPING

1 cup apricot or peach jam

2 tbsp. brandy

In a glass bowl, beat the egg whites until soft peaks form. Gradually add the sugar and continue beating until stiff peaks form.

In another bowl, thoroughly mix the flour, cornstarch, and baking powder.

Spoon half of the flour mixture over the beaten egg whites. Fold in until well blended. Repeat with the remaining half.

Fold in the ricotta cheese, cognac, and vanilla until well blended.

In a clean bowl, with clean beaters, beat the 2 egg whites until they peak. Fold into the cheesecake mixture. (This fluffs up the cake further.)

Coat an 11-by-9½-inch glass baking dish with cooking spray. Combine the breadcrumbs with sugar and sprinkle evenly over the bottom of the dish. Spoon the cheesecake mixture evenly into the dish. Bake at 375 degrees for 30 minutes. Cool.

Melt the apricot jam and brandy together and drizzle over the cooled cake. Serves 15.

Calories—167; Saturated fat—0 g.; Total fat—1 g.; Carbohydrates—30 g.; Cholesterol—5 mg.; Sodium—213 mg.; Fiber—0 g.; Protein—9 g.

FELICIA'S ROMANIAN
CHOCOLATE POTATO BALLS

PAREVE
SHABBAT
SUKKOT

There are no potatoes in this recipe. The English translation probably refers to the shape of these easy, impressive little cakes. Felicia Herscovici, a dear friend, gave me two versions of this recipe that she brought from her native Romania. The first recipe is from scratch with a lot of nuts, breadcrumbs, and cocoa cooked together. This one, she says, is the updated version. One way to top these chocolate balls is with a melted bar of bittersweet baking chocolate. When Felicia coats the balls with the chocolate, she uses a butter knife to ice the top halves. Since the balls are so moist and soft, I thought that a light and easy coating of cocoa powder and powdered sugar, topped with a cherry, was a way to avoid fat, sugar, and calories yet be elegant looking for company. Either way is delicious.

1 box Duncan Hines Chocolate Cake Mix Lower Fat Recipe
5 egg whites
1 cup water
1 cup natural unsweetened applesauce
⅓ cup brewed coffee, double strength

¼ cup rum
Heaping ½ cup coarsely chopped maraschino cherries + 9 extra cherries
3 tbsp. unsweetened cocoa powder
2 tbsp. powdered sugar

Preheat the oven to 350 degrees. Combine the cake mix, eggs, water, and applesauce. Pour into an ungreased 9-by-13-inch baking pan and bake for 31-34 minutes or until a toothpick comes out clean when inserted into the cake.

Remove the cake from the oven and pour the coffee and rum over the cake. Cool the cake while the coffee and rum soak in.

Mix the cooled cake with a spoon or with your hands (better method) and add the heaping ½ cup of cherries. Shape into about 18 balls.

On a plate, mix the cocoa and powdered sugar. Roll the cake balls into the mixture. Slice the 9 cherries in half and place each half on the top of each ball. Makes 18 balls.

Calories—148; Saturated fat—1 g.; Total fat—3 g.; Carbohydrates—27 g.; Cholesterol—0 mg.; Sodium—198 mg.; Fiber—0 g.; Protein—2 g.

Note: These freeze very well—and you can take them out of the freezer to thaw as you want them.

QUICK CHOCOLATE-CHIP CHERRY RING

PAREVE
SUKKOT
CHANUKAH

*I don't always have the time or inclination to bake a cake from scratch.
My sister Janis tested this moist cake on her Temple Sisterhood
and it was a big hit.*

**1 box Duncan Hines
  Yellow Cake Mix**
3 egg whites
**⅓ cup natural unsweetened
  applesauce**

1½ tsp. almond extract (optional)
16-oz. can light cherry pie filling
**¾ cup reduced-fat chocolate bak-
  ing chips**

Preheat the oven to 350 degrees. Grease and flour a 12-inch Bundt pan.

Mix the cake mix, egg whites, applesauce, and almond extract if using. Stir in cherry pie filling and chocolate chips

Turn the mixture into the prepared Bundt pan and bake for approximately 1 hour or until toothpick comes out clean. Serves 12.

*Calories—216; Saturated fat—2 g.; Total fat—4 g.; Carbohydrates—42 g.;
Cholesterol—0 mg.; Sodium—377 mg.; Fiber—1 g.; Protein—3 g.*

CARAMEL ROLLS

DAIRY

YOM KIPPUR BREAK-THE-FAST

These easy treats are German-Austrian in flavor. Bakery goodies in the U.S. have been largely influenced by the talents of German and Austrian bakers due to a large immigration here from that part of the world. These were a big hit at my son's graduation brunch, thanks to my sister Janis, who sent me the recipe from Pittsburgh, Pennsylvania.

Cooking spray
12 frozen dinner rolls
1 box vanilla pudding mix
   (not instant)
½ cup brown sugar

1 tbsp. cinnamon
½ cup raisins
⅓ cup crushed walnuts or pecans
4-5 tbsp. low-fat margarine

Coat a 10-inch Bundt pan with the cooking spray. Arrange as many of the rolls as will fit in a single layer.

Sprinkle the tops with the entire package of pudding mix, brown sugar, cinnamon, raisins, and nuts. Cover with a towel or plastic wrap and let rolls defrost on the counter overnight.

In the morning, dot the rolls with the margarine. Bake at 350 degrees for 20 minutes. Remove from oven and cool 10 minutes. Flip out onto serving platter and serve warm or at room temperature. Serves 12.

Calories—121; Saturated fat—1 g.; Total fat—4 g.; Carbohydrates—20 g.; Cholesterol—0 mg.; Sodium—92 mg.; Fiber—1 g.; Protein—1 g.

A CHAROSET PARTY

My dear aunt Zendra Ashkanazi has taught religious school in St. Louis, Missouri, for many years. She created a lesson plan featuring a collection of around-the-world charoset recipes, as well as interesting customs of Jews from different countries. She was thrilled to share it with me. In turn, I had one of my most fun Seders ever by preparing in advance different varieties of charoset. I brought them out on a big tray, and everyone got to taste and judge which one was his or her favorite. It really involved the children, and the adults had fun, too! So, here's a sampling of authentic charoset recipes, to give you a start on your own "Charoset Party."

NATURAL ORANGE-DATE CHAROSET
From Rhodes, a Greek island off Turkey

1 cup pitted dates
½ cup pecan or almond pieces
1 medium orange, peeled, seeded, and sectioned

½ tsp. cinnamon
2 tbsp. kosher sweet red wine

In a food processor, combine the dates, pecans, orange sections, and cinnamon. Process until the mixture is coarsely pureed. Stir in the wine. Makes 1⅓ cups.

Per 1 tbsp: Calories—49; Saturated fat—0 g.; Total fat— 2 g.; Carbohydrates— 7 g.; Cholesterol—0 mg.; Sodium—0 mg.; Fiber—0 g.; Protein—0 g.

GREEK CHAROSET

¾ cup ground walnuts
20 large dates, chopped
1 cup chopped raisins

½ cup chopped almonds
Dash grated lemon peel
Sweet red Passover wine

Combine the fruit and nuts. Add the wine to desired consistency. Serves 56.

Per 1 tbsp.: Calories—30; Saturated fat—0 g.; Total fat—2 g.; Carbohydrates— 3 g.; Cholesterol—0 mg.; Sodium—1 mg.; Fiber—0 g.; Protein—1 g.

And here are some other authentic recipes—but ones without much fuss. They come from S'fard, an Internet publication of Sephardic recipes. Their recipes are available on floppy disk and by e-mail (sefrdi@aol.com) as of this writing. The Web site is www.sfard.com. While specific charoset ingredients appear to have little special significance for Ashkenazim, for hundreds of years, Sephardim chose the ingredients of their charoset for their significance as well as their texture and flavor. Cinnamon sticks, ginger, cardamom, and turmeric roots, because of their long shapes, represented the straw the Israelites were denied; wine represented the blood marking the houses of the Israelites during the tenth plague; dates and white sesame seeds represented the Promised Land—a land of milk and honey. Figs, pomegranate seeds, and nuts were used because they, as well as the previously mentioned ingredients, are referenced in the Torah and elsewhere in the Bible.

TURKISH CHAROSET
From Izmir, Turkey, 1952

½ cup walnuts or pistachios
½ cup dried apricots
1 square inch pickled lemon (optional) or 1 tbsp. lemon juice with ⅛ tsp. salt

1 tsp. cinnamon
¼ cup kosher red wine

In a food processor, chop the nuts, apricots, and pickled lemon. Add the cinnamon and wine. Serves 16.

Per 1 tbsp: Calories—41; Saturated fat—0 g.; Total fat—2 g.; Carbohydrates—4 g.; Cholesterol—0 mg.; Sodium—1 mg.; Fiber—0 g.; Protein—1 g.

SYRIAN CHAROSET
From Aleppo, Syria, 1947

5 tbsp. Passover halvah or ground whole sesame seeds
¼ cup chopped wine-soaked orange peel (optional)
3 tbsp. minced pistachios or almonds
1 square inch pickled lemon or 1 ½ tbsp. chopped fresh lemon with ¼ tsp. salt

2 tbsp. chopped pitted oil-cured ripe black olives
2 tbsp. chopped dates
1 tsp. cinnamon
1 tsp. ground fennel or aniseed (optional)
¼ cup kosher sweet red wine

Mix all ingredients well. Serves 16.

Per 1 tbsp.: Calories—39; Saturated fat—0 g.; Total fat—2 g.; Carbohydrates—3 g.; Cholesterol—0 mg.; Sodium—9 mg.; Fiber—0 g.; Protein—1 g.

MOROCCAN CHAROSET
From Fez, Morocco, 1951

This charoset needs to be started four days before the Seder.

**¾ cup minced almonds or
    pistachios
¼ cup chopped wine-soaked
    orange peel (air dry orange
    peel 48 hours, then soak in
    kosher red wine 48 hours)
    (optional)**

**2 square inches pickled lemon or
    2 tbsp. lemon juice
    with ¼ tsp. salt
1 tbsp. turmeric
1 tsp. cumin
¼ cup kosher red wine
1 tsp. cinnamon (optional)**

In a food processor, chop the nuts, orange peel, and pickled lemon. Stir in the remaining ingredients. Serves 16.

Per 1 tbsp.: Calories—48; Saturated fat—0 g.; Total fat—4 g.; Carbohydrates—2 g.; Cholesterol—0 mg.; Sodium—38 mg.; Fiber—0 g.; Protein—1 g.

GINGER SPICED PANCAKES

PAREVE

*These contemporary ginger spiced pancakes give those pricey
Passover box mixes a run for their money.*

4 egg whites
¼ cup applesauce
2 tbsp. apple-juice concentrate
½ cup matzah cake meal
1½ tsp. peeled and minced fresh
   ginger

¼ tsp. ground ginger
⅛ tsp. cinnamon
Oil or Passover cooking spray

Whisk the egg whites, applesauce, and apple-juice concentrate until well
blended.

Stir in the remaining ingredients except the oil.

Wipe a griddle with an oiled paper towel, or coat with Passover cooking spray.
Heat the griddle over medium—medium-high heat. Drop the batter by spoonfuls
onto the hot griddle. Lightly brown about 1 minute on each side. Makes 10 pancakes.

Serving suggestion: Serve with Citrus Cinnamon Sauce (see index) or applesauce
or top with fruit.

Variation: Add diced banana to the batter.

*Calories—34; Saturated fat—0 g.; Total fat—0 g.; Carbohydrates—6 g.;
Cholesterol—0 mg.; Sodium—22 mg.; Fiber—0 g.; Protein—2 g.*

LEMON POPPY-SEED PANCAKES

DAIRY

Here is a contemporary twist on Passover pancakes.

4 egg whites
⅓ cup nonfat plain yogurt
¼ cup nonfat cottage cheese
2 tbsp. lemon juice

1 tbsp. sugar
2 tsp. poppy seeds
½ cup matzah cake meal
Passover cooking spray

In a bowl, mix all the ingredients except the cooking spray in the order listed.

Generously coat a nonstick skillet with the cooking spray. Heat the skillet over medium—medium-high heat. Drop the batter by tablespoonful on the hot skillet. Lightly brown about 1 minute on each side. Makes 10 pancakes.

Serving suggestion: Serve with Citrus Cinnamon Sauce (see index).

Calories—42; Saturated fat—0 g.; Total fat—0 g.; Carbohydrates—8 g.; Cholesterol—0 mg.; Sodium—29 mg.; Fiber—0 g.; Protein—2 g.

SEPHARDIC FARFEL PUFFS

DAIRY

This treat has Spanish origins. There is a Parmesan-cheese bread roll made throughout the year that is popular in South America. I don't think it's a far stretch to see some commonality in these two dishes. These puffs are a little like crispy mini matzah brei.

2 cups matzah farfel	**½ cup grated Parmesan cheese**
2 cups boiling water	**1 tbsp. oil**
4 egg whites	**Cooking spray**
1 tsp. salt	

Preheat the oven to 425 degrees.

In a bowl, mix all the ingredients, except the cooking spray. Coat a nonstick cookie sheet twice with the cooking spray. Drop batter by the tablespoonful onto the cookie sheet.

Place on the bottom oven rack and bake for 5-7 minutes or until the bottoms are brown. Spray the tops with cooking spray. Turn over and continue baking for another 5 minutes. These are best served hot. Makes 16.

Serving suggestion: Serve with a dairy meal or with jam.

Calories—22; Saturated fat—0 g.; Total fat—2 g.; Carbohydrates—0 g.; Cholesterol—1 mg.; Sodium—192 mg.; Fiber—0 g.; Protein—2 g.

FRIED MATZAH WITH CHILI AND TOMATOES

PAREVE

There are so many creative ways to make this basic matzah and egg recipe that Ashkenazic Jews call matzah brei. This is excellent for a low-carbohydrate meal.

3 matzahs
2 eggs
8 egg whites
½ tsp. salt
Cooking spray

½ cup chopped onions
2 tsp.-1 tbsp. chopped
   chili peppers
2 tomatoes, chopped

Wet the matzahs under cold running water. Then crumble into a large bowl.

Beat the eggs and salt and add to the matzah. Set aside.

In a nonstick skillet coated with cooking spray, add the onions and chilis and cook over medium heat for approximately 3 minutes.

Add the tomatoes and cook for another 3 minutes.

Spray the skillet with cooking spray while the tomatoes and chilis are still in it, and pour in the matzah mixture. Cook 5 minutes on each side, or cook as scrambled eggs. Serves 4.

Calories—74; Saturated fat—1 g.; Total fat—3 g.; Carbohydrates—6 g.; Cholesterol—106 mg.; Sodium—372 mg.; Fiber—1 g.; Protein—7 g.

PASSOVER INDIAN ROLLS

PAREVE

*This starts with a recipe for Passover rolls.
Serve it as a side to a meat or vegetarian meal.*

¾ cup matzah meal
¼ cup potato starch
¼ tsp. salt
¼ tsp. onion powder
Dash white pepper
1 cup water

1 tbsp. oil
3 egg whites
Cooking spray
1 tsp. minced garlic
2 scallions, chopped
3 tbsp. chopped cilantro

Preheat the oven to 375 degrees.

In a medium bowl, combine the dry ingredients.

In a saucepan, bring the water and oil to a boil. Mix into the matzah-meal mixture. Add the egg whites, one at a time, and beat thoroughly after each one. (In total, you should beat the mixture for approximately 2 minutes.) Set aside for 10 minutes.

Coat a nonstick skillet with cooking spray and fry the garlic and scallions together on medium-high heat for approximately 1 minute. Add the cilantro, stirring for 1 minute more.

Generously coat a foil-covered cookie sheet with cooking spray, and drop the matzah batter by the spoonful. Slightly flatten each and make an indentation in the center of each top.

Place ½ tsp. of the onion-garlic mixture in each indentation. Bake for 35-40 minutes or until golden brown. Pull up from foil immediately. Makes 10 rolls.

Calories—35; Saturated fat—0 g.; Total fat—1 g.; Carbohydrates—4 g.; Cholesterol—0 mg.; Sodium—77 mg.; Fiber—0 g.; Protein—1 g.

VARIETY KNISHES

DAIRY

This is a really good lunch idea to take to school or work during Passover— or year round!

KNISH DOUGH

2 cups mashed potatoes, cooled
1 cup matzah meal
3 tbsp. potato starch
½ tsp. salt
¼ tsp. black pepper
4 tsp. dry minced onions
2 egg whites

CHILI-CHEESE FILLING

1 cup grated kosher-for-Passover
  low-fat cheddar cheese
2 tbsp. minced chili pepper,
  or to taste

Cooking spray

Mix all the dough ingredients. Knead until a dough is formed. Pinch off 12 balls and flatten each ball.

Preheat the oven to 400 degrees. Mix the cheese and chilis. Place about 1 tbsp. of the filling on each dough circle. Fold the dough over and press the edges together. Place on a well-sprayed cookie sheet. Coat the tops of the knishes with the cooking spray. Bake for 15 minutes on each side or until golden. Makes 12 knishes.

Variations:

- Spinach-Cheese Filling—Mix ²⁄₃ cup frozen spinach, thawed and squeezed dry, or steamed fresh spinach; ½ cup grated kosher-for-Passover low-fat white or cheddar cheese (or feta cheese); and ½ tsp. dry dill. Place about 1 tbsp. filling on each dough circle. Fold over and follow instructions above.

- Tuna and Cheese Melt—Mix ²⁄₃ cup water-packed flaked tuna, drained, and ¼ cup grated kosher-for-Passover low-fat American cheese. Place about 1 tbsp. filling on each dough circle. Fold over and follow instructions above.

- Knish Dogs for the kids—Slice 8 reduced-fat turkey or chicken hot dogs into 3 slices and form the dough around each nugget (divide dough into 24 balls for this recipe). You can wrap the dough to have the hot-dog ends show or not— it's your choice. Bake in the same manner as above. Send these for lunch with a little Passover mustard for dipping. This is good throughout the year for kids' lunches or snacks. I have also made it with vegetarian hot dogs and it works beautifully.

Chili-Cheese: Calories—117; Saturated fat—1 g.; Total fat—2 g.; Carbohydrates—18 g.; Cholesterol—6 mg.; Sodium—256 mg.; Fiber—0 g.; Protein—6 g.

Spinach-Cheese: Calories—104; Saturated fat—1 g.; Total fat—1 g.; Carbohydrates—18 g.; Cholesterol—3 mg.; Sodium—242 mg.; Fiber—0 g.; Protein—5 g.

Tuna and Cheese: Calories—109; Saturated fat—0 g.; Total fat—1 g.; Carbohydrates—18 g.; Cholesterol—4 mg.; Sodium—272 mg.; Fiber—0 g.; Protein—7 g.

Knish Dogs: Calories—162; Saturated fat—2 g.; Total fat— 6 g.; Carbohydrates—20 g.; Cholesterol—31 mg.; Sodium—625 mg.; Fiber—0 g.; Protein—6 g.

MOROCCAN-STYLE PESACHDIGE BASTILLA

MEAT

*Bastilla is an elegant Moroccan dish that is phyllo pastry encasing
a fragrant mixture of chicken, almonds, and eggs. This Passover version is
more like a casserole but with the same aromatic flavors.
Use fresh chicken breast or leftover soup chicken to make this.*

2 lb. cooked boneless skinless
   chicken breast, cut into cubes
2½-3 cups Vegetable Broth
   recipe
1 large onion, chopped
½ tsp. ground ginger
¼ tsp. salt
¼ tsp. black pepper
⅛ tsp. cayenne pepper

1 cinnamon stick
2 whole eggs
7 egg whites
¼ cup lemon juice
¼ cup chopped parsley
¼ cup cilantro (optional)
Cooking spray
3 matzahs

TOPPING

⅓ cup slivered almonds
1 tbsp. cinnamon

1 tsp. ginger
1½ tbsp. sugar

In a large skillet, combine the chicken, vegetable broth, onion, ginger, salt and pepper, cayenne pepper, and cinnamon stick. Simmer over medium heat for approximately 25-30 minutes. Remove from heat and discard the cinnamon stick. Remove and shred the chicken pieces. Set aside.

In a bowl, beat the eggs and egg whites, lemon juice, parsley, and cilantro. Add to the sauce. Stir until well mixed. Cool. Add the chicken back to the mixture. (This mixture can be frozen and thawed until ready to use.)

Preheat the oven to 400 degrees.

Prepare the topping by toasting the almonds in a dry skillet over medium heat for 2-3 minutes or until lightly browned. Add the cinnamon, ginger, and sugar. Set aside.

Coat a 9-inch square baking dish with cooking spray. Place a matzah on the bottom of the dish. Pour half the chicken mixture over the matzah. Layer another matzah and most of the remaining sauce. Top with the third matzah and the remaining sauce. Push any chicken pieces on the top to the sides.

Sprinkle the topping mixture over all. Bake for 25 minutes or until the eggs appear set. Let stand for 5-10 minutes before serving. Serves 8.

*Calories—238; Saturated fat—1 g.; Total fat—7 g.; Carbohydrates—11 g.;
Cholesterol—119 mg.; Sodium—121 mg.; Fiber—1 g.; Protein—33 g.*

BAKED TUNA AND SMOKED SALMON SQUARES

DAIRY

1¼ cups matzah farfel
½ cup boiling water
Cooking spray
⅓ cup chopped green onions
8 oz. mushrooms, coarsely
chopped
4 cups fresh spinach
6½-oz. can water-packed tuna,
drained
2 oz. smoked salmon
½ cup low-fat cottage cheese

1 tsp. Passover mustard
1 tsp. lemon juice
4 egg whites
½ cup Passover egg substitute
2 tbsp. fresh dill or 1½ tsp. dried
dill
⅛ tsp. black pepper
2 tbsp. any grated low-fat cheese
with a strong flavor, such as
cheddar, Gruyere, or feta, or a
combination

Preheat the oven to 350 degrees.

Soak the farfel in the boiling water until the water is absorbed.

Spray a nonstick skillet with cooking spray. Over medium-high heat, sauté the green onions and mushrooms for 2-3 minutes.

Reduce heat to medium and add the spinach. Cover and cook a few minutes until the spinach wilts. Remove from heat. Chop the spinach a little while still in the skillet. Add the spinach mixture to the farfel. Mix in the remaining ingredients except the cheese.

Coat a 10-inch square baking dish with cooking spray, including the sides; pour mixture in. Top with grated cheese. Bake uncovered for 50-55 minutes. Cut into squares to serve. Serves 6.

Calories—117; Saturated fat—1 g.; Total fat—2 g.; Carbohydrates—5 g.; Cholesterol—9 mg.; Sodium—492 mg.; Fiber—1 g.; Protein—20 g.

POTATO-CRUSTED MUSHROOMS AND EGGPLANT

PAREVE

This can be a meal in itself. Serve as is, or with a tomato sauce.

Cooking spray	4 tsp. Harissa Seasoning recipe,
1 egg white	or to taste
¼ cup egg substitute	1½ lb. sliced portobello
⅔ cup mashed-potato flakes	mushrooms and peeled and
3 tbsp. matzah meal	sliced eggplant

MOROCCAN TOMATO SAUCE (OPTIONAL)

2 tsp. oil	½ tsp. turmeric
1 large onion, chopped	¼ tsp. black pepper
15-oz. can crushed tomatoes	½ cup water

Place the oven rack in the bottom position. Preheat the oven to 450 degrees. Spray a baking sheet heavily (3 layers) with the cooking spray. Set aside.

In a small bowl, mix the egg white and egg substitute. On a plate, mix the potato flakes, matzah meal, and Harissa Seasoning.

Dip the vegetables in the egg mixture, then into the crumbs. Place on the prepared baking sheet in a single layer. Coat the tops of the vegetables with one layer of cooking spray.

Bake for 5-7 minutes one each side or until the crust turns a golden brown.

To make the sauce, heat the oil in a skillet over medium-high heat and sauté the onions for 5-7 minutes until brown. Add the remaining sauce ingredients, reduce heat to low, and simmer uncovered for approximately 10 minutes.

To serve, spoon a little sauce on the side of the vegetables, or spread the sauce on the bottom of a serving platter and layer the vegetables on top. Serves 4.

Variation: For a finer crust, lightly crush the potato flakes in a plastic bag with a rolling pin or the bottom of a heavy pan.

With tomato sauce: Calories—159; Saturated fat—0 g.; Total fat—1 g.; Carbohydrates—30 g.; Cholesterol—0 mg.; Sodium—65 mg.; Fiber—2 g.; Protein—8 g.

EGGPLANT-MATZAH KUGEL

MEAT/DAIRY/PAREVE

This is a twist on the traditional matzah dressing.
The eggplant gives it a lighter taste.

5 matzahs or 2½ cups matzah
  farfel
10-oz. can chopped tomatoes
½ cup fat-free chicken broth or
  chicken-flavored pareve broth
1 lb. eggplant, peeled and cut in
  small cubes
Cooking spray
1 onion, chopped

½ lb. sliced mushrooms
1 cup diced celery
½ cup chopped red pepper
2 garlic cloves, minced
5 egg whites
½ tsp. ground sage
½ tsp. oregano
¼ tsp. black pepper

Wet matzahs under hot water from faucet, then crumble into a bowl. Mix the crumbled matzah with tomatoes and broth. Set aside.

In a saucepan, steam the eggplant with a little water over medium heat, for 7-10 minutes or until the eggplant is tender.

Meanwhile, in a skillet coated with cooking spray, sauté the onion, mushrooms, celery, and red pepper over medium heat for 5 minutes. Add garlic and sauté 1 minute more.

Drain the eggplant if any water is left. Mash the eggplant and stir into the skillet mixture.

Remove from the heat. Add the matzah mixture and egg whites and stir in the sage, oregano, and pepper.

Preheat the oven to 375 degrees. Grease a 1½-qt. baking pan and turn the mixture into the pan. Bake for 45 minutes or until lightly brown and firm to the touch. Serve with any meat dish or as a vegetarian dish. Serves 6-8.

Variation: Top with ½ cup grated low-fat cheddar cheese.

Calories—59; Saturated fat—0 g.; Total fat—0 g.; Carbohydrates—11 g.; Cholesterol—0 mg.; Sodium—49 mg.; Fiber—1 g.; Protein—2 g.

BASIL-ZUCCHINI KUGEL

PAREVE

This is a classic zucchini kugel with contemporary flavor.

Cooking spray
1 tsp. oil
½ medium onion, chopped
2 garlic cloves, chopped
1½ lb. zucchini, grated
1 cup grated carrots
½ cup matzah meal or
   dry breadcrumbs

½ cup egg substitute
2 egg whites
7-8 basil leaves, chopped
½ tsp. salt
¼ tsp. black pepper

Coat a 9-inch square baking dish with cooking spray.

In a small skillet, over medium-high heat, add the oil. When the oil is hot, sauté the onion and garlic for 4-5 minutes until lightly browned.

Remove and combine with the remaining ingredients. Spoon the zucchini mixture into the prepared baking dish.

Bake at 350 degrees for 45 minutes. Halfway through baking, spray the top of the kugel with the cooking spray. This will help to lightly brown the top of the kugel. Serves 6.

Calories—126; Saturated fat—0 g.; Total fat—0 g.; Carbohydrates—24 g.; Cholesterol—0 mg.; Sodium—249 mg.; Fiber—1 g.; Protein—7 g.

BROCCOLI AND CHEESE KUGEL

DAIRY

Here's a great, low-carb Passover matzah dish.

2 matzahs
½ cup hot water
Cooking spray
4 egg whites or ½ cup Passover
   egg substitute
1 cup skim milk

⅔ cup low-fat or nonfat shredded
   cheddar cheese
2 cups chopped broccoli
½ cup chopped green pepper
3 tbsp. chopped scallions
Paprika

In a large bowl, crumble the matzahs and soak them in the hot water for approximately 5 minutes.

Coat a 1½-qt. baking dish with the cooking spray.

Add the remaining ingredients except the paprika to the matzahs in the bowl. Mix well. Turn into the prepared baking dish. Sprinkle top with paprika. Bake at 350 degrees for 35-40 minutes. Serves 6.

Calories—78; Saturated fat—1 g.; Total fat—2 g.; Carbohydrates—5 g.; Cholesterol—8 mg.; Sodium—119 mg.; Fiber—0 g.; Protein—9 g.

APPLE-PLUM KUGEL

PAREVE

This is an impressive dessert or sweet side dish inspired by a recipe from Vicki-Bluma Olesky, an extraordinary Denver hostess and cook. Vicki-Bluma was kind enough to let me adapt this recipe, which called for more than twice the amount of eggs and sugar. With all the adjustments, it is still a winner!

1 cup matzah farfel	**½ cup raisins**
1 cup boiling water	**¾ cup plum jam**
¼ cup egg substitute	**2 tbsp. sugar**
1 egg white	**½ tsp. cinnamon**
3 apples, peeled and grated, or	**¼ tsp. salt**
4½ fresh peaches, peeled and	**1 tsp. oil**
thinly sliced	

SAUCE TOPPING

1½ tbsp. lemon juice	**2 tbsp. sweet red wine**
1 tsp. grated lemon rind	**2 tbsp. honey**

Preheat the oven to 350 degrees. Mix the farfel and boiling water, and let sit until it cools.

In another bowl, beat the egg substitute and egg white. Add the fruit, raisins, jam, sugar, cinnamon and salt, and carefully mix. Mix in farfel.

Cover the bottom and sides of an 8-inch square baking dish with the oil. Heat in the oven for 2-3 minutes. Pour the fruit mixture in the heated baking dish and bake for 25 minutes.

Meanwhile, heat the sauce ingredients in a small saucepan, or microwave just until the honey dissolves.

Spoon over the pudding and continue to bake for 25 minutes more. Serves 6.

Variation: This can be easily doubled and baked in a 3-qt. baking dish for a Seder crowd.

Calories—268; Saturated fat—0 g.; Total fat—1 g.; Carbohydrates—61 g.; Cholesterol—0 mg.; Sodium—130 mg.; Fiber—2 g.; Protein—3 g.

PASSOVER FRUIT CRISP

PAREVE

This can be easily doubled or tripled, depending on the crowd.

4 large sliced apples, plums, or pears
3 cups blueberries or raspberries or mixture

½ cup pineapple-juice concentrate

TOPPING

½ cup matzah meal
¼ cup cake meal
¼ cup potato starch
3 tbsp. sugar

¼ cup pineapple-juice concentrate
2 tbsp. pareve margarine
1 tsp. cinnamon

In an 8-inch square baking pan, combine the fruits and pineapple-juice concentrate.

Combine the topping ingredients and spread evenly over the fruit.

Bake at 350 degrees for 40 minutes.

If you want a softer topping, spoon some sauce from the baked fruit over the topping and let it sit. This is best served at room temperature. Serves 4.

Calories—425; Saturated fat—1 g.; Total fat—4 g.; Carbohydrates—92 g.; Cholesterol—0 mg.; Sodium—81 mg.; Fiber—3 g.; Protein—5 g.

INSTANT CUSTARD SAUCE OVER FRUIT

DAIRY

*Are you tired of cakes and cookies for Pesach? Here's a dessert for adults and children. It's inspired by English custard sauces.
Of course, you can spoon it over cakes, too!*

1¼ cups skim milk
**2 tbsp. instant Passover
vanilla pudding mix**

**¼ cup any pureed fruit, such as
bananas, any berries, peaches,
apricots, mangoes, or kiwi**

In a bowl, with an electric mixer (or by hand), mix the milk and pudding mix for 1 minute until it thickens. Stir in pureed fruit of your choice and spoon over any sliced fruit of your choice. Makes 1¼ cups.

Variation: If using during another time of the year, substitute calcium-fortified rice or soy milk for the milk.

Calories—68; Saturated fat—0 g.; Total fat—0 g.; Carbohydrates—13 g.; Cholesterol—1 mg.; Sodium—68 mg.; Fiber—0 g.; Protein—3 g.

TOASTED MACAROON CAKE DELITE

PAREVE

I found this recipe in a treasured cookbook—Tempting Kosher Dishes from Manischewitz Co., 1933—belonging to my grandmother, the late Mollie ("Malka") Ashkanazi. I have updated the recipe just to reduce the calories from fat.

¼ cup orange juice
1 tsp. vanilla extract
1 tsp. almond extract
¾ cup sugar
6 egg whites, room temperature
**¾ cup potato starch or ½ cup
matzah cake meal and ¼ cup
potato starch**

¼ cup toasted coconut
**¼ cup chopped walnuts or
almonds, lightly toasted, then
crushed**
Cooking spray

Blend the orange juice, extracts, and sugar.

Beat the egg whites until stiff peaks form.

In a bowl, combine the potato starch, coconut, and nuts.

Fold the orange-juice mixture into the egg whites and then into the cake-meal mixture until well blended.

Line a 9-inch springform pan with wax or parchment paper. Spray lightly with cooking spray. Or spray a 9-inch Bundt pan with cooking spray. Pour in batter. Bake at 350 degrees for 40 minutes or until cake springs back to a light touch. Cool pan, inverted, on a wire rack. Serve cake plain, with fresh fruit, or with Raspberry Coulis recipe. Serves 8.

Calories—197; Saturated fat—2 g.; Total fat—5 g.; Carbohydrates—33 g.; Cholesterol—0 mg.; Sodium—45 mg.; Fiber—10 g.; Protein—5 g.

PASSOVER CHOCOLATE CAKE ROLL

DAIRY

FILLING

1¾ cups yogurt cheese (drained 24-48 hours)
½ cup sugar
3 tbsp. chopped bittersweet chocolate

1 tbsp. Passover liqueur of your choice
½ tsp. almond extract
¼ tsp. vanilla extract

CAKE ROLL

Cooking spray
¼ cup matzah cake meal
¼ cup cocoa
¼ tsp. cinnamon (optional)
5 egg whites

⅔ cup sugar
2 tbsp. water
1 tsp. vanilla
2 tbsp. sugar

GLAZE (OPTIONAL)

¼ cup powdered sugar
1 tbsp. cocoa

2 tbsp. water or milk
½ tsp. vanilla

In a bowl, mix filling ingredients well. Set aside.

Preheat the oven to 375 degrees. Coat with cooking spray a foil-lined 10-by-15-inch baking pan.

In a bowl, mix the cake meal, cocoa, and cinnamon. Set aside.

In a medium bowl, beat the egg whites until soft peaks form. Gradually add the sugar, water, and vanilla.

Fold in the cake meal mixture a third at a time until well blended.

Spread the batter evenly to the edges of the baking pan. Bake for 10-12 minutes or until the cake springs back to a light touch.

Meanwhile, lay a dishtowel on a surface and sprinkle with 2 tbsp. sugar. Using a sharp knife, loosen all around the sides of the baked cake. Then, going in one direction, keep separating the cake roll from the foil with the knife, inverting the hot cake onto the dishtowel. Immediately roll the cake and towel into a cylindrical shape, starting with the long edge. Cool.

Unroll the cake and spread the cheese filling evenly over the cake. Either reroll in plastic wrap or glaze the top at this time, if desired. (Stand toothpicks on top of the cake so the plastic wrap does not touch the cake.) Chill the cake for 2-3 hours.

To make the glaze, combine the glaze ingredients in a small container, and microwave on high for 10 seconds. Drizzle over the cake roll.

This will freeze well. To serve, slice into 1-inch portions, and garnish with fruit slices or chocolate shavings. Serves 6-8.

Variation: Omit the glaze. Sift Cocoa Cinnamon Topping recipe over the cake before serving.

Calories—249; Saturated fat—1 g.; Total fat—2 g.; Carbohydrates—49 g.; Cholesterol—1 mg.; Sodium—105 mg.; Fiber—0 g.; Protein—7 g.

CHOCOLATE TORTE

PAREVE

Flourless chocolate tortes are popular. Nuts or lots of chocolate replace the flour to give the cake its texture. Here the fat is reduced without losing the flavor.

½ cup boiling water with
2 tsp. instant coffee
½ cup unsweetened
cocoa powder
2 tsp. vanilla or 1 tbsp. Passover
liqueur, such as Sabra
3 tbsp. bittersweet chocolate
chips

1 cup sugar
1 egg yolk
5 egg whites
⅓ cup finely ground toasted
almonds
3 tbsp. potato starch
Cooking spray

TOPPING

¼ cup Passover powdered sugar   2 tsp. cocoa

Preheat the oven to 325 degrees.

Place the boiling water and coffee in a bowl and add the cocoa, vanilla, chocolate, and sugar. Stir until the sugar is dissolved. Cool for 5 minutes. Mix in yolk.

In another bowl, beat the egg whites until stiff peaks form. Alternately fold in the chocolate mixture, nuts, and potato starch until all are completely blended.

Coat a 9-inch tube pan with cooking spray.

Carefully pour the chocolate mixture into the pan. Bake for 25-30 minutes.

Remove the cake from the oven and cool. Carefully loosen the cake from the pan by running a knife along the sides of the of the pan. Invert the cake onto a serving plate.

Mix the powdered sugar and cocoa, and sprinkle over the cake. Serves 16.

Calories—150; Saturated fat—1 g.; Total fat—6 g.; Carbohydrates—20 g.; Cholesterol—13 mg.; Sodium—40 mg.; Fiber—0 g.; Protein—3 g.

CHOCOLATE-SPICE ANGEL FOOD CAKE

PAREVE/DAIRY

This is an English-style recipe for a Passover cake.

1¼ cups potato starch	¾ cup sugar
¼ cup cocoa powder	2 oz. semisweet chocolate, minced
1 tsp. cinnamon	
¼ tsp. nutmeg	½ cup orange juice
12 egg whites, room temperature	2 tbsp. lemon juice

Sift the potato starch, cocoa, and spices together into a bowl.

In a large bowl, beat the egg whites until foamy and double in volume. Gradually, add the sugar by tablespoonfuls, beating after each addition. Continue until the whites are stiff and the sugar is used up.

Sift ⅓ of the dry ingredients onto the whites and fold in. Add the chocolate and fold in.

Add another ⅓ of the dry ingredients, then the orange and lemon juices and the last ⅓ of the dry ingredients.

Spoon evenly into a 10-inch tube pan.

Bake at 325 degrees for 45 minutes. Invert the cake pan and cool completely on a wire rack. For quicker results, invert on a rack in the refrigerator to cool.

Gently, with a sharp knife, go around the sides of the pan to loosen the cake.

Serving suggestion: Top with Cocoa Cinnamon Topping recipe or Dairy Chocolate Sauce recipe.

Variations:

- Reduce the potato starch to 1 cup. Increase the cocoa powder to ½ cup. Omit the orange juice and lemon juice and add ½ cup strong brewed coffee.

- For other holidays, replace the potato starch with the same amount of cake flour.

Calories—177; Saturated fat—1 g.; Total fat—2 g.; Carbohydrates—33 g.; Cholesterol—0 mg.; Sodium—87 mg.; Fiber—1 g.; Protein—6 g.

COCOA CINNAMON TOPPING

PAREVE

This is a versatile, sweet topping for cakes and frozen yogurt.
Its uses are only limited by your imagination.

¼ cup minus ¾ tsp. sugar
¾ tsp. potato starch

¼ tsp. cinnamon
1 tsp. unsweetened cocoa powder

Grind the sugar and potato starch in a coffee grinder briefly until a powdery texture. This creates powdered sugar. Add the cinnamon and cocoa. Sprinkle over Chocolate-Spice Angel Food Cake, Mocha Chocolate Cheesecake, or Passover Chocolate Cake Roll. Makes ¼ cup.

Per tablespoon: Calories—40; Saturated fat—0 g.; Total fat—0 g.; Carbohydrates—9 g.; Cholesterol—0 mg.; Sodium—3 mg.; Fiber—0 g.; Protein—1 g.

DAIRY CHOCOLATE SAUCE

DAIRY

Serve over cake, sorbet, or ice cream.

½ cup sugar
¼ cup cocoa
1½ tbsp. potato starch

¾ cup skim milk
1 tsp. vanilla

In a saucepan, add the sugar, cocoa, and potato starch over medium heat. Stir in the milk and continue to cook and stir until it begins to boil. Then continue to cook for 1-2 minutes longer until the mixture thickens. Remove from heat and mix in vanilla. Serves 8.

Calories—83; Saturated fat—1 g.; Total fat—1 g.; Carbohydrates—17 g.; Cholesterol—3 mg.; Sodium—31 mg.; Fiber—0 g.; Protein—1 g.

CHOCOLATE BROWNIES

PAREVE

*The rich, dense, chocolaty flavor of these brownies
will satisfy your chocolate cravings.*

Cooking spray
¾ cup sugar
¼ cup unsweetened applesauce
3 egg whites
¼ cup oil

2 tbsp. melted chocolate chips
2 tsp. vanilla
½ cup cocoa powder
⅓ cup matzah cake meal

Lightly coat an 8-inch square pan with the cooking spray.

In a bowl, mix the sugar, applesauce, egg whites, oil, chocolate chips, and vanilla. Mix the cocoa powder and cake meal, and add to the sugar mixture. Mix well.

Turn into the prepared pan. Bake at 350 degrees for approximately 20 minutes or until the top is slightly firm to the touch. Makes approximately 25 bars.

Calories—72; Saturated fat—0 g.; Total fat—3 g.; Carbohydrates—11 g.; Cholesterol—0 mg.; Sodium—25 mg.; Fiber—0 g.; Protein—1 g.

CHOCOLATE-ALMOND MACAROON MINIBITES

PAREVE

Macaroons are found all over the Mediterranean area. Iraqi macaroons are scented with orange-blossom water or rosewater. This recipe features an Italian combination of flavors. The pureed strawberries reduce the need for sugar.

½ cup toasted slivered almonds
3 egg whites
⅔ cup sugar
½ cup pureed fresh strawberries

⅓ cup cocoa powder
1 tsp. almond extract
⅓ cup toasted coconut

Preheat the oven to 375 degrees. Line two cookie sheets with parchment paper. In a food processor, mince the almonds. Set aside.

In a bowl, beat the egg whites until soft peaks form. Gradually add the sugar and continue to beat until stiff peaks form.

In another bowl, combine the strawberries, cocoa powder, and almond extract. Alternately fold the almonds, strawberry-cocoa mixture, and toasted coconut into the beaten egg whites.

Drop by teaspoonfuls onto the lined cookie sheets. Bake for 10-12 minutes. Remove cookie sheets to wire rack to cool. These will freeze well stored in a zipper bag. Makes 4 dozen.

Calories—29; Saturated fat—0 g.; Total fat—1 g.; Carbohydrates—4 g.; Cholesterol—0 mg.; Sodium—8 mg.; Fiber—0 g.; Protein—1 g.

CINNAMON MACAROONS

PAREVE

I sent a batch of these with my son as he was going off to college.
He loved them.

1 cup slivered almonds
2 egg whites
⅔ cup sugar

1 tbsp. cinnamon
1 tsp. vanilla

Line a cookie sheet with parchment paper. Toast the almonds in a 425-degree oven about 3 minutes until the nuts start to turn a light golden brown. Cool.

Reduce the oven heat to 325 degrees. In a food processor, coarsely grind the almonds.

In a bowl, beat the egg whites until frothy. Gradually beat the sugar into the whites in 3 batches until stiff, glossy peaks form. Fold in the cinnamon, almonds, and vanilla.

Drop by teaspoonfuls onto the prepared cookie sheet. Bake for 20-25 minutes. Let cool on the cookie sheet. These macaroons can be stored in an airtight container up to 4 days, or frozen. Makes 36.

Calories—44; Saturated fat—0 g.; Total fat—2 g.; Carbohydrates—5 g.; Cholesterol—0 mg.; Sodium—4 mg.; Fiber—0 g.; Protein—1 g.

PISTACHIO LIME COOKIES

PAREVE

*This contemporary recipe combines Sephardic and Middle Eastern tastes.
Pine nuts, pistachios, and cinnamon are used quite often in both communities.
Lime is found in Iraqi cuisine in the form of dried peels.*

⅓ cup coarsely chopped toasted
pistachios and/or pine nuts
1 cup matzah meal
1 cup matzah farfel
⅔ cup sugar
5 tbsp. oil
1 whole egg

2 egg whites
1½ tbsp. lime juice
1 tbsp. grated lime zest
2 tsp. grated orange zest
½ tsp. almond or vanilla extract
½ tsp. cinnamon
Cooking spray

LIME GLAZE

⅓ cup powdered sugar
3 tbsp. lime juice

1 tbsp. orange juice

Preheat the oven to 350 degrees.

In a bowl, combine all the ingredients, except the cooking spray. Coat a cookie sheet with the cooking spray. Drop the batter by teaspoonfuls onto the cookie sheet.

Bake for 10-12 minutes or until golden brown. Remove cookies to wire rack to cool completely.

Blend the glaze ingredients together and drizzle over the cookies. Makes approximately 4 dozen.

Per cookie: Calories—46; Saturated fat—0 g.; Total fat—2 g.; Carbohydrates—6 g.; Cholesterol—4 mg.; Sodium—4 mg.; Fiber—0 g.; Protein—1g.

STRAWBERRY WHIP DESSERT

DAIRY

*Are you searching for Passover desserts that aren't high in sugar,
matzah meal, or egg whites? Try this.*

1 pkg. sugar-free strawberry-flavored kosher-for-Passover gelatin
1 cup boiling water

1 cup ice cubes
1 cup halved strawberries (or raspberries)
½ cup nonfat plain yogurt

Mix the gelatin and boiling water in a bowl. Add the ice and stir until most melts and the gelatin begins to thicken. Remove any remaining unmelted ice cubes.

Transfer to a food processor or blender and add the strawberries and yogurt. Blend at high speed until the mixture is smooth.

Pour into dessert glasses. Garnish each with a strawberry or raspberries. Chill for 1 hour or until firm. Serves 4.

Calories—35; Saturated fat—0 g.; Total fat—0 g.; Carbohydrates—6 g.; Cholesterol—1 mg.; Sodium—26 mg.; Fiber—0 g.; Protein—2 g.

INSTANT CHOCOLATE-BANANA SHAKE

DAIRY

This is for kids of all ages.

6 tbsp. cocoa powder
2 bananas, peeled
¾ cup nonfat plain yogurt

3 tbsp. pineapple- or apple-juice concentrate

In a blender, mix all ingredients. Serves 3.

Variation: For a milkshake, add 1 tbsp. skim milk at a time to desired consistency.

Calories—121; Saturated fat—1 g.; Total fat—1 g.; Carbohydrates—25 g.; Cholesterol—1 mg.; Sodium—83 mg.; Fiber—1 g.; Protein—5 g.

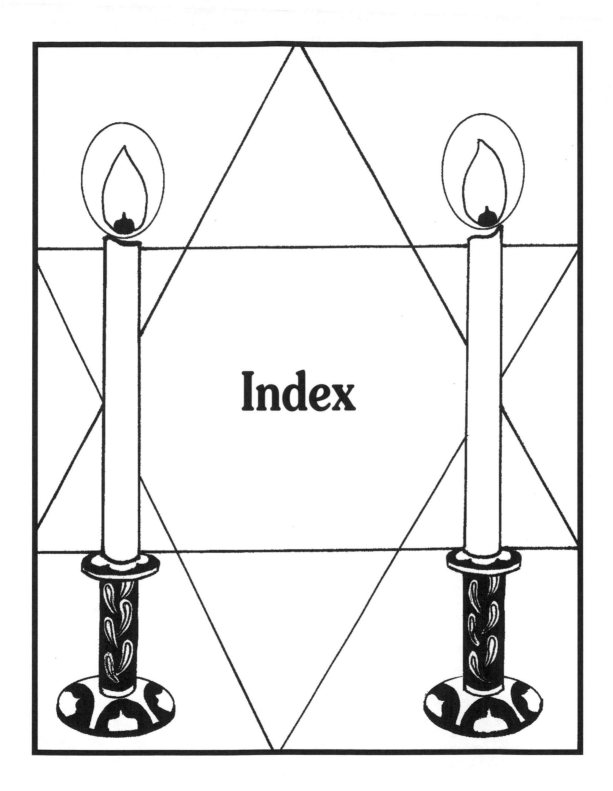

Index

APPETIZERS
Baba Ghanouj, 66
Black-Eyed Pea Salad, 57
California Hummus, 64
Chickpea Salad, 55
Confetti Whitefish Spread, 137
Grilled-Pepper Salad, 58
Hummus with Peppers, 63
Israeli Salad, 60
Lentil Pate, 71
Moroccan Carrot Salad, 59
Moroccan Eggplant, 65
Moroccan-Style Beet Salad, 55
Olivada, 70
Roasted Pepper Dip, 65
Romanian Putlejela, 67
Russian Beet Salad, 56
Smoked Eggplant Caviar, 68
Smoked-Salmon Cream Cheese, 69
Spice-of-Life Chips, 72
Tabbouleh, 61
Turkish Salad (Salsa), 62

BEEF
Adobe Cholent, 153
Kibbeh, 160
North African Style Meatballs over
Couscous, 161
Stuffed Tomatoes Syrian Style, 158
The Tax Chazzan's Great Cholent,
152

BREAD
Baked Eggless French Toast Cochin
Style, 96
Etta Chaya's Back-to-Nature Eggless
Challah, 95
Herbed Bread, 97
Russian Rye Croutons, 97

CAKES
Apple Cake, 249
Chocolate Marble Pound Cake, 269
Chocolate-Spice Angel Food Cake,
295

Chocolate Torte, 294
Felicia's Romanian Chocolate Potato
Balls, 272
Orange Sponge Cake, 265
Pineapple Honey Cake, 267
Quick Chocolate-Chip Cherry Ring,
273
Root-Beer Spice Cake, 268
Rosewater Angel Food Cake, 264
Sour-Cream Coffeecake, 270
Toasted Macaroon Cake Delite, 292

CHAROSET
Greek Charoset, 277
Moroccan Charoset, 279
Natural Orange-Date Charoset, 277
Syrian Charoset, 278
Turkish Charoset, 278

CHICKEN
Adobe Cholent, 153
Afghan-Style Chicken Hamin, 151
American Spaghetti in a Bread Bowl,
163
Best Mediterranean Chicken, 149
Brazilian-Style Arroz con Pollo, 146
Chicken and Pine Nut Salad, 148
Chicken Kasha Soup, 102
Chicken with Artichokes and Olives,
146
Chicken with Quinces or Apples, 145
Dafna's Chicken, 143
Herb Chicken in Tomato Sauce, 147
Inside-Out Stuffed Cabbage, 157
Latke Chicken, 141
Moroccan Chicken with Almonds and
Prunes, 143
Moroccan Couscous (Chicken Veg-
etable Soup), 103
North African Style Meatballs over
Couscous, 161
Shabbat Chicken in Barbecue Sauce,
142
Shashlik with Harissa Seasoning, 150
Springtime Chicken Soup, 103

Sweet and Savory Chicken, 141
The Tax Chazzan's Great Meatballs,
162

CHOLENT
Adobe Cholent, 153
Afghan-Style Chicken Hamin, 151
Iranian-Inspired Crockpot Hamin,
152
The Tax Chazzan's Great Cholent,
141

CONDIMENTS
Apricot-Tomato Chutney, 17
Curry Apricot Salsa for Gefilte Fish,
231
Harissa Salsa, 231
Harissa Seasoning, 231
Horseradish (Chraine), 233
Tunisian Tabil Mix, 232

COUSCOUS
Festive Couscous, 218
Five-Vegetable Stew with Couscous,
167
Garden Vegetables with Couscous,
180
Moroccan Couscous (Chicken Veg-
etable Soup), 103
North African Style Meatballs over
Couscous, 161

DESSERTS
Anisette Cookies, 256
Apple Cake, 249
Apple-Plum Crisp, 249
Apple-Plum Kugel, 290
Caramel Rolls, 274
Carol Joy's Microwaved Fruit Com-
pote, 239
Cheesecake in Phyllo Pouches, 262
Chocolate-Almond Macaroon
Minibites, 298
Chocolate Brownies, 298
Chocolate Mandelbroit (Biscotti), 254

Chocolate Marble Pound Cake, 269
Chocolate-Spice Angel Food Cake,
295
Chocolate Torte, 294
Cinnamon Macaroons, 299
Cinnamon Mandelbroit, 255
Cocoa Cinnamon Topping, 297
Dairy Chocolate Sauce, 297
Felicia's Romanian Chocolate Potato
Balls, 272
Hamantaschen, 253
Honey Date Orange Cake, 266
Instant Chocolate-Banana Shake, 301
Instant Custard Sauce, 292
Italian Cheesecake, 271
Lemon Cream Pudding, 257
Lemon Poppy-Seed Cream-Cheese
Bars, 258
Mocha Chocolate Cheesecake, 260
Moroccan Dates Dipped in Chocolate,
242
Moroccan Oranges Rimonim, 241
Orange Sponge Cake, 265
Passover Chocolate Cake Roll, 293
Passover Fruit Crisp, 291
Pineapple-Apricot Strudel, 249
Pineapple Honey Cake, 267
Pistachio Lime Cookies, 300
Pita Blintzes with Syrup, 251
Quick Chocolate-Chip Cherry Ring,
273
Rice Pudding, 256
Root-Beer Spice Cake, 268
Rosewater Angel Food Cake, 264
Sour-Cream Coffeecake, 270
Strawberry Whip Dessert, 300
Sugarless Pineapple Cheesecake, 259
Toasted Macaroon Cake Delite, 292
Truffles (Kartoshka), 252

EGGPLANT
Austrian-Hungarian Eggplant Goulash,
183
Baba Ghanouj, 66
Eggplant and Tomatoes, 199

Eggplant-Matzah Kugel, 288
Fish in Tomato-Cumin Sauce with
    Eggplant, 133
Moroccan Eggplant, 65
Potato-Crusted Mushrooms and
    Eggplant, 286
Romanian Putlejela, 67
Smoked Eggplant Caviar, 68
Stuffed Eggplant, 173

EGGS
Creamy Egg Salad, 185
Fried Matzah with Chili and Tomatoes,
    282
Tortilla de Patata Frita, 185

FISH
Bahian Fish Muqueca, 136
Baked Salmon Gefilte Fish, 126
Baked Tuna and Smoked Salmon
    Squares, 286
Confetti Smoked Whitefish Spread,
    137
Fish and Vegetable Platter, 130
Fish in Tomato-Cumin Sauce with
    Eggplant, 133
Grilled Halibut in a Citrus Vinaigrette,
    137
North African Poached Fish, 135
Pasticcio di Tonno, 131
Pickled Tuna Salad, 132
Poached Herb Salmon, 129
Salmon in Phyllo, 127
Salmon Pie in a Potato Shell, 128
Sea Bass in Tomato Sauce, 133
Smoked-Salmon Cream Cheese, 69
South African Gefilte Fish, 125
Tuna and Cheese Melt Knishes, 284
Tunisian Pasta with Tuna, 90

FRUIT
Apple Cake, 263
Apple-Plum Crisp, 249
Apple-Plum Kugel, 290
Avocado-Grapefruit Salad, 84

Carol Joy's Microwaved Fruit
    Compote, 239
Cherry Dairy Kugel, 227
Chilled Apple Soup, 120
Citrus Cinnamon Sauce, 234
Cold Apple-Beet Borscht, 119
Cranberry-Apple Kugel, 228
Curry Apricot Salsa for Gefilte Fish,
    231
Flower-Scented Fruit Compote, 240
Fruit 'n' Carrot Salad, 84
Greek Charoset, 277
Instant Chocolate-Banana Shake, 301
Instant Custard Sauce over Fruit, 292
Israeli Baked Apples, 244
Lemon Waldorf Salad, 85
Melon Fruit Salad, 240
Moroccan Charoset, 279
Moroccan Dates Dipped in Chocolate,
    242
Moroccan Oranges Rimonim, 241
Natural Orange-Date Charoset, 277
Passover Fruit Crisp, 291
Peaches 'n' Cream Kugel, 226
Peach Soup, 121
Pineapple-Apricot Strudel, 249
Strawberry Whip Dessert, 301
Summer's Fruit in a Cloud, 242
Sweet Apples in Date Sauce, 243
Syrian Charoset, 278
Turkish Charoset, 278
Watermelon-Ade, 245

GRAINS
Arroz Brasileiro (Brazilian Rice Pilaf),
    215
Brazilian-Style Arroz con Pollo, 146
Cornmeal Latkes, 219
Egyptian Rice Pilaf, 214
Fava Beans with Rice, 176
Iraqi Rice, 213
Kasha Varnishkes, 217
Lentil and Rice Stuffed Peppers, 168
Mamaglia, 219
Mushroom Barley Pilaf, 215

Onion and Chive Polenta, 171
Orzo Rice Pilaf, 216
Polenta-Stuffed Peppers, 169
Rice Pudding, 256
Rice-Stuffed Zucchini, 172
Syrian Mejadarra (Lentils and Rice),
 175
Tabbouleh, 61
Vegan Cornmeal Latkes, 220

KNISHES
Chili-Cheese Knishes, 283
Knish Dogs, 284
Spinach-Cheese Filling for Knishes,
 284
Tuna and Cheese Melt Knishes, 284
Variety Knishes, 283

KUGELS
Apple-Plum Kugel, 290
Basil-Zucchini Kugel, 289
Broccoli and Cheese Kugel, 289
Cherry Dairy Kugel, 227
Cranberry-Apple Kugel, 228
Eggplant-Matzah Kugel, 288
Onion-Vegetable Kugel, 223
Peaches 'n' Cream Kugel, 226
Roasted-Garlic Potato Kugel, 224
Romanian Zucchini Kugel, 224

LAMB
Iranian-Inspired Crockpot Hamin, 152
Kibbeh, 160
Shashlik with Harissa Seasoning, 150

LATKES
Broccoli Latkes, 194
Cornmeal Latkes, 219
Italian Butternut-Squash Latkes, 195
Low-Fat Classic Potato Latkes, 206
Vegan Cornmeal Latkes, 220

PASSOVER RECIPES
Apple-Plum Kugel, 290

Artichokes for Stuffing, 189
Austrian-Hungarian Eggplant Goulash,
 183
Austrian Mushroom Sauce, 234
Baked Salmon Gefilte Fish, 126
Baked Tuna and Smoked Salmon
 Squares, 286
Basil-Zucchini Kugel, 289
Braised Carrots and Leeks, 191
Braised Fennel and Artichokes, 190
Broccoli and Cheese Kugel, 289
Caramelized Onions, 193
Carol Joy's Microwaved Fruit Com-
 pote, 239
Charoset Party, 277
Chicken and Pine Nut Salad, 148
Chicken with Artichokes and Olives,
 146
Chili-Cheese Knishes, 283
Chilled Apple Soup, 120
Chocolate-Almond Macaroon
 Minibites, 298
Chocolate Brownies, 298
Chocolate-Spice Angel Food Cake,
 295
Chocolate Torte, 294
Cinnamon Macaroons, 299
Citrus Cinnamon Sauce, 234
Cochin-Style Okra, 198
Cocoa Cinnamon Topping, 297
Cold Apple-Beet Borscht, 119
Coleslaw with Lime and Cilantro, 83
Confetti Smoked Whitefish Spread,
 137
Creamy Potato Chili Soup, 117
Dairy Chocolate Sauce, 297
Eggplant and Tomatoes, 199
Eggplant-Matzah Kugel, 288
Fish and Vegetable Platter, 130
Fried Matzah with Chili and Tomatoes,
 282
Fruit 'n' Carrot Salad, 84
Garlic Mashed Potatoes, 208
Ginger Spiced Pancakes, 280

Gourmet Matzah Balls, 105
Greek Charoset, 277
Greek Salad, 79
Grilled Pepper Salad, 58
Herb Chicken in Tomato Sauce, 147
Herbed Cucumber-Fennel Salad, 81
Herbed Home Fries, 208
Honey-Almond Sauce, 235
Horseradish (Chraine), 233
Instant Chocolate-Banana Shake, 301
Instant Custard Sauce over Fruit, 292
Israeli Baked Apples, 244
Israeli Salad, 60
Italian Butternut-Squash Latkes, 195
Italian Pesto Sauce, 88
Knish Dogs, 284
Latke Chicken, 141
Lemon Cream Pudding, 257
Lemon Poppy-Seed Pancakes, 280
Lemon Waldorf Salad, 85
Low-Fat Classic Potato Latkes, 206
Melon Fruit Salad, 240
Mixed Green Salad with Honey-Mustard Dressing, 75
Moroccan Carrot Salad, 59
Moroccan Charoset, 279
Moroccan Chicken with Almonds and Prunes, 143
Moroccan Dates Dipped in Chocolate, 243
Moroccan Eggplant, 65
Moroccan-Style Pesachdige Bastilla, 285
Natural Orange-Date Charoset, 277
North African Poached Fish, 135
Passover Chocolate Cake Roll, 293
Passover Fruit Crisp, 291
Passover Indian Rolls, 282
Peach Soup, 121
Pistachio Lime Cookies, 300
Poached Herb Salmon, 129
Potato-Crusted Mushrooms and Eggplant, 286

Potatoes with Caper-Dill Sauce, 206
Potato Shell, 128
Red Cabbage with Orange, 196
Roasted-Garlic Potato Kugel, 224
Roasted Turkey Tzimmes, 155
Roasted Vegetables with Sephardic Taste, 204
Romanian Coleslaw, 82
Romanian Putlejela, 67
Romanian Zucchini Kugel, 224
Rosewater Angel Food Cake, 264
Russian Beet Salad, 56
Russian Sweet and Sour Zucchini Salad, 80
Salmon Pie in a Potato Shell, 128
Sara's Spinach Pie, 181
Sea Bass in Tomato Sauce, 133
Sephardic Farfel Puffs, 281
Sephardic Portuguese Zucchini Soup, 116
Shashlik with Harissa Seasoning, 150
Smoked Eggplant Caviar, 68
South African Gefilte Fish, 125
South African Vegetable Tzimmes, 203
Spinach-Cheese Filling for Knishes, 284
Springtime Chicken Soup, 103
Strawberry Whip Dessert, 300
Sweet and Savory Chicken, 141
Sweet Apples in Date Sauce, 243
Syrian Charoset, 278
The Tax Chazzan's Great Meatballs, 162
Toasted Macaroon Cake Delite, 292
Tortilla de Patata Frita, 185
Tuna and Cheese Melt Knishes, 284
Turkish Charoset, 278
Variety Knishes, 283
Vegetable Broth, 101
Vegetable-Stuffed Tomatoes, 86
Watermelon-Ade, 245
Zahava's Marinated-Vegetable Salad, 76

PASTA
American Spaghetti in a Bread Bowl,
163
Barria Brusca, 87
Italian Pesto Sauce with Pasta, 88
Kasha Varnishkes, 217
Orzo Salad, 92
Pasta Salad Col D'Var, 89
Sesame Noodles, 90
Tunisian Pasta with Tuna, 90

PEPPERS
Grilled-Pepper Salad, 58
Hummus with Peppers, 63
Lentil and Rice Stuffed Peppers, 168
Polenta-Stuffed Peppers, 169
Roasted Pepper Dip, 65
Roasted Vegetables with Sephardic
Taste, 204
Sugar Snap Peas with Roasted Pep-
pers, 197

POTATOES
Creamy Potato Chili Soup, 117
Crusty Browned Potatoes, 205
Garlic Mashed Potatoes, 208
Glazed Sweet Potatoes, 203
Herbed Home Fries, 208
Low-Fat Classic Potato Latkes, 206
Picnic Potato Salad, 81
Potatoes with Caper-Dill Sauce, 206
Potato Shell, 128
Roasted-Garlic Potato Kugel, 224
Roasted Vegetables with Sephardic
Taste, 204
South African Vegetable Tzimmes,
203

RICE
Arroz Brasileiro (Brazilian Rice Pilaf),
215
Brazilian-Style Arroz con Pollo, 146
Egyptian Rice Pilaf, 214
Fava Beans with Rice, 176

Iraqi Rice, 213
Lentil and Rice Stuffed Peppers, 168
Orzo Rice Pilaf, 216
Rice Pudding, 256
Rice-Stuffed Zucchini, 172
Syrian Mejadarra (Lentils and Rice),
175

SALADS AND DRESSINGS
Avocado-Grapefruit Salad, 84
Black-Eyed Pea Salad, 57
Carrot-Beet Salad "Bi Tahini," 78
Chicken and Pine Nut Salad, 148
Chickpea Salad, 55
Coleslaw with Lime and Cilantro, 83
Fruit 'n' Carrot Salad, 84
Greek Salad, 79
Grilled Pepper Salad, 58
Herbed Cucumber-Fennel Salad, 81
Israeli Salad, 60
Lemon Waldorf Salad, 85
Mediterranean Broccoli Salad, 77
Mixed Green Salad with Honey-
Mustard Dressing, 75
Moroccan Carrot Salad, 59
Moroccan-Style Beet Salad, 55
Orzo Salad, 92
Pasta Salad Col D'Var, 89
Pickled Tuna Salad, 132
Picnic Potato Salad, 81
Romanian Coleslaw, 82
Russian Beet Salad, 56
Russian Sweet and Sour Zucchini
Salad, 80
Sesame Noodles, 90
Tunisian Pasta with Tuna, 90
Turkish Salad (Salsa), 62
Vegetable-Stuffed Tomatoes, 86
Zahava's Marinated-Vegetable Salad,
76

SAUCES
Austrian Mushroom Sauce, 234
Citrus Cinnamon Sauce, 234

Curry Apricot Salsa for Gefilte Fish, 231
Curry Sauce, 179
Dairy Horseradish Sauce, 233
Honey-Almond Sauce, 235
Orange-Blossom Syrup, 236
Moroccan Tomato Sauce, 287
Rich 'n' Dark Chocolate Syrup, 235
Tax Chazzan's Sauce, 158

SOUPS AND ACCOMPANIMENTS
Algerian Lentil Vegetable Soup, 109
Algerian Split-Pea Soup, 108
Ashkenazic Split-Pea Soup, 107
Brazilian Black Bean Soup, 111
Brown Lentil Soup, 109
Chicken Kasha Soup, 102
Chilled Apple Soup, 120
Cold Apple-Beet Borscht, 119
Cream of Artichoke Soup, 118
Creamy Potato Chili Soup, 117
Gourmet Matzah Balls, 105
Israeli Tomato Noodle Soup, 113
Lucie Prenzlau's Vegetable Soup, 114
Moroccan Couscous (Chicken Vegetable Soup), 103
Peach Soup, 121
Sephardic Black Bean Soup, 111
Sephardic Portuguese Zucchini Soup, 116
Soupe à la Grecque, 106
Springtime Chicken Soup, 103
Vegetable Broth, 101
Vegetable Rice Soup, 112
Vegetarian Moroccan Harira Soup, 110
Vegetarian Mushroom Barley Soup, 115

TURKEY
American Spaghetti in a Bread Bowl, 163
Inside-Out Stuffed Cabbage, 157
Kibbeh, 160

The Lighter Holipshkes (Rolled Stuffed Cabbage), 156
Roasted Turkey Tzimmes, 155
The Tax Chazzan's Great Meatballs, 162

VEGETABLES
Artichokes for Stuffing, 189
Black-Eyed Pea Salad, 57
Braised Carrots and Leeks, 191
Braised Fennel and Artichokes, 190
Broccoli and Cheese Kugel, 289
Broccoli in Lemon-Soy Sauce, 193
Broccoli Latkes, 194
Caramelized Onions, 193
Cochin-Style Okra, 198
Eggplant and Tomatoes, 199
Indian Carrot Curry, 192
Israeli Salad, 60
Italian Butternut-Squash Latkes, 195
Moroccan Carrot Salad, 59
Moroccan-Style Beet Salad, 55
North African Green Beans in Tomato Sauce, 196
Potato-Crusted Mushrooms and Eggplant, 286
Red Cabbage with Orange, 196
Rice-Stuffed Zucchini, 172
Roasted Vegetables with Sephardic Taste, 204
Russian Beet Salad, 56
Russian Sweet and Sour Zucchini Salad, 80
South African Vegetable Tzimmes, 203
Sugar Snap Peas with Roasted Peppers, 197
Sweet Pumpkin and Chickpeas, 190
Vegetable-Stuffed Tomatoes, 86
Zahava's Marinated-Vegetable Salad, 76

VEGETARIAN ENTREES
American Spaghetti in a Bread Bowl, 163

Austrian-Hungarian Eggplant Goulash,
183
Creamy Egg Salad, 185
Dolmas (Stuffed Grape Leaves), 174
Falafel Two Ways, 182
Fava Beans with Rice, 176
Five-Vegetable Stew with Couscous,
167
Garden Vegetables with Couscous,
180
Grilled Veggie Sandwich, 184
Lentil and Rice Stuffed Peppers,
168
The Lighter Holipshkes (Rolled Stuffed
Cabbage), 156

Onion and Chive Polenta, 171
Polenta-Stuffed Peppers, 169
Rice-Stuffed Zucchini, 172
Sara's Spinach Pie, 181
South African Malaysian Vegetable
Curry, 178
Stuffed Eggplant, 173
Stuffed Tomatoes Syrian Style, 158
Sweet and Sour Israeli-Style Goulash,
183
Syrian Mejadarra (Lentils and Rice),
175
Tortilla de Patata Frita, 185
Vegetarian Seneyeh with Apricot-
Tomato Chutney, 176